[   ]

PRAISE FOR *BEYOND THE GREEN ZONE*

"An independent American journalist, Dahr Jamail went to Iraq several times since our invasion 'to try to challenge the distortions of the mainstream media.' He succeeded brilliantly. *Beyond the Green Zone* is a collection of his reports on such subjects as American disinformation about how we captured Saddam Hussein, the battles of Fallujah, and the U.S. campaign to bring freedom and democracy to Iraq. His observations of the gratuitous cruelty of American soldiers toward innocent Iraqis are particularly devastating."

—Chalmers Johnson, author,
Nemesis: The Last Days of the American Republic

"*Beyond the Green Zone* is essential reading for anybody who wants to know what is really happening in Iraq. It is a book that reports what Iraqis endure and what has happened to them during the occupation."

—Patrick Cockburn, Middle East correspondent for the
Independent, author of The Occupation: War and Resistance in Iraq

"Dahr Jamail is the real deal: a reporter who not only has the guts to go where the danger is but the courage to open his heart to the people he finds there. In his radio reporting and now his new book, Jamail goes beyond the Green Zone and beyond most people's comfort zone of denial."

—Laura Flanders, radio host and author,
Blue Grit: True Democrats Take Back Politics from the Politicians

"This book pierces the miasma of ignorance, mendacity, and embedded egotism that has shaped most coverage of Iraq in the American press. It is a passionate and deeply insightful look at the reality of war and occupation, and also an example of international journalism at its best."

—Stephen Kinzer, former foreign desk chief, *New York Times*,
and author, *All the Shah's Men*

"Dahr Jamail does us a great service, by taking us past the lies of our political leaders, past the cowardice of the mainstream press, into the streets, the homes, the lives of Iraqis living under U.S. occupation. He is a superb journalist, in the most honorable tradition of that craft, in the tradition of Heywood Broun, John Reed, I. F. Stone. If what he has seen could be conveyed to all Americans, this ugly war in Iraq would quickly come to an end."

—Howard Zinn, author, *A People's History of the United States*

"Dahr Jamail's *Beyond the Green Zone* is the response to the embedded, propagandistic corporate media empire that played a crucial role in making the invasion and occupation of Iraq possible and helps ensure its continuation. While the powerful media conglomerates were embedded on the ground with the invading and occupying forces—and ideologically with the men running the war—Jamail embedded in the blood-soaked streets of Fallujah and Sadr City with the suffering people of Iraq and uncovered the horrors of this war of 'liberation.' With trademark bravery and a quiet and humble commitment to telling the stories of those forced to live on the other end of the barrel of the U.S. foreign policy machine gun, Jamail ensured that the history of the Iraq occupation would not be written exclusively by self-proclaimed victors and the powerful. Simply put, Dahr Jamail is the conscience of American war reporting, the quintessential unembedded reporter."

—Jeremy Scahill, *New York Times* best-selling author of *Blackwater: The Rise of the World's Most Powerful Mercenary Army*

"Even more notable than Dahr Jamail's extraordinary courage as an independent American journalist in wartime Iraq is his wide-open heart on the beat of the war's central human realities. While U.S. media coverage routinely skitters along the surface of Iraqi suffering, Jamail repeatedly dives into its actual horrors—relentlessly and compassionately exploring the terrible results. Along the way, he lets us know about the inspiring kindness and unsung bravery of people who continue to endure a hellish daily ordeal.... *Beyond the Green Zone* tells us what the big American media are apparently incapable of reporting in any sustained way. For an easier spin, read the *New York Times* or the *Washington Post*. For a true story too real and awful for mainstream news, read this book."

—Norman Solomon, author,
War Made Easy: How Presidents and Pundits Keep Spinning Us to Death

BEYOND THE GREEN ZONE

BEYOND THE GREEN ZONE

DISPATCHES FROM AN UNEMBEDDED
JOURNALIST IN OCCUPIED IRAQ

DAHR JAMAIL

FOREWORD BY AMY GOODMAN

Haymarket
Books

Chicago, Illinois

T 120002

First published in 2007 by Haymarket Books
P.O. Box 180165
Chicago, IL 60618
773-583-7884
info@haymarketbooks.org
www.haymarketbooks.org

Trade distribution:
In the U.S. through Consortium Book Sales, www.cbsd.com
In the UK, Turnaround Publisher Services, www.turnaround-psl.com
In Australia, Palgrave MacMillan, www.palgravemacmillan.com.au

This book was published with the generous support of the Wallace Global Fund.

Cover design by Josh On
Cover image by Dahr Jamail

ISBN-13: 978-1931859-47-9

Printed in Canada by union labor on recycled paper containing 50 percent post-consumer waste in accordance with the guidelines of the Green Press Initiative, www.greenpressinitiative.org

Library of Congress CIP Data is available

2 4 6 8 10 9 7 5 3 1

CONTENTS

FOREWORD BY AMY GOODMAN
AND DENIS MOYNIHAN   XI

INTRODUCTION   1

1. ENTERING IRAQ   7

2. PEERING INTO AN ABYSS   33

3. GROWING FURY AND UNREST   53

4. KEBABS IN FALLUJAH   67

5. CRAVING HEALTH AND FREEDOM   85

6. GOING "HOME"   101

7. REENTERING THE INFERNO   107

8. SARAJEVO ON THE EUPHRATES   127

9. RAIDING MOSQUES, TORTURING IRAQIS   143

10. THE AFTERMATH IN FALLUJAH   159

11. SHATTERED DREAMS   175

12. "NOBODY HERE LIKES THE OCCUPIERS"   191

13. LEAVING THE VOLCANO
FOR THE EYE OF THE HURRICANE   209

14. SPIRALING INTO OCCUPIED IRAQ   217

15. OPERATION PHANTOM FURY   229

16. INTO OBLIVION   241

17. DYING FOR DEMOCRACY   259

18. COMING "HOME"   277

AFTERWORD   283

NOTES   293

ACKNOWLEDGMENTS   303

INDEX   307

This book is dedicated
to the people of Iraq

Dahr Jamail is an independent journalist—an unembedded journalist. He comes from a conservative, Republican, Texas family. In
2003, he was working as a volunteer mountain-rescue ranger in
Alaska. As he eloquently writes in this, his first book, he quit the
wilds of Alaska, driven into the heart of the war zone in Iraq, dis-
gusted and outraged at the U.S. invasion and occupation, and at the
dominant U.S. media's abysmal coverage of it. Dahr Jamail's story
demonstrates the power of genuine, independent journalism, and
what one person, through a simple act of courage, can accomplish.

What do you know about Fallujah, and when did you know it? The
two U.S. military sieges of Fallujah, in April and November of 2004,
stand among the most violent and devastating attacks on a civilian
population in recent decades. Americans know very little about them,
and what little most managed to learn came from journalists embedded with U.S. troops. Central to Dahr Jamail's dispatches are those he
wrote in and around Fallujah. The scale of the destruction and loss of
life, juxtaposed with the absolute failure of the Western media to
cover the plight of the Fallujans, fuels his tireless reporting.

His vivid description of the trip he took on a medical-supply run
into Fallujah in April 2004 is an excellent example of such work.

Dahr accompanied English human rights activist Jo Wilding, among others, into Fallujah in order to cover the siege, bringing medical supplies into the embattled city, and ferrying out the wounded. The harrowing journey is described by Dahr and captured on film in the excellent documentary about Jo Wilding by British filmmaker Julia Guest, titled *A Letter to the Prime Minister*. The bus inches along from Baghdad to Fallujah. It navigates U.S. military roadblocks and Fallujan militia roadblocks. In Fallujah, the keffiyeh-clad militiamen cheer the bus, firing off their Kalashnikovs into the air. Dahr describes the scenes of desperation and death at the clinic, without basic supplies or electricity, as women and children are brought in, shot by U.S. snipers who targeted anything that moved.

Jamail knew enough of the inherently flawed embed process, how the lives of the journalists depended on the very soldiers they were tasked with covering. He also knew that the invasion and occupation of Iraq was proving to be especially lethal to unembedded journalists, with attacks from the "coalition" forces, the local resistance, criminals, and the small percentage of combatants from foreign lands. Dahr Jamail, with scant resources, made his way to Iraq, embodying the words of Dr. Martin Luther King, Jr.: "There comes a time when one must take a position that is neither safe, nor politic, nor popular but one must take it because one's conscience tells one what is right." As Dahr puts it, "I felt that I had blood on my hands because the government had been left unchecked." That is the role of the media, to be the check on power. To be the fourth estate, not for the state. Dahr Jamail's journalism, his work, comprises a series of stories woven into a coherent history—of people on the ground, at the target end, in the crosshairs of U.S. foreign policy, and resisting it.

And Dahr does not miss a beat. Immediately after arriving in Iraq, he goes to a hospital, beyond the Green Zone, as his title declares, meeting and interviewing doctors, patients, the parents of injured children. Shortly thereafter he is pursuing the multinational corporation Bechtel, which had contracts to rebuild (among other things) Iraq's potable water supply and delivery systems. While government and military spokespeople fed misinformation and propaganda to a compliant press corps, Dahr deployed his scant resources to travel to several villages and cities, to actually visit the water treatment plants and interview the managers. In Hilla, plant manager Salman Hassan Kadel said of Bechtel, "We ask of them that instead of painting buildings, they give us one water pump, and we will give service to more people." Despite the dismal performance, which cost people their lives through waterborne illnesses, Bechtel, before abandoning Iraq, received over $2.3 billion in contracts.

In late November 2003, General Peter Pace claimed that fifty-four insurgents had been killed in Samarra. "Mainstream" reporters repeated the claim as fact. Dahr headed to Samarra, began interviewing witnesses, local leaders, doctors. It turns out that eight civilians were killed, none of whom were combatants. This is what it means to be an investigative journalist.

Jamail's consistent, strong reporting gained him an increased audience and interviews. A global public desperate to make sense of the war connected with his blog posts. We started having him on our *Democracy Now!* news hour regularly. Others began using his work as source material.

Pulitzer Prize–winning journalist Seymour Hersh praised him at the Third Annual Al-Jazeera Forum in Doha, Qatar, describing how his editors stripped Hersh's mention of Jamail: "There is a young journalist here, Dahr Jamail, whose stuff has been very prescient, and I've four or five times included the brave accounts of some of his work in my stories.... It's not just at the *New Yorker*, it's at the *New*

York Times where I worked very happily for a decade—the first thing you cut out is any mention of anybody else. That's such a disagreeable aspect of our profession, the competition. Rather than credit a competitor we'll ignore the story."

John Pilger, filmmaker and journalist for many decades and across many war zones, says about Dahr Jamail: "For me, he is the finest reporter working in Iraq. With the exception of Robert Fisk, Patrick Cockburn, and several others, mostly freelancers, he shames the flak-jacketed, cliché-crunching camp followers known as 'embeds.' He has reported from the besieged city of Fallujah, whose destruction and atrocities have been suppressed by Western broadcasters, notably by the BBC."

Dahr's words were used to form part of a script for a play called *Fallujah*. Its London production merited a dismissive review in the *New York Times*, written by Jane Perlez, on May 29, 2007. Perlez wrote, "The denunciations of the United States are severe, particularly in the scenes that deal with the use of napalm in Falluja, an allegation made by left-wing critics of the war but never substantiated." Perlez wrote that Jamail was Canadian, as well. Jamail repeatedly attempted to get a correction to the two points from the *Times*. The *New York Times* corrected the bit about Jamail's nationality, but failed to correct the larger point, that the use of napalm was never substantiated (even though, as Fairness and Accuracy in Reporting noted, the *Times* editorialized against the U.S. military's use of white phosphorous).

While "napalm" itself was not necessarily used, white phosphorous was, and, as Dahr notes, military people use the two terms interchangeably, as the horrific effects of the banned chemical weapons are identical. The substance clings to the skin and infiltrates the lungs, burning its victims alive. Jamail, following the November 2004 attack on Fallujah, dubbed by the U.S. "Operation

Phantom Fury," began hearing firsthand accounts on the chemical attacks, and received photos of corpses with burned skin, some with flesh burned off to the bone. He described his findings on *Democracy Now!* on November 29, 2004.

Far from being an unsubstantiated allegation, it was clear that white phosphorous had been used as a weapon that had killed civilians. Italian television channel RAI did a documentary about it. *Democracy Now!* premiered the documentary, translated into English (it actually aired on *Democracy Now!* before it aired in Italy, in November 2005). Following that broadcast, *Democracy Now!* had Lieutenant Colonel Steve Boylan of the U.S. Army on from Baghdad, denying they used white phosphorous. Lieutenant Barry Venable, however, contradicted that to the BBC, acknowledging the use, forcing a retraction of the earlier denial.

If Jane Perlez or any other reporter at the *New York Times* is interested in pursuing unsubstantiated allegations of weapons in Iraq, they are well positioned, as there was no bigger booster of the lies of Iraq's weapons of mass destruction than the *Times* itself. Front-page stories by the *New York Times* duo of Judith Miller and Michael Gordon still need a full review and public exposure by the *Times*, in addition to their tepid mea culpa—better put, "kinda culpa"—that appeared one day, buried on page A10. President Bush could not have had a better ally than the *New York Times* in selling the war to the U.S. public.

Dahr spent his months in Iraq in the hospitals, in the morgues, in the neighborhoods, in the mosques. He took the time to learn the names of the dead from the mourning family members, names you would otherwise never see in print. He was shot at, covering some of the most covered-up conflicts in Iraq. As an unembedded reporter, he was exposed to threats of violence from all sides. Often literally in the sights of the U.S. military, he also had to be careful interviewing people in the streets as their stories tumbled out, one after another, their anger increasing against an occupying force whose country he came from.

Dahr Jamail is truly courageous. He has taken great risks in the service of the truth. He has tirelessly told the stories of the victims, proud people in dire straits, writing with poignancy and immediacy, with eloquence and accuracy. If only the corporate networks would devote a small percentage of their resources to the type of reporting that Dahr Jamail accomplishes with next to nothing. The prospect of such a media system depends on the demands and activism of the public, a public that holds the networks, the reporters, and elected officials accountable, and a public that supports independent media.

INTRODUCTION

In 2002, while winter began to settle across the United States, the drumbeat for war became deafening. Living in Anchorage, Alaska, I spent much of my free time reading the news from abroad or getting it via alternative online outlets such as Media Lens, *Democracy Now!*, and Media Channel. The cheerleading for war feebly disguised as "journalism" that corporate media television stations and newspapers in the United States spewed was intolerable. The overwhelming evidence was already available. There were not and had not been "weapons of mass destruction" in Iraq for years. The make-believe link between Saddam Hussein and 9/11 was a chimera. The excuse given later, that of "liberating" the people of Iraq, held even less truth.

Nevertheless, illusions were maintained by a media in the United States that had sunk to being little more than state stenographers giddily scribbling and announcing the diktats of George W. Bush and his administration. Thousands of years of Iraq's rich history were cursorily omitted from the media and replaced by the graphic of a U.S.-installed dictator with a bull's-eye on his forehead.

The worldwide protests of February 15, 2003—the largest in human history—Bush brushed aside as a "focus group."[1] Watching this occur enraged me, particularly since after 9/11 the one paper in Anchorage, Alaska, which I had been freelancing for, fired its editor because our content had become "too political." My mind was a pressure cooker. I wondered, what could be done to stop an illegal war of aggression against a country that had been suffering more than twelve years of economic sanctions that had already killed over one million people?

Nothing.

The United States invaded Iraq in March 2003. Coverage by most of the mainstream media worsened. Rather than showing the true face of war, television coverage more closely resembled a weapons manufacturer's show, complete with brilliant graphics of fighter jets, missiles, attack helicopters, and interactive maps of Iraq that could have been taken straight from a video game.

The news I followed from the media of other countries, such as the *Independent* and the *Guardian* newspapers in the U.K., *Le monde diplomatique* in France, Al-Jazeera in Qatar, and outlets in Greece and Italy, portrayed a different reality. While shown for the propaganda stunt it was in many foreign media outlets, the stage-managed toppling of one of Saddam Hussein's statues in central Baghdad captivated uninformed Americans watching news, which by then closely resembled the state-controlled media of an authoritarian regime. The disparity in reportage between many foreign outlets and those in the United States was nothing less than news reporting on the one hand and flag-waving on the other. The occupation began and quickly lurched toward chaos, violence, and suffering. Rather than being explored and explained by most media in the United States, the mayhem of war was portrayed as one dimensional, and described with slogans like "Operation Iraqi Freedom" and other rhetoric so familiar to the peoples of the Third World.

Formerly repressed currents of Iraqi religious, political, and social strata emerged and began to breathe life back into the complex patterns of the social fabric of Iraq after the dictator was removed. The multilayered quilt of tribal and religious societies resurfaced.

I spent the summer of 2003 volunteering as a rescue ranger for the National Park Service on the highest mountain in Alaska, Denali, climbing, pondering, and listening to radio reports at night in my tent. I listened as Iraqis were quickly pulled into the undertow of a violent upheaval against an occupation they had not sought. While climbing on icy slopes during the day, I wondered what I might do to bring the information I found reported in other countries back to the uninformed, horribly misled population of my own country.

I would like to say that I decided to go to Iraq for philosophical reasons, because I believe that an informed citizenry is the bedrock of any healthy democracy. But I went to Iraq for personal reasons. I was tormented by the fact that the government of my country illegally invaded and then occupied a country that it had bombed in 1991. Because the government of my country had asphyxiated Iraq with more than a decade's worth of "genocidal" sanctions (in the words of former United Nations Humanitarian Coordinator for Iraq Denis Halliday).[2] The government of my country then told lies, which were obediently repeated by an unquestioning media in order to justify the invasion and occupation. I felt that I had blood on my hands because the government had been left unchecked.

My going to Iraq was an act of desperation that has since transformed itself into a bond to that country and so many of her people. There were stories there that begged to be heard and told again. We are defined by story. Our history, our memory, our perceptions of the future, are all built and held within stories. As a U.S. citizen complicit in the devastation of Iraq, I was already bound up in the story of that country. I decided to go to learn what that story really was.

While the vast majority of the reporting of Iraq was provided by journalists availing themselves of the Pentagon-sponsored "embed" program, I chose to look for stories of real life and "embed" myself with the Iraqi people. The U.S. military side of the occupation is overly represented by most mainstream outlets. I consciously decided to focus on the Iraqi side of the story.

The story of the many oppressed peoples of the world is rarely recorded by the few who oppress. We are taught that the truth is objective fact as written down by the conquerors.

Truth is more than fact. Before his testimony against the flooding of his traditional life and homeland in James Bay by Hydro-Quebec (for power shipped to the United States), François Mainscum, a Mistassini Cree hunter, was asked to place his hand on the Bible. He had left his bush camp only a few days before he appeared in court. "When I was told to touch the book, my first reaction was to wonder what this book is for," he said, "Until I was told to touch it, the book, so that I could speak the 'truth.'"

He spoke with his translator at length, and finally the translator looked up at the judge. "He does not know whether he can tell the truth. He says he can tell only what he knows."[3]

There are roughly 27 million people in Iraq. Each of them has his or her own story about what has happened in Iraq during the U.S. occupation. Their stories define them, and us. They belong in our history, our memory, our perceptions of the future.

This book contains some of those stories.

Berkeley, California
Summer 2007

Alleged looter, who was pulled from his car and beaten by men dressed as Iraqi police, as well as un-uniformed men who claimed to be Iraqi police, who then took his vehicle, November 2003.

CHAPTER 1

ENTERING IRAQ

The high-paid speechwriters, spin doctors, and the press conferences gauged to conceal and rebuff in the name of higher principles like "national security," the well-groomed, dispassionate news anchors, the noncommittal hypocrisy of "balanced reporting," the sentimentalities following accidents, the pharmaceutical ads that arouse fear in the name of healing and relief, the Sunday preachers, the titillation of interruptions ("We're out of time, I have to cut you off") before any satisfactory conclusion can be reached, and above all else the whitewash from the White House.... The unrelenting bombardment of the people with the toxins of hypocrisy, TV's own weapon of destruction of the masses, may indeed call for sanctions and censorship—not by the government but of the government—because TV hypocrisy evokes a subliminal response of disgust and impotent anger, alienation from civic participation, existential worthlessness, degradation of the citizen's innate intelligence, dignity, and perception of truth, igniting a powder keg of terrible rage.
                                               —James Hillman, A Terrible Love of War

JANUARY 2005

The thundering explosion jolted me into consciousness, and I saw the curtains flowing in, as if a strong wind were blowing into my room. My door blasted open, splintering the wood frame where it had been locked shut. The windows, too, concussed open, but thankfully none of them shattered. Small chunks of concrete from the ceiling were strewn about the floor as white dust particles hovered, suspended in frozen time.

I looked out my window and saw that, although there was shattered glass lying outside many of the nearby buildings, the Australian embassy across the way, which I thought had been bombed, remained intact.

I quickly threw on some clothes, grabbed my camera, and ran into the hall—it was filled with so much dust it was difficult to see. Chunks of white plaster from the ceiling and broken glass were tossed about the hall. I pulled my shirt up to cover my nose, squinting to peer through the dust. Sirens wailed outside and the whining grew louder as they approached from across Baghdad, while I clumsily made my way upstairs to the roof.

The suicide car bomb detonated near the base of a large tan building across the street, which was home to many Australian soldiers. From atop this multistory building, snipers guarded their nearby embassy. Two smoldering bits of a vehicle sat near the building and two bodies lay in pools of blood across the street. Adjacent to the Australian outpost, the right ceiling of a small building that was under construction had collapsed—the gray concrete slumped down tiredly onto the floor beneath. A small date palm between the two buildings stood limply; half its drooping, green fronds closest to the bomb still smoldered.

Despite being heavily fortified with concrete barriers, concertina wire, sand bags, and sand barriers, the outpost had chunks blown out of its concrete facade. Tan camouflage netting and plywood that covered many of the windows hung limply out of the openings they had once covered.

It was eleven days before the January 30, 2005 elections. The chaos and violence had been unrelenting since the U.S. siege of Fallujah had begun a little more than two months earlier. This month, January, already looked as though it would be one of the bloodiest of the entire occupation for occupation forces, with more than four being killed every single day as resistance attacks continue unabated. Car bombs, uncommon earlier in the occupation and unheard of in Iraq prior to the invasion, had become a daily event.

I was on the roof just minutes after the blast when the Iraqi police began to arrive en masse. Across the street from the blast, a woman covered in her black *abaya* stood near one of two bodies lying in a pool of blood, screaming hysterically. She was quickly pushed inside one of the white-and-blue pickup trucks of the Iraqi police, and driven away.

Other policemen stood over the two bodies, which appeared to be piles of clothing on the pavement—but with their limbs contorted and stretched into unnatural positions. Black smoke plumes languidly drifted down the street in the early morning stillness, away from the putrid fires of the burning rubber and shattered steel of the spent weapon. Police ran about in pandemonium, yelling orders and barking at journalists. There was nothing much else for them to do. I watched them eventually load the two bodies into a vehicle, perhaps to be driven to a morgue.

This was a smaller car bomb and it didn't leave a crater like so many of the others do. Nevertheless, in buildings hundreds of yards away from the blast, the glass was shattered and portions of wall were crumbled. It was like being in a massive earthquake, but with the tremors consolidated into one large, abrupt shake.

About twenty minutes later, several truckloads of Iraqi soldiers showed up, many of them wearing their usual black masks. It was by now common for the majority of the Iraqi security forces to cover their faces to avoid reprisal attacks against their families by the resistance. Plus, many of them were members of the resistance themselves, since the security forces had long since been infiltrated. Other "security" forces were common criminals opting for anonymity in the violent chaos that now prevailed on the streets of Baghdad, while others concealed their identity because they were likely members of death squads.

After another fifteen minutes, the U.S. military showed up with ten Humvees, a Bradley, and an M-1 Abrams tank. The Abrams puked black smoke from JP-8 fuel out its rear as the rattling treads ground across the crumbling pavement. A gray curb popped into dust beneath the behemoth as it promptly stopped and swung the huge barrel of its cannon down the street to ward off would-be suicide bombers. They resealed the street even though it was already secured by the police. A few soldiers began stringing their concertina wire across the road while the rest aimed their guns down the street from inside their vehicles.

Two Apache helicopters arrived and commenced rumbling in circles around the area like large, wrathful insects, their blades chopping angrily at the gray morning haze. Jill Carroll, a freelance journalist living in a nearby hotel and currently working for the *Christian Science Monitor*, shuffled up beside me. We nodded to one another awkwardly while grimly shaking our heads.

I watched an old woman who lived just across from the bombing. She walked aimlessly around in her small yard, stopping to slowly pick up rubble from her wall, which was damaged in the blast. After a while, she glanced at the bloody entropy in her street, dropped the block of concrete in her hands, and shuffled back into her home.

Her stoicism and resignation was emblematic of Iraqis throughout the country. Most of them had long since surrendered hope that the occupation would bring positive change in their lives.

It was another of those moments when I wondered what the hell I was doing in Iraq. I was completely burnt out, but the catastrophe that the U.S.-led occupation of Iraq had become staggered haphazardly into an unknown, increasingly bleak future. Requests for news and radio dispatches continued to pour in, and I went along regardless of my weary numbness.

Past the shrapnel-pocked buildings in the bomb's path, the polluted brown waters of the Tigris River lazily eased past, my gaze fixed on them until the noise of the chopping blades of the Apaches faded.

Half an hour later, another large car bomb detonated in eastern Baghdad at an Iraqi police headquarters, killing eighteen people. The explosion echoed across the capital city. Shortly after this, three more huge explosions rumbled across the center of Baghdad. In a span of just ninety minutes, five car bombs detonated, killing at least twenty-six people. One of the car bombs detonated outside a bank where Iraqi police were waiting to collect their salaries, killing at least ten of them. Another car bomb detonated at the airport, killing two guards. A military installation was also attacked, killing two U.S. soldiers and two civilians.

As I began to make some calls to let folks know I was alive, Iraqis around my hotel compound began sweeping up glass. Hanging up the phone, I marveled at how hardened I'd become after four trips and nearly eight months in Iraq. I knew I had to leave soon. I had to leave, even though the disintegration afflicting the country at this point was exponentially worse than it was during my first trip to Iraq.

NOVEMBER 2003

My first trip to Iraq began when I landed at the Queen Alia International Airport in Amman, Jordan. As we taxied to the gate, we passed three green-and-white bodies of Iraqi Airways jets that had seen better days. Their aged, rusted fuselages sat idle, a reminder of pre-sanctions Iraq, when the country was actually functioning.

I had just left Lebanon, where I visited cousins, most of whom I'd never met. My great-grandfather, a Christian from Beirut, had left there for the United States in 1904. Now, Jordan was the last step for me in my preparations to enter Iraq. It was also the first step toward having my life altered more dramatically than I could ever have predicted.

For seven years leading up to that flight, I had lived in Alaska, working as a mountain guide and volunteering on rescue patrols on Denali, while doing social work and freelance writing in the off season. Paying attention to politics and the foreign policy of the U.S. government was a new experience for me that had only begun shortly before the buildup to the invasion of Iraq.

I was astounded that the invasion and occupation of Iraq took place, despite having the facts in advance that it was a war for oil, for Western corporations like Bechtel and Halliburton, and geostrategic positioning of the U.S. military. It was glaringly obvious that the media was simultaneously being manipulated by the powers that be and participating actively as mouthpieces for the very government they were meant to hold accountable.

The choice for me was either to stay in Alaska and suffer the frustration and impotence of watching all this happen or take a risk to get the information I knew to be the truth out to others. Having had some experience at freelance reporting, I decided that the one thing I could do was go to Baghdad to report on the occupation myself. I saved some money, bought a laptop, a camera, and a plane ticket, and, armed with information gleaned via some connections made over the Internet, headed for the Middle East. Following the suggestions given by a Lebanese man who had just emerged from Baghdad, I found a hotel in Amman where I would stay, a driver who would take me to Baghdad, and a couple of contacts in Baghdad.

That first step out of Queen Alia Airport into the Middle Eastern desert with my backpack, which had accompanied me to the summit of Denali several times, was just a bit surreal.

The al-Monzer Hotel in Amman is a hole-in-the-wall place with some of the friendliest staff one could hope for. Staying there was a stroke of luck and assured me bottomless cups of tea through the anxiety-ridden days as I organized my journey into Baghdad. However, sitting in the hotel in Amman was a waiting game. Bursts of activity, such as hiring a car and driver to go to Baghdad, were followed by drawn-out hours of waiting—and thinking.

The news from the Iraqi drivers was that the trip in would be no problem. "One just has to be careful around Fallujah, because the resistance is strong there and the area around the city is extremely volatile, due to ongoing U.S. military operations," one of them told me.

The day before I was to head in, on November 21, 2003, the Palestine Hotel in Baghdad was attacked by rockets that were hauled in and launched from a donkey cart. I had planned to stay at the al-Fanar Hotel, which happened to be right across a small street from the Palestine, so I waited one more day, trying to find other accommodations.

I met an Iraqi university student named Sabah, who was staying at my hotel in Amman. He'd read the fear on my face and tried to distract me by teaching me small facets of his culture. "Don't cross your legs like you do in the West," he said with a smile. "Showing the bottoms of your shoes is considered offensive in Iraq."

Sabah also told me that he had a friend, a young Iraqi woman he met at university. "American soldiers broke into her parent's house looking for resistance fighters. Why they [fighters] would have been at her parent's home made no sense whatsoever. Nevertheless, the family dog began barking noisily at the Americans, so one of the soldiers shot the dog. Then the mother began yelling at the soldier for shooting the dog, so the soldier then shot the mother."

I'd heard stories like that already. Sabah stared at me, willing me to respond, but I had no response except to frown and shake my head.

(Much later in the occupation, in early 2006, Sabah was kidnapped while working as a translator for a British freelance journalist and his Iraqi driver. The three were discovered by chance when U.S. soldiers raided the house where they were being held captive by an armed group. The British journalist was eventually released into British custody. Sabah and the driver, however, were held in Abu Ghraib for over a month and treated appallingly before finally being released.)

That evening, I met James Longley at the Internet café of our small hotel. An independent filmmaker, James was on his way to a film festival in Russia. I let him know I was on my way to Baghdad and in need of a translator.

"Why don't you use mine," he asked me, "He's great—his name is Akeel and he's a really big guy, so that'll help with your security, too." Under any other circumstances, this would be considered a funny remark. But in this situation, I drew comfort from this fact.

Learning about Akeel, as well as meeting with a couple from the United Kingdom who inexplicably wanted to share the car into Baghdad "for the experience," helped quash my worries over not having a fixer and entering Baghdad alone. It was the first of a seemingly endless succession of serendipitous experiences around my relationship to Iraq.

The night of the third day of waiting, I met Hussein, our plump, brusquely energetic Iraqi driver, who knew as much English as I did Arabic. He was in his late twenties and very proud. "I am driver!" he boasted while shaking our hands in the hotel. His pride was to prove justified as our trip progressed. We departed at 10:00 p.m. sharp, winding through the streets of Amman, and then east toward the border, as the cool desert air flowed through our open windows.

Driving into Baghdad at this point in the occupation was our only option, as Baghdad International Airport had been closed to nonmilitary and non-NGO (non-governmental organization) traffic. While the road was dangerous due to thieves and clashes between the Iraqi resistance and U.S. military, it was still quite passable with a little luck.

As we exited Amman and headed directly toward the Iraqi border, a brilliant lightning display loomed ahead and bright bolts flashed across the black Iraqi sky.

Hussein popped in one of his Arabic pop-music tapes, turned up the volume, and the reality of what I was doing settled in more deeply as the tinny music blared through his speakers. The number of kilometers on the sign posts toward the border of Iraq continued to decrease while sand blasts blurred the view from time to time.

The border was in total chaos. Rows of cars and freight and fuel trucks jockeyed for position across the sand-covered highway. Hussein, in what I later found to be typical Middle Eastern fashion, rode the bumper of the car ahead with ferocious tenacity, stomping the gas and then the brake pedal so as not to allow what felt like more than three inches between our vehicles at any time.

Nevertheless, our time waiting to obtain the necessary stamp in our passports (no visas were required for Iraq until summer 2004) was relatively short at the crowded, smoke-filled border station. In less than three hours we were set to leave.

It struck me that we didn't encounter a single U.S. soldier at the border. Essentially it was wide open, with no car searches, and anyone carrying anything could access Iraq. For all the rhetoric from the Bush administration that violence occurring in Iraq was due to foreign influences, the U.S. military was doing next to nothing to guard the borders.

It would not have been difficult for anyone to walk the hundred yards on either side of the gate and cross into Iraq in total darkness undetected.

Hussein promptly stomped on the gas pedal and we sped along the highway. We had been told that our safety depended on speed. Due to the current state of anarchy and widespread lawlessness in Iraq, Hussein explained, there were no highway police and there were prowling bandits. We cruised at between 100 and 120 mph, ripping down the road across the desert of Iraq, honking and flashing our lights to urge other cars out of the way.

As the sun rose, I stared out at the vast, seemingly never-ending expanses of desert. This was the real Iraq I was finally seeing, verdant farmlands near the mighty Euphrates River. Goatherds lounging under groves of date palms contrasted with the bleak desert landscape.

As we approached Ramadi, in the distance to the northeast, there were thick, black columns of smoke. Later in Baghdad, I would learn that an oil pipeline just outside of Kirkuk had been torched recently by saboteurs.

Shortly after that, as we neared the outskirts of Fallujah, I noticed Hussein quietly wrapping his keffiyeh—the usually red or black checked scarves so commonly worn in the Middle East—around his face to provide full cover, as well as to make him appear to be a mujahedeen. As we sped past the outskirts of Fallujah, several Apache helicopters circled above Humvees and Bradleys that were parked near a grove of date palms. I spotted a group of soldiers, prostrate, with their guns aimed into the grove.

We continued on toward the capital city of Iraq, home to seven million people, whose beginning dates back to at least the eighth century. It was known as "*Dar al-Salam*" (house of peace) and was the center of the Muslim world, as well as being a center for knowledge and commerce.

By the time we entered Baghdad, there were U.S. military vehicles everywhere.

Massive M-1 Abrams tanks rumbled down the streets, the black JP-8 smoke billowing from their exhaust obfuscating the aging white-and-orange civilian vehicles rolling sheepishly behind them.

We passed a bus that had crashed into a guardrail, and saw the wreckage on the side of the road being scrutinized by dozens of people. Two wounded men with blood-stained shirts lay on the ground as a patrol of four Humvees slowed down, only to pass by. Many of the Iraqis watched the U.S. soldiers perched atop their vehicles, as if they were expecting them to pull over to lend a hand. The stares turned to glares as the patrol regained speed and quickly rolled past the crowd around the crumpled bus.

I watched intently as Baghdad slipped past my window. Bombed buildings stood randomly about the capital city, and its roads were clogged with honking vehicles. I marveled at the countless number of gutted buildings, victims of the rampant looting that engulfed Baghdad just after the invasion.

Tank blasts from the invasion of Baghdad left holes punched through the concrete walls of a tall communications tower that stood near the bank of the Tigris River, just across from the so-called Green Zone, the U.S.-controlled area in central Baghdad where Saddam Hussein's Republican Palace sat. A huge banner for the U.S.-controlled television station Al-Iraqiyah hung on the side of the building facing the bridge across the Tigris River near the Green Zone. Beneath the banner were several holes blasted by U.S. tanks. It was from this bridge that a tank shot at the nearby Palestine Hotel on April 8, 2003, killing José Couso, a cameraman working for the Spanish television channel TELECINCO, and Taras Protsyuk, a Ukrainian cameraman working for Reuters. The U.S. military claimed they were being fired upon by snipers, but video footage taken before, during, and after the shelling of the hotel by the tank showed no such evidence. On that same day, the Al-Jazeera office and Abu Dubai television bureau had been attacked by U.S. forces, killing Al-Jazeera correspondent Tareq Ayoub.[1] The tone had been set from the beginning by the invaders: Iraq was no place for independent journalists who opted not to "embed" with the U.S. military.

Since Baghdad was not carpet-bombed, the buildings that stood in disrepair were even more accentuated. This augmented the fact that there was no reconstruction. With all the billions of dollars supposedly allocated for reconstruction, why wasn't anything happening? It was a festering question that continued to gain prominence in Iraqi minds.

We passed coils of concertina wire on the sides of the road and in the median. This wire often stretched for city blocks. Huge concrete blast walls lined portions of streets, and armed Iraqi guards or U.S. soldiers milled about entrances to various compounds. Intersections were absolute chaos. With no functioning traffic lights, cars moving in opposite directions often inched past one another in the middle, causing major gridlock.

◆ ◆ ◆ ◆

Inside the Agadir Hotel in central Baghdad, the marble-floored lobby with silk window curtains had a 1970s feel to it—remnants of an aura of elegance from better days.

An Iraqi man, perhaps in his early sixties, stood inside the lobby. He wore a white button-down dress shirt and a smart black bow tie, with black slacks. His gray mustached face watched the doors of the hotel. He seemed tired—a combination of disquieting uncertainty and wariness—as he stared out the doors, as if waiting for something.

He insisted on hauling my cumbersome backpack to my room. I tipped him awkwardly. He paused before saying softly, "*Shukran*" (thank you), turned on all the lights in my room, and left, quietly closing the door behind him. Preoccupied as I was, I could not fail to notice the man's gentleness of manner and his dignity, traits that I was to encounter again and again during my stay, in Iraqis of all kinds, surviving amid the occupation.

I turned and looked out the window at the bombed-out telephone exchange across the street. Each of the two floors had a massive hole punched through them by a bomb—metal bars within the concrete pushed downward and out, like an upside-down flower. Rubble lay around the base of the empty building, its innards looted long ago. Young children played under the wreckage as beat-up cars drove by on the nearby street. Next to this, several donkeys stood about listlessly underneath date palms on a patchy yard.

The next evening, when I returned from having dinner, I met Akeel, who was waiting for me in the lobby of my hotel. A twenty-five-year-old who had earlier worked as a translator with other independent journalists and filmmakers, Akeel was eager to get back to work. A large man with a powerful build, Akeel later told me he was recruited by the Ba'ath Party to be in the military. He had resisted it by eventually shooting himself in the leg to avoid military service. While certainly no fan of U.S. foreign policy, he had an interest in American pop culture and music, such as music videos with scantily clad women and whatever the hit song of the week happened to be.

"We can cover whichever stories you like, Daher," he promptly told me. "Just tell me what you want to do, because we have to show people what's happening in Iraq."

I asked him if we could go to a hospital to talk with doctors about their situation. I wanted to find out if they had received any relief since the invasion. Akeel walked over to the front desk to use the phone to call a doctor friend of his. The line was dead, as usual. I asked the manager when he thought it would be functioning. He frowned, held up his hands and said, "Only the Americans know these things."

The next morning Akeel met me in the lobby and we caught a cab to go to the Italian Red Cross field station located near Baghdad Medical City, formerly known as Saddam Medical City. Inside the hospital we visited burned women, men, and children. A six-year-old boy was being treated for burns from a fire caused by the oil used to heat his home. His small hands grasped a yellow balloon provided by the doctors as they changed the dressing around his legs. Leaking wounds left stained shades of red and yellow through damp gauze. Both his feet were twisted—not from pain but from congenital deformation. His father looked at me wearily while he told Akeel, "We think his mother was exposed to some of the munitions used by the Americans in their previous war against us."

According to the Italians who ran the burn unit, lack of electricity had led to a 300 percent increase in the number of burn victims in Baghdad because people had started using fire to generate heat in their homes.

We caught a taxi and as it began to drive us away we noticed several bodies being unloaded from the back of an ambulance. Akeel directed the taxi driver to stop. He opened his door and asked one of the men unloading a body what had happened. Akeel quickly got back into our taxi and informed me, "They were killed by Americans while they were walking down the road," adding bitterly, "Do you think all these people, these innocent people being killed by the Americans, don't have families that are now joining the resistance?"

At this point, merely seven months into the occupation, the Iraqi resistance was already conducting as many as thirty-five attacks per day on occupation forces, according to Lieutenant General Ricardo Sanchez, commander of U.S. forces in Iraq, who made the announcement to reporters at a press conference on October 22, 2003.[2] (In less than half a year, that number would double.)

Driving across Baghdad later that afternoon, we passed a petrol station with lines of cars leading up to it, two cars thick and at least two miles long. People sat in their cars, or often walked alongside, pushing the car to save what was left of their gas.

Nearer the station, men with plastic tubs of petrol stood on the circular turnabouts with a siphon hose or cut plastic bottle to use as a funnel. They bought the gas at the petrol stations, later reselling it for a little more. This was possibly one of the fastest-growing job markets in Iraq since the occupation. Unemployment remained nearly as high as the estimated 32 percent it was during the sanctions, even according to the U.S.-backed Iraqi Ministry of Labor.

As Akeel and I were walking toward a small kebab restaurant, we watched a man being pulled from his car and beaten savagely by Iraqi police and other men carrying Kalashnikovs, who were not in uniform. The thin man held his feeble arms over his head to thwart the blows from the rifle butts, finally slumping to the ground, blood running from his skull, while a melee of kicks assaulted his body. The police told us he was a looter. We saw two of them get in the man's car and drive it away.

Akeel lit a cigarette and took a long drag. He exhaled slowly through his nose while glaring at the armed men as they drove away. "You can see that right now, with the police and the new regime that we have right now, they are dealing with the people more harshly than during Saddam Hussein's regime. You can see these police kicking people in the street, and they are saying they are looters, but no one knows the truth. We have the pictures, our proof, that guy with the blood on his head, but what use are they? This is the same terrorist regime at work now as what we had with Saddam. These are the same people, except they are behaving more harshly now."

◆ ◆ ◆ ◆

I was still settling in and getting a feel for life in occupied Baghdad— the usual power cuts, traffic jams, and fuel shortages—when an event in Samarra, 77 miles north of Baghdad, caught my attention.

On November 30, 2003, U.S. military officials reported a raging firefight between U.S. forces and Iraqi resistance fighters.[3] Reports suggested a large, highly organized ambush on U.S. troops within the city by mujahedeen and fedayeen fighters. The fedayeen were a paramilitary organization loyal to the deposed dictator. U.S. forces responded fiercely by killing fifty-four Iraqis, according to General Peter Pace, who was at the time vice chairman of the Joint Chiefs of Staff. General Pace went on to issue a threat: "They attacked and they were killed, so I think it will be instructive to them."[4]

Shortly after mainstream media in the United States posted Pace's account, holes started appearing. The Western media posted the number of dead as fifty-four "insurgents" without questioning their sources. Meanwhile, local media in Baghdad as well as outlets like Al-Jazeera, were reporting very different figures from the hospital in Samarra—eight killed, including an Iranian pilgrim, and fifty Iraqis wounded.

During the days immediately following the battle, as people began digging deeper for facts, the U.S. military steadfastly held to its figures, while residents from Samarra became more certain of their unchanging version of what occurred that Sunday. It was a scenario I would see repeated time and time again in Iraq. (Later in the occupation, on December 2, 2005, the U.S. military admitted to planting pro-U.S. articles in Iraqi newspapers, something which came out during a briefing with Senator John Warner of Virginia, who was head of the Senate Armed Services Committee.[5])

The area of Samarra was inhabited as long ago as 5,500 B.C. by a prosperous people with a highly organized social structure. More recently, in the year 836 A.D., the capital of the Caliphate was moved from Baghdad to the new city of Samarra by Caliph al-Mu'tasim. During this time, the original pre-Islamic settlement in the area was replaced with the new city, and Samarra would remain the capital of the Muslim world until 892, when it was returned to Baghdad by al-Mu'tamid. The city boasts the Great Mosque of Samarra, with its famous spiral minaret, which was built in 847 and was one of the old world wonders. An important figure in the history of Samarra is Saladin al-Ayoubi, the 12th-century Islamic general and warrior who fought during the Crusades. Samarra is a key city in Salah ad Din province, which is named after Saladin, who was from the area around the city. He was renowned in both the Muslim and Christian worlds for his leadership and military prowess, as well as his chivalrous and merciful character. The Arabic name Samarra is a fusion of the words "*Surra Min Ba'a*," which means "joy to those that see it."

I went to Samarra four days after the bloodshed to interview people who witnessed the incident. I was accompanied by two foreign journalists I'd met at the Agadir, a French journalist named Erik, and Attila, a large Hungarian with a high-pitched voice. The three of us teamed up and hired an unemployed engineer named Omar, who volunteered to drive us and work as our interpreter. It was safe enough so that we were able not only to stay in the same unguarded hotel, but to travel around together in the same vehicle. The threat of being kidnapped had yet to even cross our minds.

When we arrived in Samarra, we found residents consistently telling the same story. U.S. soldiers were guarding a delivery of money to the bank in Samarra when two resistance fighters began shooting at them from afar. Jumpy U.S. soldiers responded by opening fire, killing eight civilians and wounding fifty others while riddling the city center with bullets. Erik had contacted a local sheikh who was willing to be interviewed, so we decided to head to his home after our first cursory interviews.

Before the invasion, Iraq had moved steadily toward a culture of urban social formations with tribal dimensions. But because of the policies of the U.S.-led occupation, which focused on tribes, and the lack of social support resulting from the destruction of the state, many people were pushed to reactivate their tribal links. Thus, tribes gained prominence as they once again began to govern the traditional society of interlinked families that share Iraq's common culture, and sheikhs were once again of paramount importance in the local communities. It became apparent while interviewing Sheikh Abbas Naqshabandi in his home that U.S. soldiers had been waging a campaign of fear and intimidation in Samarra for quite some time prior to this tragic day. After we removed our shoes and were shown in, the sheikh entered, a large man with a gray beard and flowing green robes. He was one of the spiritual and political leaders of Samarra, as well as the head of one of the city's seven largest families. He shared with us that he had been concerned for quite some time about tensions between the U.S. military and the people of Samarra.

The sheikh told us he had advised the military to remain outside the city. The military had taken his advice and left the city several weeks prior to the bank incident. However, collective punishment, such as water and electricity cuts, were soon imposed, along with cuts in food and medical aid shipments. Sheikh Naqshabandi told us that U.S. forces began raiding homes within the city during the night. The sheikh added, "They committed atrocities in these houses they were entering in the night. They were detaining so many innocent people—this is sure to come back at them like a boomerang."

His report was similar to a statement made by Ismail Mahmoud Mohammed, the U.S.-appointed police chief of Samarra, who, just after the incident at the bank, asked a reporter with the *Financial Times*, "Were the French happy under the Nazis? It is the same thing here." He went on to say that the occupation forces had long since gone too far in their provocations of the residents of Samarra.[6]

Sheikh Naqshabandi told me an old Arabic proverb about how the people of a city always know more about their home than anyone else. He said because Samarra consists primarily of seven large families, the people there knew everything that occurred. He continued, "So where are the other forty-six bodies the U.S. speaks of? So all these forty-six other bodies are flying? The Americans took them in their tanks? Where are they? Show them to me."

The sheikh asked, "So what are the people to do? It [the attack] is not an action, what you have seen is a reaction. If the occupation power continues to hurt and humiliate the people here, every man will become a bomb." (At the time the sheikh made that statement suicide bombings were rare in Iraq, yet in less than one year more than one was to occur every single day.)

Sheikh Naqshabandi, wanting to underscore his point, added, "There were no fedayeen among these killed. The people who were killed are normal citizens, poor people. There are only eight dead people here. So why are we seeing this incorrect number on the television? The people who attacked the Americans in retaliation are not an organized group, do not belong to any organization, not to Saddam's regime or to any new organization. They are only defending their freedom, their city, their families, and their holy places."

The military, backed by U.S. Central Command, maintained that Iraqi "insurgents" wearing fedayeen uniforms attacked two separate convoys that were carrying new Iraqi currency for deposit at Samarra banks. The fighters used mortars, grenades, and automatic weapons. The military claimed that more than one hundred "insurgents" were believed to have taken part in the "ambush," and by the end of the confrontation U.S. forces claimed to have killed fifty-four attackers.[7]

Within days of this incident, the *New York Times* published a story about the Pentagon awarding a contract to a private company (SAIC) to study how the Department of Defense (DOD) could more effectively use propaganda for "effective strategic influence" in the "war on terror." This propaganda campaign (which would eventually come back to haunt U.S. secretary of defense Donald Rumsfeld) was referred to by the DOD as a "tactical perception-management campaign." The title of the new document produced by SAIC was "Winning the War of Ideas."[8]

We stayed for lunch with Sheikh Naqshabandi at his insistence and then we went to the city center, where the violence had occurred, to interview witnesses.

In a short time, we arrived at the bustling city center in the shadow of the magnificent al-Askari Shrine, one of the most sacred Shi'ite shrines in the world. The shrine is believed to contain the remains of al-Hadi and Hassan al-Askari, the tenth and eleventh Shia Imams, and is located next to the shrine of the twelfth Imam, Muhammad al-Mahdi, better known as the "hidden Imam." (Many Shia believe al-Mahdi to be the ultimate savior of mankind, and the core of the Shi'ite religious worldview. While the stories of the first eleven Imams are historical, the story of the twelfth Imam is simultaneously mystical and miraculous. Muhammad al-Mahdi was born in 868 A.D. When the eleventh Imam, Hassan al-Askari, died in 874 A.D., the seven-year-old al-Mahdi declared himself to be the twelfth Imam and went into hiding. The Shi'ites believed that he hid himself in a cave below a mosque in Samarra; this cave is blocked by a gate that the Shi'ites call *Bab al-Ghayba*, or the "Gate of Occultation.")

We interviewed people who were willing to speak with us, and it did not take long for a crowd to gather. Talib, a thirty-one-year-old resident of the city, angrily told me, "At an American checkpoint I was dragged from my car and they put their shoes on my chest. Why do they use these actions? Even Saddam Hussein did not do that! They are not coming to liberate Iraq!"

An angry mob began to grow around us at the city center, so we quickly walked to the shrine, hoping to diffuse the situation. Inside the grand courtyard, it was quiet. A couple of women in their black *abayas* were praying near the shrine. We stood quietly under the sparkling gold dome of the mosque, gazing at the ornate walls of the shrine for some time before going back to the street for some tea at one of the countless stalls near the entrance.

A man who had been in his tea stall and witnessed most of the incident spoke for so many of the people I met in Samarra when he said, "The Americans say the people who fought them are al-Qaeda or fedayeen. We are all in this small city living here. Why have we not seen these foreign fighters and strangers in our city before or after this battle? Everyone here knows everyone, and none have seen these strangers. Why do they tell these lies?"

While Iraqis did not believe that foreign fighters were in the resistance, they were convinced foreigners were carrying out terrorist attacks. Meanwhile, the U.S. military estimated that a maximum of 6 percent of the attacks being carried out against them were by "foreign fighters." The words I heard most often from people in Baghdad when one of these attacks, slaughtering innocent Iraqis, was carried out was, "No Iraqi would do such things." A case in point was two car bombs that detonated in the Al-Dora area of Baghdad during 2004. Several Iraqis were killed, and more than ten wounded by the bombs that detonated just five minutes apart. When the injured and dead were taken from the scenes to Yarmouk Hospital, the hospital was car bombed. At least eight people died in the hospital car bombing.

There was another consistent fact reported to me by the sheikh, officials in the hospital of Samarra, and all the eyewitnesses I interviewed on the streets. They recounted that many civilians, when fired upon by U.S. soldiers, ran to get their guns in order to protect themselves. They said there were only two mujahedeen who lived near the city who had attacked the Americans.

We were surrounded by throngs of nervous and very angry Samarra residents when we revisited the scene of the attack after taking our tea. A rusty old taxi driving by slowed, and a man yelled at us out the window, "All the media is not telling the truth. They are lying, all of them! Don't talk to them. I did so many interviews with the media and nobody is telling my truth! Nobody [journalists] has reported what I told them. Why should you even talk to them? They are lying all the time, so don't talk to them."

I stood near a building riddled with bullets and spoke with people who crowded around, anxiously waiting to tell their story. Shell casings littered the ground near the wall of a home. A man in his early forties exclaimed with his hands in the air, "If the Americans can shoot every child walking in the street, it means the end of this planet." In just one week I had already become familiar with the hands-in-air gesture made by frustrated and shocked Iraqis. To me, it signified the despair that was spreading across the country, a plea to anything or anyone who would listen.

Another man showed me a parked car scarred with 112 bullets. He told of a U.S. soldier who had gone crazy and fired his weapon everywhere, even up at the sky at electrical wires running above the street. Two of the wires had been shot through and were crudely spliced back together. "They shot a lot of bullets to cut these wires," he said. "The American soldier was laughing and shooting the wires. Are they fedayeen wires? Were the wires attacking the Americans? He was laughing like a crazy man!"

Another man approached me with the two children of his brother, killed by U.S. gunfire, by his side. "This little boy and girl, their father was shot by the Americans. Who will take care of this family? Who will watch over these children? Who will feed them now? Who? Why did they kill my brother? What is the reason? Nobody told me. He was a truck driver. What is his crime? Why did they shoot him? They shot him with 150 bullets! Did they kill him just because they wanted to shoot a man? That's it? This is the reason? Why didn't anyone talk to me and tell me why they have killed my brother? Is killing people a normal thing now, happening every day? This is our future? This is the future that the United States promised Iraq?"

Pointing to a building, then over toward a road, another man wanted me to know there were U.S. soldiers who had been killed, which was not reported by the media. "There is blood on top of that building, and there were only American soldiers up there. And over here on this road, everybody saw three dead U.S. soldiers on the ground, burning and bleeding."

Near the hospital of Samarra, about a five-minute drive from the city center, there was a small mosque with fresh cement covering an area near a window. In the nearby hospital parking area sat two incinerated cars. A man on crutches told the story of what had happened here, a good distance from the battle downtown. "One man in the mosque was shot and killed by the Americans from a tank," he said, pointing with one of his crutches to a hole in the wall of the mosque where a shell from the tank had struck. "Nobody knows why they burned all these cars, and why they were shooting here. American troops used small guns from a tank to shoot the mosque because they hate Islam. There is no other reason. This happened at five o'clock, and the battle had ended at three o'clock."

Another man standing in the small crowd exclaimed angrily, "There was no battle here, only a tank that came and destroyed hospital cars and shot the mosque. What is the reason for this?"

It was outrage, which I was already seeing as common among Iraqis outside of the Green Zone, where the supposedly "secure" U.S. headquarters in Iraq is located in the middle of Baghdad. Thus, most Iraqis lived in what was referred to by the U.S. military as the "Red Zone," designated "unsafe" areas.

The central portion of Samarra had remained without electricity and water since the incident took place several days earlier. All the men I spoke to believed they were being subjected to deliberate collective punishment from the U.S. military.

Was it possible for every resident of Samarra to be telling the same uniform lie, with all the same details? Or was it possible that the U.S. military, desperate for some form of good news to broadcast to the world and its troops about the occupation of Iraq, used an attack on its forces in Samarra as part of a "tactical perception-management campaign"?

As the crowd continued to grow in size and emotion, we decided it was time to jump in the car and head back to Baghdad. The sun was beginning to set, and soon it would be too risky to be out on the open highways.

Driving slowly out of the city, Omar lit a cigarette. He said to himself, "It's time for me to take my wife out of this country. This place is falling apart. This, what we have seen just now, can only go one direction because we know the Americans don't plan to leave. The fuse of Iraq is burning quickly now." I was reminded of the lightning I had seen in the sky on my way to Iraq.

Most of the drive to Baghdad found us in silence. A few Bradleys rumbled past us on the dark street as Omar pulled up to the Agadir. After paying him for the day's work, we thanked him and walked up the steps into our hotel. (That was the last time I would ever see Omar.)

Iraqi woman whose two sons were killed by U.S. soldiers during a home raid in village near Ramadi. The family claimed the U.S. military returned the day after the killings and apologized for raiding her home due to "bad information." December 2003.

CHAPTER 2

PEERING INTO AN ABYSS

There were several independent foreign journalists staying at the Agadir Hotel. Each morning we would gather on the second floor of the hotel for breakfast, to talk and make plans for the day.

I was continuing to send emails to friends back in Alaska about what I was seeing. Before long, these were to evolve into a Web log of the occupation. Each evening in my bare room of two single beds, a small wooden table, and a broken refrigerator, I would sit and write about the day's events I'd witnessed, attach a few digital photographs, and email them out to a list of around 130 friends. It seemed a small thing compared to the exposure that would have been possible had I been using established news outlets.

While the security situation was unstable and the frequency of attacks on occupation forces was slowly increasing, kidnapping had yet to appear during the occupation. The group of us at the Agadir were able to share drivers, interpreters, and cars, as well as walk down the streets during the day and even into the early night. On my braver days, I would even take taxis around on my own.

Cracking gunfire echoed periodically across Baghdad, but, typically, it was limited to nighttime. I had only been in Baghdad two weeks, but it was clearly apparent that most Iraqis I'd spoken with were ready for the occupiers to leave their country, despite the occupation being less than eight months old. People were happy to have Saddam Hussein gone, but the slow yet steady decline in the infrastructure and ongoing chaos was already wearing on people's patience.

The occupation authorities in the Coalition Provisional Authority (CPA), led by L. Paul Bremer III, were growing concerned about civil unrest. Bremer, the highest-ranking U.S. civilian in Iraq, was answerable only to Secretary of Defense Donald Rumsfeld. He was in charge of Iraq's entire civil administration, a responsibility that would come back to haunt him. He had served as an assistant to Henry Kissinger in the mid-1970s, had been active in the U.S. Foreign Service during the Reagan administration, then went on to become the managing director at Kissinger Associates Inc., a worldwide consulting firm founded by Henry Kissinger. Prior to his appointment at the CPA, Bremer was chairman and CEO of Marsh Crisis Consulting, a risk and insurance services firm.

Some colleagues and I were having breakfast on December 5, 2003, when several Humvees and Bradley fighting vehicles rumbled down the street below. They pulled over and briskly off-loaded roughly a dozen soldiers, along with a couple of plainclothes covert-ops types with bomb-sniffing dogs. I watched them sweep the street for explosives. It was common knowledge in Baghdad that Iraqi resistance groups planted roadside bombs in piles of rubbish, animal carcasses, empty kerosene cans, and virtually any other clutter along the street. Medians were also a favorite spot. I'd learned in no time to watch carefully where I was walking in the capital city.

One group of soldiers slowly continued down the street toward the nearby National Theater, where black flame marks streamed up toward the sky out its windows, broken from when the building was looted and burned after the fall of Baghdad. Most of them were young guys. They didn't even look like they needed to shave. One soldier in particular caught my eye as he was walking down the street. He was looking wildly in all directions, his helmet tilted off to the side from constantly swiveling and jerking his head. He peered up at us and then quickly swung around toward the street, his M-16 rifle pointing at the traffic creeping down the chaotic avenue. The chinstrap of his tan helmet was loose, and when he twitched his left shoulder his head appeared to jerk toward the left. This seemingly uncontrollable nervous ticking continued incessantly as he shuffled down the street, often walking backward, holding his gun while turning around quickly to look over his shoulder.

Hamoudi, who worked full time as Attila's interpreter and driver, watched the soldier with me from the open balcony. He leaned over to me and said, "Look at that poor bastard. It is clear to anyone with eyes that he has mental problems from being here doing this shit job." We both watched him and the other soldiers fade into the distance of the wide but cluttered street.

Following this sweep, a small group of people started to assemble down the avenue in the other direction, in nearby Firdos Square, where the infamous stage-managed toppling of one of Saddam Hussein's statues had occurred on April 9, 2003. Attila, the large war-weary Hungarian journalist I'd recently traveled with to Samarra, Hamoudi, a few of our colleagues, and I decided to go see what the demonstration was about. Demonstrations had been banned by the occupation authorities unless they had a permit from the CPA. This had effectively put an end to all anti-occupation marches, so we knew this at least had to be an interesting charade.

Roughly five hundred people, who conveniently lined up on the street in front of the journalist-filled Palestine Hotel, were preparing to march the few blocks toward Firdos Square. Out in front was a line of young children, roughly ten years of age, carrying small bouquets of flowers. Following them were two drummers and a very bad trumpet player who blew the same terrible song over and over as the procession made its way down the street. Many in the crowd carried banners that read, "Thank You CPA for Freeing Iraq," and others of similar content, while armed guards buffered the small group from the public. As they marched past concrete blast barriers that had "Troops Out Now" and "America go home!" spray painted in red in English on them, the tiny procession wasn't too convincing to the few onlookers who were present. (This was the first of many stage-managed "demonstrations" I was to witness in occupied Iraq.)

Walking back to our hotel, we passed a small, decrepit petrol station with two lines of cars stretching as far as we could see, waiting for gas. There was a separate line for black marketers, who were lined up with their jerry cans and plastic jugs awaiting their chance. The black market was burgeoning. Those who could afford the extra cost were less willing to wait in the ever-lengthening lines as the gas crisis worsened. The black marketers took their plastic jugs to the petrol stations, filled them, walked down the street a few meters and used siphons and plastic funnels to pour gas into the empty tanks of those able to pay a little extra. Everyone from small children to elderly men on crutches were doing this. Meanwhile short-tempered Iraqis were jamming their cars toward the pumps, some having slept overnight in their cars in order to keep their place in line.

"And the Americans try to tell us this war was not about our oil," yelled a man while pushing his car. He agreed to talk with us as long as we stayed out of his way. "Even under that bastard Saddam we never had benzene shortages!" I'd seen these lines all over Baghdad. Gas lines were so thick in some areas that traffic would often get choked down to a single lane, further aggravating the already impossible chaos of Baghdad's auto congestion.

Some of the men we spoke with in the fuel line were aware of the fact that Halliburton subsidiary KBR had just been caught by the Pentagon for grossly overcharging them by importing gasoline into Iraq from Kuwait at $2.65 per gallon. Iraqi concerns were able to do the job for just under one dollar per gallon. Halliburton, which had Dick Cheney as its chairman and CEO from 1995 to 2000 before he relinquished his position in order to become vice president of the United States, was unabashedly looting the Pentagon. By this time, Cheney's old company, which he still had financial ties with, had obtained billions of dollars of contracts in Iraq. (No one knows exactly how much money has been contracted in total, but as of the time of this writing, Halliburton's overall contracts for LOGCAP and oil infrastructure rebuilding have totaled approximately $20 billion in Iraq. Total expenditures on U.S. corporations operating in Iraq on reconstruction and other services is about $50 billion. LOGCAP is a Logistics Civil Augmentation Program with the U.S. Army Corps of Engineers, which is Halliburton's largest government contract. Under this contract, Halliburton is responsible for providing supplies and services to the military on a global basis. Services include construction of military housing for troops, transporting food and supplies to bases, and serving food.)

It's worth noting that it was Dick Cheney, as defense secretary in 1992, who spearheaded the movement to privatize most of the military's civil logistics activities. Under Cheney's direction, $9 million was paid by the Pentagon to KBR to conduct a study to determine whether private companies like KBR should handle all the military's civil logistics. KBR's classified study conveniently concluded that greater privatization of logistics was in the government's best interest. Shortly thereafter, on August 3, 1992, Secretary Cheney awarded the first comprehensive LOGCAP contract to KBR. The *Washington Post* reported, "The Pentagon chose [KBR] to carry out the study and subsequently selected the company to implement its own plan."[1] Three years later Cheney became CEO of Halliburton.

The manager at this particular petrol station told me that one month earlier he used to receive nine tankers of fuel per day. At present, he was receiving one, and the fuel price at the pump had risen three times in recent weeks. Petrol had skyrocketed to 1,250 ID per liter just three weeks earlier; in some places, black market petrol averaged less than one-twelfth of that. Now, one U.S. dollar bought 1,900 Iraqi dinars (ID). The tattered currency notes still bore the bust of the former dictator.

The gasoline crisis was driving up the cost of everything. A man named Yassir in the gas line told me, "Before the invasion we used to pay two thousand per kilo for sheep, but now it is more than seven thousand ID. How can we afford to live like this when we see no signs of the jobs they promised us?" The thirty-three-year-old unemployed mechanical engineer was hoping to drive his car as a taxi to generate some income. "The cost of our cooking fuel is up by fifteen times what it was before the invasion."

I wondered to myself what would happen in the United States if a fuel crisis struck and drove the cost of food, fuel, and basic living necessities through the roof? How would the normally placid people of Anchorage, my town in Alaska, react if the price of gas went from its $1.70 to $20.40 per gallon in a few weeks' time? What would we witness on the streets?

◆ ◆ ◆ ◆

That evening as I sat in my room writing about the day, the electricity was cut yet again. After every other cut, the hotel staff took a while to get the generators going. I sat in the dark of my room, which was dimly illuminated by the screen of my laptop. Even in the short time I'd been in Baghdad, there had been a decline in the electricity supply.

Someone knocked gently on my door in the darkness. Having become justifiably paranoid, I asked who it was before opening the door to welcome Hamoudi. The usually cheerful interpreter would appear at the hotel in the morning, at times looking very depressed. He had started driving his car as a taxi to provide for his wife and several relatives prior to and during the invasion. From the time we met, he and I talked often.

This evening, again, he seemed to be down. He told me he had this bad feeling about where his country was headed. "Even Saddam, despite the sanctions, got our electricity back up in three months after they bombed us in 1991," he said despondently, "The Americans are sending the message that they don't care about the Iraqi people, and we are starting to get this message. They have destroyed our country and have no intention of putting it back together, Daher." I was beginning to like the way Iraqis pronounced my name in Arabic, with a softer "D" and an "h," breaking it into two syllables, unlike the English pronunciation in a flat, single syllable.

"People are frustrated, very tired, and many are quite hopeless experiencing this now after going through the sanctions," he explained. "The largest tragedy of the invasion and occupation is the devastation of the people of Iraq. We were hoping for relief, but so far it has only been more suffering."

It was nearing 9:00 p.m., the time most people commenced their self-imposed curfew. After 9:00, the streets were ruled by criminal gangs and the resistance. "I must go home to my wife," he said. We stood and I gave him a hug and walked him to the door.

"See you tomorrow morning, Hamoudi," I said to him as he walked down the hall. From the darkness I heard him reply, "*Insh'Allah* (God willing), Daher, *Insh'Allah*." I was to grow very, very used to *Insh'Allah*. An integral part of common parlance for Arabs and Muslims everywhere, the term *Insh'Allah* in occupied Iraq had come to embody the mix of fear, hope, uncertainty, insecurity, and despair that Iraqis experienced on a daily basis under the U.S. occupation.

The next day, Hamoudi, Attila, Akeel, and I went to visit a farmhouse in Ramadi, where we were told atrocities had been carried out by U.S. forces. A group of men and small children converged on us as we stood looking at the scene of destruction. They were quiet until we started asking them questions. I was silently led back up to the road where a small pile of bullet casings from a .50-caliber machine gun were pointed out to me.

The story began to piece itself together as we walked through the area. On November 23, just after the sun had set and it was time to break the daily fast during Ramadan, a family had laid out their evening meal and were preparing to sit down to share it.[2] No sooner did they sit down than U.S. troops descended upon them, crashing in through the doors on either side of the house, and ordering the inhabitants to exit immediately.

The men of the family were a forty-five-year-old civil rights lawyer of the village and father of six, Ibrahim Ahmed Oday, his thirty-five-year-old brother, Sabah Ahmed Oday, and their brother-in-law Hammed Nawf Half, a twenty-eight-year-old father of two small children. Their hands were tied and they were forced to lie face down in the mud, as a soldier stood over them, guarding them at gunpoint. All the women and children were made to stand off to the side, within view of the men.

After being shown the utter destruction of this farmhouse, we entered the living room on our way out. Among the debris on the ground were shattered white plates with uneaten food on them.

Khalil Ahmed, the thirty-year-old brother of two of the victims and cousin of a third, wept as he pointed to the food. "You can see the food in this room. They couldn't break their fast. They died hungry." According to Khalil, once the family had been ordered out of the house, U.S. troops stormed the house through each of the two doors, and opened fire on one another in panic and confusion from across the empty home. Shortly thereafter, one of the soldiers walked out the front door, blood covering his uniform. When the soldier guarding the men saw this, he immediately executed the men by shooting them all in the back.

We could see the bloodstains in the dirt where this had occurred. After the family had been removed, the home had been heavily damaged by Humvees with machine guns, Bradley fighting vehicles, many foot soldiers, and helicopters. The outer walls looked like Swiss cheese. Still in a state of shock, Khalil calmly continued, "These men were executed, rather than being treated as prisoners of war. So the U.S. military are criminals for killing them this way."

We heard from eyewitnesses that they had seen two of the soldiers arguing over whether or not to kill the rest of the family—the children and the women. One of them refused to do this, or the carnage would have been even greater.

"I want the whole world to hear of this crime. God does not accept this. They had already tied their hands and had them on the ground. They could have taken them and questioned them and found out the truth for themselves. But instead they just killed them." Khalil continued with conviction. "The Americans are the ones who create the terrorists. They say they will kill all the terrorists in the world, but they are actually creating more terrorists."

The mother and sister of two of the men who had been killed were both injured. Samah Khalil, the seven-year-old daughter of Ibrahim, had gauze-covered shrapnel wounds on her forehead. She told me her father was looking straight in her eyes as they executed him.

The day after the massacre, some GIs had returned to apologize to the family. They had come to tell the remaining members of the family that they had been given wrong information and attacked the wrong home. It was a microcosm of the entire U.S.-led war on Iraq, even with a similar song and dance about faulty intelligence leading to the attack. Here, the "intelligence" apparently had been convincing enough to the soldiers for them to execute three men, destroy their home, and terrorize their family. As with the invasion of the country, far more effort was spent obtaining and acting on the intelligence needed to wage an aggressive, destructive attack than in making amends for harm done.

The soldiers presented the grieving family with a cake. So much for U.S. soldiers "winning hearts and minds" of Iraqis.

The family was also given a form to fill out, if they so chose, to claim damages for property and loss of life. The form was from the 82nd Airborne Division, al-Ramadi, to be returned to Robert B. Hamilton, foreign claims commissioner. Months later, after much negotiating and help from outside groups, the family was compensated for their dead—at less than five hundred dollars per body.

Just before we left, a lawyer appeared with a stack of at least fifteen folders, each containing copies of submitted claim forms. "After they have done all these horrible things—killing all these people, destroying all their property, they come the next day and say, 'We are sorry.' What will the word 'sorry' do for us?"

(Several months later, a colleague of mine visited a U.S. Army forward operating base and spoke with a lieutenant colonel about the incident. According to the military, a tip led the army to conduct a home raid where several rocket-propelled grenades (RPGs) were found. During the raid, a grenade was thrown at the soldiers, who then opened fire. The lieutenant colonel claimed that he had footage of the cache of weapons found, though he never produced that footage. "No formal report was made on the incident," he explained.)

Back in Baghdad, we were served another pro-occupation demonstration staged by the occupation forces. Our street was swept yet again for bombs, and shortly after we saw it fill up with throngs of Iraqi police. Every intersection was blocked off as police with automatic weapons lined the street.

Some Iraqi police entered our hotel and told Baha, the front desk manager, they would protect the hotel and guests if the staff was willing to pay. Baha leaned over and whispered to me in English, "This is bullshit, just like Saddam. The bribes haven't stopped at all." The cops left and Baha produced a Kalashnikov and handed it over the desk to the lobby clerk. I'd gotten to know Baha a little better than the other clerks. A kind Christian man, he was leaving to get his son out of a nearby school and bring him home to be on the safer side. He glanced at me on the way out and said, "This is dangerous, these things."

A large group of people with all kinds of colorful banners marched by, waving flags, while Apache helicopters circled overhead. This was the most heavily guarded and controlled demonstration I'd witnessed thus far. Our little clique of journalists used handheld radios to communicate with each other. On one of these we could hear U.S. soldiers directing the crowds.

As the procession progressed, we saw several fundamentalist Islamic groups walk past, loudly calling for an Islamic-ruled Iraq. Not only were they loud, they were also the largest among the marching groups. An Islamic Iraq similar to Iran was not the goal of forces driving the Bush administration to invade the country in 2003, but clearly political, social, and religious tides were rapidly taking Iraq in that direction.

Jo Wilding, a British activist staying at the Agadir, had been in Iraq since before the invasion. She was attempting to chronicle the effects of the invasion and the subsequent occupation on the Iraqi people. An upbeat, passionate person, she often used a great sarcasm and biting sense of humor to drive her points home. Since she had visited Iraq during the horrific sanctions, I'd already learned much from her about the conditions, history, and people of Iraq in the few times I had talked with her.

A young American freelance journalist, David Enders, was also staying at our hotel. An easygoing and soft-spoken fellow, he was always busy with his stories. He and Jo had hired a retired Iraqi Army captain, Harb al-Mukhtar, as an interpreter and driver to take them to Ramadi on December 11, the morning of my birthday. While Dave was interested in interviewing a U.S. commander in Ramadi for a story, Jo wanted more information on the farmhouse attack, as did I, and she invited me along for a follow-up visit.

I had met Harb a few days before this second trip to Ramadi. At that time, he had been finishing up his work with a depleted uranium (DU) study team from Japan. He'd taken them all over southern Iraq with their Geiger counters to measure what he said were extremely high levels of radiation in particular locations. DU munitions are used during combat because they are extremely effective. Made of radioactive heavy metals that can effortlessly cut through armor, they leave a radioactive dust upon impact that filters through the air, water, and ground, contaminating everything it touches.

Uranium is a heavy metal and a radioactive poison whose toxicity is not debatable, even according to the director of the U.S. Army Environmental Policy Institute, who stated in a report mandated by Congress, "No available technology can significantly change the inherent chemical and radiological toxicity of DU. These are intrinsic properties of uranium."[3] In fact, even the primary U.S. Army training manual stated, "NOTE: (Depleted Uranium) Contamination will make food and water unsafe for consumption."[4] Nevertheless, hundreds of tons of DU munitions were used in the prior Gulf War, and the Pentagon admitted to using much more during this war. The effects on the Iraqi people had already been shown to be devastating.

In his mid-fifties, his short brown hair beginning to gray, Harb seemed to always have a cigarette and drank more Iraqi tea than I thought humanly possible. I immediately warmed up to his tendency toward laughter yet consistent emotional honesty. He was eager to help.

The information I'd gleaned during my first visit to Ramadi was basically that Ibrahim Oday, his brother, and his cousin had been brutally executed by soldiers during a raid on their home. All three had been shot in the back of the head, execution style, at point-blank range, in the presence of their families. I couldn't understand why the death certificate issued by the coroner stated that the men had been killed by "shrapnel." Nor could I find any explanation for the Iraqi doctor who had performed the autopsy failing to sign the death certificate.

We loaded into Harb's small white sedan in front of the Agadir. The Baghdad traffic, already rendered impossible by the gas queues clogging the streets, was worsened that day by the closing of two main bridges over the Tigris by the U.S. military. But finally we made our way onto the highway west to Ramadi. On the way, Harb stopped on the highway for directions to the farmhouse, and a car he waved down stopped to help. When they heard where we were headed, they told us to follow and took us most of the way to the destroyed home. Harb proudly leaned over toward the middle of the car to say, "This is the Iraqi! I am so pleased that you get to see the true spirit of the Iraqi people, such as this man!" He beamed with pride as he drove to a police checkpoint on the outskirts of Ramadi, sixty miles west of Baghdad.

After asking further directions, we had an Iraqi policeman, Hussein, hop in to take us the rest of the way. He refused to tell us his real name, and said he was a friend of the family we were going to visit. On the way, he told us how the Americans were trying to use Iraqi police to conduct raids on homes, but the neighbors wouldn't give them any information, even if the families being raided were truly part of the resistance. One of Hussein's neighbors had been arrested by U.S. soldiers, beaten, and tortured. He told us, "None of us trust them," and said that he had no interest in helping the occupying powers.

As Hussein talked, we passed the usual assortment of Humvees, armored personnel carriers, and a few helicopters buzzing above the palm trees. We passed the lush, verdant farms bordering the blue waters of the Euphrates River and the desert of rural Iraq before arriving at the wrecked home.

The old stone farmhouse had huge holes blasted through the walls. Scorch marks from flames stained the yellow paint above each window black, pieces of wall lay crumbled on the ground from heavy weapons fire, and pockmarks left by bullets studded every wall of the house. A small white car parked outside, similar to Harb's, was riddled with bullet holes. An empty black shoe sat on the ground outside the driver's door.

We talked at length again with Ibrahim's brother and his cousin, and were told that the doctor had written the death certificate under duress while soldiers stood over him.

We surveyed the devastated home. Blood in the bathroom was pointed out to us as that of an American soldier's. According to the family, the soldiers were the only ones inside the house at the time of the shootings. I had heard from witnesses on my first visit that two groups of soldiers entering from either side of the house had shot at each other in panic. It seemed they had killed some of their own. At the same time, the conflicting reports from the military and the family caused me to doubt both accounts. Could there have been so much confusion the soldiers didn't realize they were fighting each other? What we did know for sure was that the three men were dead and the family was shattered, and the U.S. military would never provide us with any information to refute the family's account.

We talked some more with the family members, and met Ibrahim's only son, a boy of nine, who kept watching us with stern eyes. Many children crowded around as we went about collecting more information, their sad, wary eyes following us. Inside a nearby home a child wept, its whimpering carried by the wind through the date palms and out into the vegetable fields.

We learned the names of the lawyer representing the family and the two doctors respectively involved in the autopsy and the manufactured death certificate, and set off to find them. Before we got far, however, Hussein, the policeman who was still with us, insisted on buying us sodas and some sweets at a small roadside stand, as is customary in Iraq.

We failed to track down the first doctor. He was nowhere to be found at the General Hospital, where they suggested we go to his nearby home. A man answered the front gate to tell us the doctor was not home. I'd visited the place during my last trip and had met with the same result. This man wouldn't open the door all the way. He let us know that the doctor would be at the hospital later, obviously another deflection. At one point, when Hussein stepped out of the car, Harb leaned over to me and whispered, "This policeman is a spy for the Americans. Be careful what you say. He probably speaks English, but won't show it."

We decided to leave the house when we figured that the doctor wasn't interested in talking to the press, either because he had been paid or because he had been threatened by the occupation forces, both common practices in Iraq at this point in the occupation. We shook off our police "friend" and proceeded to one of the U.S. bases where Dave had an appointment.

On the way I asked Harb, "Why do you say he is a spy?"

"Because he raved about the Americans, and I could tell he was afraid. Nobody here, especially in this area, is happy with them. But he has his job to keep and he needs his money." Already I could sense that nobody trusted any Iraqi working for the Americans in any capacity, way, or manner. Occupation is a dangerous business. Multiple invisible lines dividing the people in Iraq widened daily. The seeds of internal violence that were being sown did not take long to germinate.

We came to the wrong gate of the base. Four soldiers pointed their guns at us as we walked toward them. After shouting that two of us were American, they lowered their M-16s, fingers still on the triggers. Their nervousness was palpable. One of them gave us directions to the front gate, repeating, "Stay to the left of the road near the entrance. If you go to the right, you'll be shot."

I marveled at how scared they were, despite being the ones with the biggest guns.

We made our way to the front gate. This U.S. base in Ramadi is, like so many of the others in Iraq, within the compound of a former palace of Saddam Hussein.

Harb parked about two hundred feet away from the gate and let us out. As we approached the gate, the soldiers standing there started waving to us to get back. We brandished our passports, trying to indicate to them that we have an appointment with the commander. When one of the soldiers raised his gun to his shoulder to sight us, we hastily pocketed our passports and walked away. As we reached the car, three Humvees sped past us and blocked off the road between us and the base. Several soldiers jumped out and one of them yelled, "Get the fuck out of here, the base is on lockdown!" They ordered us to get in our car and wait at a distance of more than three hundred feet. There was a possibility the base might open up soon.

There wasn't much choice so we followed their instructions. After a few minutes of waiting in the car, we felt the sickening thump of a large explosion from a direction that seemed like the other side of Ramadi. My immediate thought was that this had to be a suicide car bomb, though I had no idea yet what one sounded like. Harb began to drive away, saying, "I don't think we'll be visiting the base today." Two medical choppers rumbled low over our heads as we drove back into Ramadi.

We found out later, in fact, that a suicide bomber had breached the security of another U.S. base in the city before detonating, killing one soldier and injuring fourteen others. This was the third suicide bomb attack on a U.S. base in Iraq that week. It had occurred inside "Champion Main," a sprawling compound that housed "Task Force All American," another base located inside one of Saddam Hussein's former palaces.

We drove into Ramadi hoping to find the other doctor, who had a clinic in the city. For the last many days, there had been neither electricity nor running water. This was part of the collective punishment that the town was being subjected to as penalty for the number of anti-American attacks on patrols and military camps. I was amazed at the shortsightedness of these tactics employed by the occupation forces. How would Iraqis cope with neither water nor electricity? What would the consequences be for these people, as well as for any U.S. patrols that rolled through the city from then on?

The trip to the second doctor's clinic proved equally futile. We were told by his colleague that he had gone to Jordan for an indefinite period.

Not ones to give up easily, we decided to make another attempt at an interview with the base commander for Dave. But our naive optimism took flight even as we slowed near one of the gates to ask the soldiers if the base had opened. His bark of a response, "Don't stop" and the gun pointed at the car were enough to dissuade us from any further inquiry.

We decided to head back to Baghdad, but Harb was determined to salvage some mileage out of the trip and, in a bid to get us some information, pulled off the road in a few places for quick interviews with passersby.

From a crowded sidewalk in the afternoon sun, a store owner yelled in our direction, his hands in the air, "Is this the freedom? We have no human rights now! No respect! We are being attacked and killed by the Americans!" When they noticed our notepads, a crowd gathered around us in no time, their furious comments and questions flying from all directions. "They are cutting our water and electricity because they hate us! We can't live like this. Do they think this is helping them? Helping their cause?"

We stopped a few blocks down the street for some black market gas because the lines at the petrol stations were several miles long.

One of the men filling our tank with his plastic jug of fuel said, "Do you think this is the resistance you are seeing? This is not the resistance. The resistance is coming. You wait!" (In less than five months, fighting in nearby Fallujah would erupt with an intensity never before seen in the occupation.)

Immediately after the capture of Saddam Hussein, U.S. forces raided the al-Shahid Adnan Kherala Secondary School for Boys and detained sixteen schoolchildren for having a "pro-Saddam Hussein demonstration." December 2003.

CHAPTER 3

GROWING FURY AND UNREST

I used to have intermittent conversations with Baha Mikhail each time I passed through the hotel lobby. He was one of my windows into the way average Iraqis were struggling to survive amid the ruins of their former lives.

"It has become impossible now, Daher," he told me, "I have to choose between coming to my job, which I must have, or going and waiting in line for eight hours in the morning to get gas. And of course I cannot afford to buy it on the black market. And if I fail to appear at my job one day, our manager deducts four days' wages instead of one, as he should. This is our new democracy, and there is nothing to stop him from treating us this way because he knows there are no other jobs for us."

In a futile bid to control the chaos and line-cutting, the U.S. military tried to guard the petrol stations. Another more effective but wasteful method that they used was to cut open the jugs in which the black marketers stored the fuel they wanted to sell.

There was a gas station down the road from my hotel. I saw some Humvees pull up near a group of black marketers selling fuel. The men held their hands in the air as the soldiers walked away with their fuel-filled plastic jugs and put them inside cars sitting in a traffic jam. Some of the jugs were simply sliced open with knives as the hapless black marketer watched forlornly. These attempts to force or restore order took away a desperate source of livelihood from very needy Iraqis reeling under the impact of unemployment more severe than during the sanctions, eliminating the only alternative access to fuel for those who could ill afford to wait in the enormous queues. Whatever the goal, these tactics only angered Iraqis, limiting mobility and decreasing Iraqis' security.

◆ ◆ ◆ ◆

The evening of December 12, 2003, I accompanied Baha to his shoe store. What was once a thriving shoe company with two large factories and a chain of twenty stores in Baghdad had been reduced to one outlet. This last shoe store was all that remained of the family business. After the invasion and fall of Baghdad, the store had been looted. He wanted me to use photographic evidence and tell his story to people back home. The Coalition Provisional Authority had failed to offer the due compensation. This had forced Baha to seek employment as a day clerk at the hotel for wages that were not enough to support his family.

Baha's was but one example of the way the occupation had affected the vast majority of Iraqis who used to own small businesses. We pushed our luck driving into the empty gloominess of Old Baghdad, where the shell of the store remained. Looted buildings stood vacant, the outer walls above most windows seared black from flames set during the orgy of destruction that engulfed Baghdad during its "liberation" the previous spring. The man that Baha was selling the store to was waiting when we arrived. Glumly, Baha handed him the store key in exchange for a small amount of cash. The store had become a liability and he could not afford the rent anymore. I looked on as he collected some papers in boxes and a few shoes the looters had not been interested in, along with the mandatory picture of Saddam Hussein that had been hanging on the wall. He did not want to have to come back there, he said.

There was very little evening light left when Baha drove me to the factories that the family still owned, though only notionally. They had been totally vandalized and laid to waste. There was no money to restore them and no possibility of selling them because there was no administration to authorize an appraisal and evaluation or to carry out the requisite paperwork.

After a desultory walk inside one of the dusty buildings, we were on our way back to the hotel in the car when an acquaintance of Baha's waved us over. A fortnight back, the man's father had left for Basra to fetch his retirement money but he had not returned. The family had contacted the people who he was supposed to have met in Basra and found that he had never turned up. Baha commiserated with his friend. His old car was filled with our silence as we drove into the ruddy setting sun en route to the Agadir.

At 8:30 p.m. on December 13, members of the Kurdish Patriotic Front, popularly known as the Patriotic Union of Kurdistan (PUK), led American soldiers to Saddam Hussein's hideout at a farm compound in the village of Adwar, ten miles from his hometown of Tikrit. The disoriented dictator was pulled out of the infamous "spider hole" without a single shot being fired. Kurdish leader Jalal Talabani was the first to break the news, the same night, to the Islamic Republic News Agency of Iran. The next morning there were open celebrations and revelry in the largely Kurdish northern region of Iraq. Most of us in Iraq came to know of the course of events several hours before the U.S. leaders in Baghdad formally announced that Saddam Hussein had been taken into custody.

The media, too, was ahead of the administration in broadcasting the news that it was a special intelligence unit of the PUK led by Kosrat Rasul that had led the U.S. troops of the 4th Infantry Division to the deposed dictator. PUK spokesman Nazim Dabag had apprised Reuters on the night of the capture itself. The next morning, a Kurdish wire service announced the news, followed in quick succession by the *Sunday Herald* in Scotland, Agence France-Presse, Al-Jazeera, the *Sydney Morning Herald*, and the Australian Broadcasting Corporation News online.[1]

On December 20, the British *Sunday Express* quoted an unnamed intelligence officer in the Middle East as saying, "Saddam was not captured as a result of any American or British intelligence. We knew that someone would eventually take their revenge, it was just a matter of time."[2] It was a member of the al-Jabur tribe who betrayed Saddam, because his daughter had been raped by the dictator's son Uday. The man disclosed Saddam Hussein's location to the PUK, a group that had fully cooperated and even fought alongside the United States through the invasion and ongoing occupation. The PUK then handed over the drugged dictator to the U.S. forces. (Nevertheless, it would prove a bargain like so many others—where the Americans would fail to hold up their end.)

Predictably, the American administration chose not to respond, either to the aforementioned PUK statements or to the various press accounts of the lead-up to the arrest of Saddam Hussein.

On the afternoon of December 14, we were glued to the television set that sat in the lobby of the Agadir, watching images of Saddam Hussein having his hair checked for lice by a U.S. soldier, then his throat checked with a wooden tongue depressor. We looked on as the images were run over and over, even though it is a violation of the Geneva Conventions that they were shown publicly. The hypocrisy was underscored by the fact that the United States had invoked this very clause of the Geneva Conventions when U.S. troops were captured by Iraqis during the invasion.

The immediate reaction of the Iraqis around me, as we watched the television, was a mixture of relief, joy, shock, and a nagging anxiety that the formerly all-powerful dictator might still manage to return to power. After having lived under his U.S.-backed brutal rule for decades, many Iraqis still remained hesitant to openly express their happiness at Hussein's detention.

Not long after this, at the 5:00 follies, otherwise known as the daily press conference in the Green Zone, a jubilant Paul Bremer announced, "Ladies and gentlemen, we got him," to a loud round of applause from Western journalists.[3] The media were already beginning to fall in line with the American-led propaganda and declaring that the arrest was going to be a huge morale booster for the U.S.-led coalition, that attacks on U.S. forces were sure to decline, and making other similarly baseless comments.

In reality, compared to recent months, attacks on U.S. forces would only drop marginally in the coming months, and by April 2004 would increase by over 100 percent and continue to escalate.[4] Rather than acknowledging that the capture of Saddam Hussein had caused an acute escalation in the ongoing violence, once again the corporate American media capitulated to the U.S. military and chose only to parrot the "success" of the "capture."

In my report to electroniciraq.net that day, I stated that it was the PUK that had led the Americans to Saddam Hussein, and compared the media blitz to the much-hyped pulling down of Saddam Hussein's statue earlier in the occupation. Both were publicity stunts temporarily useful to politicians in Britain and in the United States.

A few celebratory demonstrations occurred across the capital city, but not everyone was pleased with the news of the dictator's capture. Once again the story on CNN, ABC, NBC, CBS, and even the BBC had little in common with the word on the street.

Akeel and I set out to conduct some random street interviews. Faisal, a twenty-one-year-old university student, told us, "I feel terrible. Really, I thought there was a chance to improve my life. But now, with the occupation, I have no hope. I feel the resistance will be worse now, because people will feel more desperate." When we asked why he felt that way, he replied, "Because as long as the Americans are here, there will be increasing resistance. Who wants to have their country occupied?"

Aziz, a taxi driver, was both skeptical and prophetic. "You wait and see. It will become much worse. What other hope does the resistance have to get the Americans out of here now? Fighting against them is truly the only way. It will be worse now for the Americans here."

Only too aware that none of the Western media outlets would air any pro-Saddam opinion from Iraq, we chose an area of Baghdad where we were confident we would find formidable support for him. Under gray skies that were darkening swiftly with the approaching night, Akeel and I, along with Attila and Hamoudi, drove to the Abu Hanifa mosque in the al-Adhamiyah neighborhood of the capital city.

"I don't believe them . . . this is another American lie," said Khalil, a chagrined twenty-one-year-old merchant, "That man is not Saddam." It did not take too long for others to crowd around us when they found out that we were journalists. I noticed that Akeel stepped into a brisker pace of translation in order not to miss any of the comments flying at us from the infuriated men. Khahlil's next comment was one that I heard repeatedly in the context of Hussein's capture. "They show us this to get our minds off the terrible situation here— with no gas, no electricity. They don't want us to talk about how terrible it is here."

We could hear the sound of gunshots while the angry crowd surrounding us grew even larger. "Even if they arrest Saddam, there are three million more who will begin to fight, you wait," said a man who called himself Mustafa. We noticed that men continued to gather in front of the mosque, "If Saddam dies, the resistance won't stop. He is just one man. We will fight now."

Akeel, who had been recruited by the Ba'athists when he was barely out of high school, had always been ambivalent about the former dictator. There existed in his mind some degree of confusion between his sense of nationalism and his feelings for the dictator.

The heartfelt outpouring of support for the detained dictator that he was witnessing roused his youthful nationalism and so overwhelmed him with emotions that he began to weep. Some of the men around us noticed this and before we knew it they had lifted him off the ground and atop their shoulders. His hands still clutching my mini recorder, he pumped his fist in the air leading the chant from that precarious perch, "In our soul, in our blood, we will sacrifice for you, Saddam!"

My nervousness grew in direct proportion to the growing frenzy of the crowd that kept swelling to fill the streets, its chant echoing off the buildings. The situation seemed more volatile than a spark igniting petrol fumes. The crescendo kept rising as the men chanted, thrusting fists of hand grenades into the air. One man in a black outfit including a black face mask appeared from nowhere. Around his chest were strapped six sticks of TNT. The red and yellow wires from them were taped together and ran to an ignition switch on his side. He carried an RPG launcher and was immediately hoisted onto another man's shoulders. The chant grew more fervent. Kalashnikovs rattled off countless rounds as the crowd burgeoned in strength from tens to hundreds to thousands and took over the streets.

Akeel, now back to us and his senses, found us a cab and we gingerly made our way out of the neighborhood.

◆ ◆ ◆ ◆

Things were already going poorly for the occupiers. According to the Department of Defense, by December 2003, U.S. soldiers reported to be sick, injured, or dead from the invasion/occupation numbered over ten thousand, a figure that kept rising, alarmingly, by the day. Resistance attacks on Americans were averaging over thirty per day, which amounted to an average over over 1.3 soldiers killed per day.[5]

But, it was far worse for Iraqis. One of the doctors I interviewed at the Baghdad medical center informed me that the number of Iraqi children dying from malnutrition and disease had doubled since the invasion, and natal mortality among women had tripled. Fear of kidnappings led to most children being kept at home. Women faced a constant threat of rape and abduction from criminal gangs on the rampage. Gunfire at all hours of the night and day had become familiar and commonplace in most areas of Baghdad.

It was gut-wrenching to witness the heavy toll that a dictatorial regime, multiple wars, sanctions, and now the occupation had taken on this ancient land. Environmentally, Iraq was a disaster area. Most people I knew, including myself, had the "Baghdad cough" from the impossibly high levels of pollution in the capital city. Many areas in southern Iraq were uninhabitable due to the presence of contaminated soil and water from the use of depleted uranium munitions by the U.S. military during the 1991 Gulf War. The scars of war were visible everywhere: on the buildings, the landscape, and the people.

On December 17, Mishi, a Hungarian journalist also staying at the Agadir, accompanied me and Akeel to the al-Amiriyah district of

Baghdad. Mishi, a gaunt filmmaker with a thick Transylvanian accent, would eventually share my room as both of our funds ran low. We had decided on this day to visit the Amiriyah bomb shelter, which had been targeted during the 1991 Gulf War.

Three hundred and thirteen Iraqi women and children had been killed at Amiriyah in the notorious incident on February 13, 1991, when two U.S. laser-guided "smart bombs" sequentially struck the shelter, incinerating everyone inside. U.S. officials claimed it was being used as a communications center, but Western reporters, including BBC correspondent Jeremy Bowen, who was one of the first television reporters to reach the scene, did not find any evidence of military use of the bunker.[6]

Entire families were vaporized by the blasts, and as we toured the cavity of the building underneath the gaping hole in the ceiling blasted by the first bomb, we photographed black patches of human skin that had been burned into the walls in places. There was a child's hand burned into one wall, and in another, the imprint of a woman holding her baby. These impressions generated by the searing flash of the second bomb were similar to the infamous shadow of a Japanese boy seared into the pavement by a U.S. atom bomb blast in 1945.

The shelter, now a museum to memorialize the dead civilians, had been looted in the chaos that ensued after the fall of Baghdad.

On our way back to the hotel, we happened upon countless U.S. military vehicles surrounding the al-Shahid Adnan Kherala Secondary School for Boys. The main road we were on was blocked by at least ten Humvees and several Bradleys. We jumped out of our taxi to investigate.

Walking toward the front gate, I noticed a huge M-1 Abrams tank parked on one of the side streets near the school. Two helicopters slowly hovered back and forth above us. The school had been sealed off completely by forces from the First Armored Division, the doors locked from within. Soldiers and Iraqi police entered with photos of students taken during a small pro-Saddam demonstration the previous evening.

I addressed the first soldier I came upon. "I'm an American journalist. Can you please fill me in on what is going on here?" The moment he started to talk, another soldier in a Bradley behind us began yelling. Turning around, we noticed a soldier gesturing for him to be silent.

"I can't talk to you," he explained, then walked away.

Closer to the school, we encountered two Humvees mounted with loudspeakers. An Iraqi translator was instructing the crowd that gathered in front of the school, "You must not attend the demonstration tomorrow that is to be held here! Please disperse and go away!"

I finally learned what was happening from a U.S. soldier from Wisconsin, who requested anonymity. "Apparently some students of the school had held a pro-Saddam demonstration the previous day and the IPs [Iraqi police] were there," he says, to "catch the kids who were throwing rocks at a Humvee patrol as it passed their demonstration. Aside from that, it was nonviolent and nobody got hurt." I asked if any weapons had been fired. "No. Some kids were just throwing rocks." I probed further, asking if he knew which kids to talk with from last night.

"We had some IP here last night who took photos. They are going through the school now to identify the kids in the pictures." I was startled by his response to my question as to why the U.S. military is involved in detaining school kids. "Anyone who stands in the way of American interests here will be arrested."

As we approached the front entrance of the school, we saw that the students were being held inside. All the doors were sealed and had security guards outside of them. Students crowded behind the door bars waiting to be released. We watched a group of soldiers, surrounded by Iraqi police, bring out a group of boys with their hands cuffed with plastic ties behind their backs. As we watched, several Humvees with machine guns surrounded a large canvas-covered troop transport truck, into which sixteen students were loaded and driven away, guarded by tanks in front and behind. The arrests were a preemptive move intended to prevent any demonstration taking place in the same area tomorrow.

Shortly after the students were driven away, the doors were unlocked, releasing the frightened students, who flocked out the doors. The youngest seemed to be about ten years old, with none of the students older than eighteen years. The children, many of them in tears, were running out just as we arrived at the school gate. Others seemed enraged, kicking and shaking the front gate. We were soon surrounded by frenzied students, yelling, "This is democracy? This is freedom? You see what the Americans are doing to us here?"

One student was crying as he told us, "They took several of my friends! Why are they taking them to prison? For throwing rocks?" The boys closed in on us, threatening to beat us up because we were Westerners, when Akeel stepped in to block them with his large frame. They called him a traitor for being with us. Mishi and I quickly walked away to diffuse the volatile situation, while Akeel stayed behind to explain to the boys that we were journalists trying to report the truth.

By the time Akeel caught up with us, we were a few blocks away, with a smaller group of students who had agreed to talk with us. They could not believe that their friends had been taken away for throwing rocks.

There was a lot of commotion and total chaos as the tanks—Bradleys, and Humvees that were guarding the perimeter of the school—began to exit down the street. Several young boys with tear-streaked faces picked up stones from the wayside and hurled them at the armored vehicles driving past. The stones occasionally clanged the metal before falling impotently to the ground. After a couple of such "clangs," two soldiers, one atop each of two Bradleys, opened fire with their M-16s above our heads as we quickly dove into the backseat of a nearby taxi. A soldier on another tank, behind the first, was also firing randomly above our heads. Children and pedestrians started running helter-skelter, trying to find cover inside the stores. None of us could believe what we were seeing. Mishi pulled out his small video camera and recorded short glimpses of the soldiers terrorizing the crowd. In between the rattling gunshots, he perched his camera over the seat and filmed the chaos.

I saw a small boy holding a huge stone, standing at the edge of the street. He glared at the Humvees and Bradleys as their treads rattled loudly across the pavement. A soldier riding atop another passing Bradley pulled out his pistol and aimed it at the boy's head, keeping him in his sights until his vehicle rolled away toward the bright sun.

As we regrouped, one student asked us, "Who are the terrorists here now?"

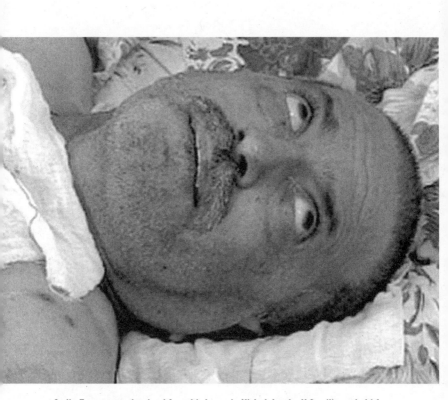

Sadiq Zoman was detained from his home in Kirkuk by the U.S. military, held for one month, then dropped off at Salahadeen Hospital in Tikrit by U.S. soldiers. He was comatose with electrical burn marks on this feet and genitals, the back of his head was bashed in, and he had multiple bruises on his legs, chest, and back. January 2004. Photo: Unknown photographer.

CHAPTER 4

KEBABS IN FALLUJAH

On December 19, 2003, nearly a fortnight after the event, the Coalition Provisional Authority released its official statement about an attack on Paul Bremer's convoy. The civil administrator announced that he had survived an "impromptu" attack on December 6. The CPA at that point was still unwilling to acknowledge that the Iraqi resistance was already a well-coordinated, sophisticated movement backed by an efficient intelligence system. The official line from the U.S. government, therefore, projected this and other attacks as random unorganized incidents.

Less than two months earlier, on October 26, 2003, U.S. Deputy Defense Secretary Paul Wolfowitz, the number two civilian in the Pentagon, was nearly killed when between eight and ten rockets slammed into the heavily defended al-Rashid Hotel where he was staying. The future president of the World Bank narrowly escaped death when the rockets reached the eleventh floor, just one floor beneath his own.

At this point, we were delivered what was soon to become the refrain of the official U.S. line on attacks by the resistance. It was first mouthed by Brigadier General Martin Dempsey, commander of the First Armored Division, (and echoed later by Secretary of State Colin Powell, and repeated ad nauseam in the following years on occasions that marked each "tipping point" or "turning of the corner" for the occupation). Dempsey told reporters, "If we look back at some of what we might describe as more sensational attacks, I think you'll see it's usually the case that they follow some positive event in the lives of the Iraqi people." He added, referencing a recent lifting of the curfew that shrouded Baghdad, "This is another example of that. We take three steps forward and they try to pull us one step back, and in fact it doesn't work."

Dempsey told reporters he didn't believe Wolfowitz was the target of the attack. "I think this . . . probably took a couple of months to prepare. His travel itinerary certainly wasn't known at that point in time."[1] This was the exact line taken by Pentagon officials to describe the attack on Bremer. In that instance, the press was told that the attackers probably didn't know that it was the CPA head's convoy that they were attacking. It may have been pure coincidence that the rockets were aimed at the side of the hotel where Wolfowitz was and had missed his room by a few yards. A coincidence similar to the attack the day before on the al-Rashid Hotel, when a U.S. Army Black Hawk helicopter guarding Wolfowitz in Tikrit was hit by RPG fire, which wounded some of its crew. According to U.S. officials, this was certainly another opportunistic, random, and desperate attack.

This same propaganda was recycled to describe the attack on Paul Bremer's convoy on December 6, 2003, the day Secretary of Defense Donald Rumsfeld visited Iraq.

Coalition spokesman Dan Senor let reporters know at a press conference that there "was no evidence of a planned assassination attempt on Bremer" and that "it was probably a random kind of attack." To reinforce the point further, he elaborated, "Attacks occur there all the time and he happened to drive through it."[2]

(Three months after Bremer was attacked, General John Abizaid, the top-ranking U.S. general in the Middle East, was attacked by a flurry of RPGs that struck his convoy when he went visiting Major General Charles Swannack in Fallujah. General Abizaid, commander of all U.S. forces in Iraq, was confident that the group who carried out the attack was not representative of the rest of the people in Fallujah.[3])

◆ ◆ ◆ ◆

Every day on the streets of Baghdad, I was witnessing the deterioration of conditions in Iraq. I had been in Iraq for barely a month and had seen the steady rise in the number of people begging on the streets. Women sent their children after me, with their hands stretched out as I walked to an Internet café or to buy some food. There were times when I had a child grabbing onto either arm as I walked. This grew worse when the temperatures dipped as the winter months set in.

On a cold, wet, rainy day, I sat in the lobby of the Agadir talking with Baha. Staring out the window at the falling rain he said, "See how there are fewer cars now? Fewer people can afford the petrol. And now people will be freezing in their homes."

Meanwhile, there was also an escalation in the number of murders and kidnappings. After the pro–Saddam Hussein demonstrations following his capture, in which more than forty Iraqis were killed by the Americans, Baghdad had settled back into a hesitant, tense quiet. Piercing this relative calm would be random bombs and sporadic gunfire, a long since normalized aspect of night in Baghdad.

◆ ◆ ◆ ◆

Christmas Eve in Baghdad was a surreal experience for a Westerner. After a day of interviews, Akeel and I arrived back at the

Agadir to find the lobby filled with people flurrying around discussing the attack on the big hotel. We obtained enough sketchy details to send us out once again, in the direction of the most heavily fortified hotel compound in Baghdad, that of the nearby Sheraton/Palestine hotel complex. We did so purely by trial and error since accurate details are hard to come by in such situations.

We asked a U.S. soldier, who did not know what happened, but directed us toward the French embassy down the street, where we had been told the attack took place. He seemed quite friendly, so I asked where he was from. "I'm from California," he said. I could tell he wasn't sure if I was an American, due to my beard and the keffiyeh wrapped around my neck. To continue the conversation, I said, "I'm from Alaska. How are you doing, man?" He replied, "Hanging in there brother, hanging in there. I was born in Anchorage, but now I live in San Diego." I told him to keep hanging in there and he thanked me. As we began to walk away, I heard him say, "Merry Christmas." I swung around and wished him the same, and saw him smiling at the instance of normalcy amid the chaos of war-torn Baghdad.

We eventually reached a small field outside the hotel complex and were met by several Iraqi police manning a small checkpoint. They told us the attack had been launched from the field situated between the Tigris and the hotel. One of them, who was smoking a cigarette and eyeing us nervously, filled in the details, "At approximately 8:30 p.m., a car pulled up near a palm tree in this small field. Two men got out of the car calmly and unloaded a small Russian-made Katusha missile. By the time it had launched and slammed into the top floor of the hotel, we realized what was happening and started shooting at them. We had a big gun battle, and shot over one hundred and twenty rounds at them, but they managed to escape."

Walking down an unlit side street back toward my hotel, we stopped at a tea vendor about two blocks from where the missile had been launched. Akeel didn't think the guards' story really stacked up and so he asked the tea man what he had heard. There had been no shell casings around where they said they had fired one hundred and twenty times, and the guards had not been able to tell us what type of car it was, even though they said they had shone their spotlight on it. The tea man confirmed our hunch when he said he had heard the huge missile explosion, but no bullets at all.

Stories of incompetent, hastily trained Iraqi police abounded, as did stories of resistance fighters joining the police as infiltrators, which is probably what the men that we had talked with outside the hotel had been. (The trend of infiltration into both the Iraqi police and army by members of the resistance increased exponentially in the coming months. What we had just witnessed of the collaboration between the Iraqi police and the Iraqi resistance at the Sheraton Hotel incident was but a prelude to infiltration on a massive scale to occur in the "security" forces.)

◆ ◆ ◆ ◆

On Christmas evening, as I sat typing in my room, several large explosions echoed from down the street, and I heard others from all directions in the city. Sporadic gunfire broke out, and an ambulance raced past in the direction of a few of the deep explosions.

Earlier in the evening, there had been news of three more U.S. soldiers killed and many more wounded by another roadside bomb. The number of wounded and dead soldiers as a direct result of the invasion and occupation was by then nearly eleven thousand. The soldiers were in a position where they could trust no one, least of all those who were supposed to be helping them. They were in Iraq fighting an ill-defined war, fighting for their own survival, not knowing where or when the next roadside bomb, suicide car bomb, or human suicide attacker would be hitting them. Though no amount of stress and anxiety justified the commonly adopted U.S. policy of indiscriminate firing in every direction and killing innocent Iraqis, I was beginning to understand what made such actions inevitable.

As the new year approached, Akeel and I teamed up with some other journalists to share the cost of a minivan to Samarra. One of them was Christian Parenti, a journalist who writes for the *Nation* magazine. Christian had been in Iraq twice before, and the two of us got along well, discussing the manifold aspects of the occupation and how it was bound to affect the United States on home ground. Christian, quick-witted and quite focused on his work, had worked with Akeel on his two previous trips. (He and I would meet again in Iraq, and our friendship would continue long after we'd both left.)

The first thing we saw in Samarra was a U.S. patrol of Humvees rolling up the main road toward the Golden Mosque. We all shook our heads as we watched the patrol. It was lined with Iraqi police walking between the Americans and the crowds of scornful-looking Iraqis on the sidewalks. "Human shields," I said to Akeel, "They're using the Iraqis as human shields." He nodded sullenly.

We conducted a number of sidewalk interviews to get a sense of the general mood in the town. Samarra was being subjected day and night to home raids and home demolitions by the U.S. military. En masse detentions had become the norm. At the time of our visit, a very strict night curfew had been imposed. We heard from a man at a tea stall, who said he knew of several people picked up and detained for being out too late. Nobody knew where they had been taken. "I know some people who were detained eight months ago, and still none of us know where they are. There is no civilization here anymore. All of Iraq wants the United States out now."

We inquired around if it would be possible to see a home that had been demolished, the collective punishment the Americans were practicing in the town at the time. A man known as Abu Mohammed accompanied us to the outskirts of Samarra to show us his brother's home, which had been turned into a heap of broken concrete and a pile of debris out of which a few twisted metal bars reached toward the sky.

Early in the afternoon of December 18, a large military convoy had been passing near the home when an IED (improvised explosive device) exploded under a Stryker vehicle.

We saw a large black scar of scorched earth thirty-two feet away from the spot where the IED had blown up. In retaliation, the soldiers had opened fire randomly at the surrounding homes. We noticed that bullet pockmarks peppered the walls of nearby homes, particularly the one directly across the road from where the Stryker vehicle had been hit.

An old man emerged from this home to take us inside, where he pointed out bullet holes in the walls and a television set that had been destroyed, with a bullet hole in the wall behind it. He recollected, "We were having lunch, and lay on the ground as our home was shot. There was nothing else we could do." He told us that soldiers had not only raided and searched the home, but also occupied it until nightfall. "They just stayed here to scare us, there was no other reason. They demanded information that we do not have," he said.

Four days later, we returned and were told the troops finally left at nightfall, but tanks and bulldozers arrived outside the house. The tanks sealed off the area while the bulldozers demolished the house, which was still under construction, because it was closest to the spot where the IED had exploded. When the neighbors asked the soldiers why they were destroying an empty home, they were told, "We are just following orders." Another home, a little way down the road, had also been demolished by the bulldozer after the family had been forced outside, carrying with them the few valuables that they could. While walking back to the minivan Christian turned to me and said, "And the Americans wonder why the resistance is growing like a wildfire."

On New Year's Eve 2003, a car packed with explosives detonated as a U.S. patrol passed on Palestine Street near Mustansiriyah University. Many of us staying at the Agadir jumped into a taxi and sped to the scene. On reaching the street I saw at least one Humvee flipped upside down and another completely incinerated. Concertina wire had been strung across the street. Soldiers, tanks, Bradleys, and Humvees had been positioned in such a way as to seal the entire area completely.

Soldiers were moving from building to building, pulling out all the men from shops, homes, and even some of the nearby college dorms. Inside the sealed perimeter, there already stood a group of at least twenty-five men; most would soon be detained. Several of them were college age, or even younger, and a few of them looked like street beggars in ragged clothing. The entire group looked confused. Some of the men stared listlessly at the ground as they waited anxiously to find out what the occupation soldiers would next do with them. This was the first time I'd witnessed a mass detention.

I stood by the concertina wire and watched soldiers lead more men out of the buildings. Their hands had been bound with plastic ties. A young, blond-haired soldier near me saw an Iraqi man on the outside of the concertina wire fence staring at him, and yelled, "What the fuck are you looking at, motherfucker?" He pointed his gun at him, "Get the fuck out of here. You like what you see? I said fuck off!"

Akeel quietly requested the Iraqi to please just walk away, as he stood glaring at the soldier.

Such mass detentions were not isolated incidents. Whenever a patrol was hit, the military would first seal the area for several blocks around and then, in a house-to-house search, known as a cordon search, pull all the males out for questioning, often carting them off to prison. Any male was fair game.

Another policy in force here was the ban on photography. The military did not encourage any photography of the wreckage of their hardware caused by the Iraqi resistance, but we were still hoping to shoot some pictures. The first soldier we came upon said to us, "Sure you can take pictures. Then I'll take your camera."

On the second night of the new year, there were reports of explosions from the al-Dora region of Baghdad. On January 3, 2004, some of us decided to go and check into the incident. This time, Akeel and I teamed up with two Polish Radio journalists. As we drove across the scenic farmlands of al-Dora, with its palm groves and green fields, we encountered a man who knew of witnesses willing to report on a roadside bomb attack that had killed and injured many U.S. soldiers.

Continuing down the road, we came upon a deep crater. Not far away, black skid marks were visible near a partially burned palm tree. Off the side of the road we saw small pieces and parts of a Humvee, a huge bloodied green handkerchief, a field dressing with bloodstains on it, and some bullet casings. Down in the dirt where the Humvee must have struck the palm tree sat a U.S. grenade splattered with blood.

While we were exploring the scene, we were joined by farmers who had been working in their fields at the time and witnessed the aftermath of the strike. According to them, many more soldiers arrived after the attack and immediately detained fifteen men from nearby homes. Even as we stood talking to them there was a huge explosion in the distance.

One of the men slapped his hands together, as if dusting them off, and said, "America finished!" His gesture of slapping his hands together, as if to dust them, is common in Iraqi and Arab culture. It means, roughly, "completely finished."

This al-Buaitha area of al-Dora is all farmland, with wide open fields lined with rows of palm trees and, in the village, the dwellings of farmers.

An old man stood beside a stone house pointing out to us a large crater and shrapnel scars that marked the facade. Huge chunks had been ripped out of a nearby date palm. Its red innards look like splayed veins. Other parts of the tree were scarred with holes that had shrapnel permanently embedded in them.

Hamid Salman Halwan, the owner of the home, told me, "Two nights ago, they bombed here from 6:00 to 9:00 p.m., and resumed bombing at 4:00 a.m. I think it was jets shooting missiles, because I could hear the engines. Last night they bombed some more in this area. I suppose they think resistance fighters are hiding in the fields here." The family had been eating dinner when the bombing began. Though they were in a room close to ground zero of the blast, a dividing wall had protected them from the shattered glass and shrapnel from the explosion. Hamid's wife said that the children were so afraid of all kinds of sounds that they now had trouble sleeping at night. The family hadn't slept in their home since the bombing for fear of another strike on their home. "We don't know why they bomb our house and our fields," she said, "We have never resisted the Americans. There are foreign fighters who have passed through here, and I think this is who they want. But why are they bombing us?"

U.S. Army Brigadier General Mark Kimmitt, the ever-obedient chief military spokesman for the CPA, told reporters at that time that Operation Iron Grip (whose goal was to disrupt and destroy cells of Saddam Hussein "regime loyalists," according to the Department of Defense) had sent "a very clear message to anybody who thinks that they can run around Baghdad without worrying about the consequences of firing RPGs, firing mortars. There is a capability in the air that can quickly respond against anybody who would want to harm Iraqi citizens or coalition forces."[4]

Hamid's family took us out to show us a plethora of unexploded mortar rounds sitting in their fields. The white bombs protruded halfway out of the hardened mud as children played nearby and pointed to them excitedly. I counted nine small tails of the mortar rounds sticking into the air in one small section of the field.

We asked if the family had made any effort to get the Americans to come and clean up their plantation of unexploded ordnance. Hamid's brother said with a very troubled look, "We asked them the first time and they said 'Okay, we'll come take care of it.' But they never came. We asked them the second time and they told us they would not remove them until we gave them a resistance fighter. They told us, 'If you won't give us a resistance fighter, we are not coming to remove the bombs.'" He held his hands in the air and said, "But we don't know any resistance fighters!" In a somber tone, he added, "We will have to leave this land because we cannot farm our fields with bombs in them."

A little farther on, another farmer invited us to his home, where we sat drinking tea in the setting sun. His three-year-old son, Halaf Ziad Halaf, walked up to us with a worried look on his face and said, "I have seen the Americans here with their tanks. They want to attack us."

Halaf's uncle leaned over to me and said, "The Americans are creating the terrorists here by hurting people and causing their relatives to fight against them. Even this little boy will grow up hating the Americans because of their policy here."

The next morning, Harb's brother Ghazwan rang me in my hotel room and asked me to meet him downstairs. When I did, in his usual blunt manner he instructed me to get in his aged Toyota 4Runner and, without any explanation, began driving me across Baghdad.

"American soldiers detained a man from his home in Kirkuk on July 21 of last year, and one month later, on August 23, they dropped him off in a comatose state at the hospital in Tikrit. He is still in a coma," Ghazwan said, after informing me that he was taking me to meet the man, Sadiq Zoman, and his family. We slowly made our way through traffic and passed a seemingly endless military convoy that held us up for nearly an hour. He handed me a medical report written by a Lieutenant Colonel Michael C. Hodges, an M.D.

According to that, and other military documentation Ghazwan gave me, Zoman had been transferred to the 28th Combat Support Hospital on August 11, 2003. Once there, according to Hodges' report, he had been treated for a heart attack and heat stroke. The document mentioned nothing, however, about the severe physical trauma Zoman had sustained, which I was about to see for myself.

On August 23, the Army transferred Zoman from the Combat Support Hospital to the civilian Salahadeen Hospital in Tikrit. The Red Crescent of Tikrit had posted photos of him on buses around Tikrit in the hope that someone would recognize him. Miraculously, a friend saw one of the pictures and contacted the family, who finally located him on September 4, 2003.

We arrived at a quiet two-story house and were welcomed inside by Zoman's wife, Hashmiya. Her face appeared stony under her black *hijab*, and she was obviously still in shock from what had happened to her husband. Their daughters were tending to him and stepped aside as we entered. Fifty-seven-year-old Zoman lay on a thin bed staring at the ceiling. His gaunt body bore clear signs of torture: electrical point burns on the soles of his feet and his genitalia, bludgeon marks on the back of his head and a badly broken thumb. In addition, his daughters told me they had found whip marks across his back and legs and other bruises along the length of his body.

From eyewitness accounts of other neighbors who had been detained along with Zoman, his family had pieced together that Zoman was first held at the Kirkuk Airport Detention Center, then transferred in a healthy condition to the al-Kaahd school, which the Army had converted into a detention facility. On August 6, he was moved to a base in Tikrit, where he had been severely beaten.

Zoman had nine daughters and was a member of the Ba'ath Party. Although the raid on his home netted the army no bombs or weapons of any kind, according to Rheem, his nineteen-year-old daughter, "They smashed in our front door, broke most of our furniture, and took money, gold, and jewelry, along with my father." She told me she had been horrified when she first saw her father in September. "He had whip marks all across his back and electrical burn marks all over his body, and has to this day been completely unresponsive to anything we do." Hashmiya, who was waving a paper fan to keep her husband cool in the absence of electricity, added, "We make his food with a blender because it must be liquid. But with no electricity there is no blender, so sometimes there is no food for him."

Zoman's family had received no explanation, nor any compensation for his situation from either the U.S. military or the CPA. They were almost destitute, having had to sell everything for his treatment. Aside from his bed and a few random pieces of furniture, the home was mostly empty. With tears in her eyes, Hashmiya told me, "Is it fair for any man's family to be made to suffer like this? Is it right that his daughters must see him like this? Our lives will never be the same again."

Back at my hotel that night, I emailed editors at many major newspapers in the United States. I managed to send out a total of 150 emails with a short message about this story. I urged each editor to send their own reporter to cover this story, adding that there were countless stories like this one waiting to be reported. I didn't feel the need to cover it myself; I just wanted the information to be made public. Having neither a large audience nor having had a piece published in a well-known publication, I felt the best plan would be to just feed the story to some established outlets in the hope of it getting covered.

I did not receive a single email or call in response.

More than four months later, on April 28, 2004, the Abu Ghraib "scandal" was "reported" by mainstream media in the United States after they were forced to do so by investigative journalist Seymour Hersh. Shortly after, I wrote up Zoman's story for the *NewStandard*, an Internet site I was a correspondent for at the time. Covering the U.S. portion of the story while I chased leads in Iraq, my editor Brian Dominick contacted the public affairs officer for the 4th Infantry Division, which was in charge of Zoman. Major Josslyn Aberle told Brian that Zoman's injuries were not inflicted by soldiers from the 4th Infantry Division or other army units involved in capturing and holding Zoman. She said the types of injuries described by Zoman's family and doctors, "just absolutely would not be tolerated" by the military.

Aberle insisted that Iraqi detainees were treated well because of the need to establish credibility among the Iraqi people. She failed to mention that it was also a violation of international law to torture prisoners. Rather helpfully, she added, "When you have an instance of a detainee being allegedly abused or treated improperly, that makes us no different than the former regime."

◆ ◆ ◆ ◆

In mid-January Mishi, Harb, and I went to Fallujah to follow up on some story leads.

On the way, we stopped in Old Baghdad to have a delicious traditional breakfast called *kahi*—a deep-fried sugary dough with a light cheese on top of it, drenched in syrup. We stood in the small fire-warmed bakery where two old Arab men turned out dozens of kahi every few minutes, relishing our breakfast and washing it down with glasses of strong Iraqi tea.

The road to Fallujah was controlled by multiple resistance groups and had grown increasingly dangerous, but we made it to the city without incident. No U.S. patrol could ever travel for more than half an hour through the streets of Fallujah without being hit by a roadside bomb because most inhabitants of the city supported the resistance, which was already fiercely opposing occupation forces there. We passed a wall with graffiti on it that read, "Stealing from the Americans is acceptable, and killing them is even better!"

We were in Fallujah to meet with a law professor named Sheikh Hajji Barakat. But we soon found out that the sheikh had been being detained by U.S. soldiers for the past three months and was being held at Abu Ghraib prison. The detention continued despite the fact that the U.S. commander in charge of Fallujah had already admitted to the sheikh's family that the man had been found innocent. Each time the family sought his release, they received the same promise: tomorrow.

"Sheikh Hajji Barakat," extolled his cousin Khamis, "is a great, honorable man. He even told the Americans his seven sons are involved in the resistance. This doesn't mean that their father is guilty. But they have detained him illegally anyway." It was apparently yet another example of collective punishment.

We sat outdoors in rural Fallujah, in the farmlands that support the city. Lush, green fields of onions and cucumbers lined with date palms stretched into the distance. The crystal blue waters of the Euphrates ran close to the farmlands and we could see a beautiful local mosque bathed in sunlight. Sitting outside drinking tea in the cool afternoon, we met with quite a few of the sheikh's relatives.

Omar, the twenty-year-old nephew of the sheikh, had been detained as well, but released later. He recounted his interrogation. The soldiers had asked him if he was Sunni, when he had last seen his mother, and other odd questions before releasing him. He also told us that when the U.S. troops came to take him into custody, they had smashed the door to the house, taken away papers and passports, the manifest for the family car, and all the money in the house. Omar mentioned that the soldiers who had questioned him in the prison wore civilian clothing and had threatened to release German shepherds on him. Khamis, the sheikh's cousin averred, "We need to have a vote in Iraq, and then have the Americans leave. The Americans are good for removing Saddam, but now they are behaving worse than Saddam. We have three hours of electricity a day, no security, and no running water at all." They were forced to carry buckets of water from the Euphrates when the electricity was cut. He said that there was no authority they could complain to about the electricity and water, or even the detentions. "We used to be humiliated by Saddam [Hussein], but now it is worse. We have no medicine for our children. It is the same for all of us, and we are running out of food." Two little boys whose father was in jail sat with us, listening to the conversation, as Khamis continued, "We used to believe the Americans

and Europeans would bring justice to Iraq. Instead they have taken it
out of Iraq."

The sheikh was one of fourteen brothers, all of whom had fled
Iraq after being tortured by Saddam Hussein for standing up against
him. After the United States invaded Iraq, the sheikh and one of his
brothers had returned from Saudi Arabia, where they had sought
refuge. Now the sheikh and his brother sat in prison, detained by
U.S. soldiers.

The mood lightened with some jokes about the irony of their
plight, a common phenomenon among Iraqis when discussing horrible events. On the table stood a pitcher that Khamis said contained purified water from the nearby Euphrates. Both Khamis and
Harb told me that according to Iraqi tradition it is believed that, if
one drinks water from the Euphrates River, he will return to Iraq.
With deep intention, I poured myself a cool glass and drank as some
Apache helicopters flew low over the fields in the distance.

Iraqi man holds up a bloody bandage from a wounded U.S. soldier after a roadside bomb attack on a U.S. patrol in Khaldiya, near Fallujah. As was common, young Iraqi boys and men celebrated at the sites of attacks against U.S. forces. January 2004.

CHAPTER 5

CRAVING HEALTH AND FREEDOM

JANUARY 2004

Hayda Hakeem gripped the wheel of the rented, beat-up, white-and-orange Passat that he used as a taxi. As we rattled down the street, I noticed two of his fingers were stubs, shaking on the steering wheel. We were proceeding to a press conference in the Green Zone. I was with Hannah, a translator working with the Polish Radio team at my hotel. Hannah was studying French literature when the invasion occurred, and had since withdrawn from university to work as a translator. She was brave, extremely smart, and experienced. Her ability to find sources and stories was as good as any interpreter I ever worked with, and her translation was top-notch.

"I have just returned to Iraq after spending fourteen years in an Iranian prison because I fought in that war," Hayda told us, "I am saddened to see this country now as compared to how much better it was when I left it—even during a time of war." We found he could not afford his own vehicle, and he paid the owner of the car a cut of what he made.

"I have to support my two handicapped sisters, since they have no medical support anymore. We have no heater. It is cold at night. Our parents died while I was in the prison in Iran." Hayda refused the tip I tried to give him. When I insisted, he began to put the car in gear to drive away, so I thrust the bills on the passenger seat and quickly shut the door.

Earlier, I'd spent the day interviewing Ayad Hashim at my hotel. He used to work as an engineer prior to the invasion, and now worked as a taxi driver in an attempt to feed his family of five. Given the appalling employment situation, this was one source of income still available to Iraqi males. It was a condition that reinforced the prevalent notion that "every car is a taxi in Baghdad."

Hashim had been saving money for a long time to build the first home for his family. It was this home in the al-Saidia area of Baghdad that incurred severe damages at the hands of the U.S. troops. "All the damage was caused by the U.S. Army. The army was using my house for watching people, for various jobs, for sleeping inside. In the process they destroyed my home." Conceding the inevitability of the situation, he said he was fully aware that things like this occurred during times of war, but he was angry because he had yet to receive one Iraqi dinar of compensation.

The occupation forces had drawn up an elaborate list of details that Iraqis had to furnish in order to file claims for losses and damages incurred by them because of the invasion. These were, verbatim (including the mistakes):

- Proof of ownership of the property in question.

- Medical bills/Doctors written assessment of the injury.

- Additional witness statements.

- Proof of negligence of US Soldiers
  (statement of soldier, or identifying unit)

- Two written estimates of damages by a certified repair shop, engineer, auto dealer, or other professional as required by the nature of your claim.

- Requested amount in US dollars and Iraqi Dinar.

- Exact date and time of accident.

- Proof of Identity.

- Agency agreement.

- Death certificate (if applicable).

- Address and phone number where you can be reached.

This list of demands made it next to impossible for most Iraqis to actually file a claim.

To make matters worse, claims had to be filed within thirty days of the incident's occurrence.

In addition, most people in Iraq could ill-afford to visit a doctor to get a written assessment and seldom were the injuries singular or restricted to one individual. Getting written estimates of damages was also a problem because of the cost involved, coupled with the fact that in Iraq repair shops and auto dealers conducted their business without being "certified." For Iraqis who were likely to file claims for destroyed houses, there no longer existed any "address and phone number where [they] can be reached," other than the streets and camps where they currently resided. Most did not own phone connections and those who did had to contend with dead lines, since the communications infrastructure in Iraq was largely destroyed.

However, Hashim was able to procure all the details and documents that the army required. The folder he showed me contained all the documents that had been requested. He had it all. But when he presented the set to the CPA, he was given their printed response, which he showed me. "Your claim is denied. The FCA (Foreign Claims Act) requires proof of negligent or wrongful acts on the part of U.S. government employees. Accordingly, there is no evidence of negligence on the part of U.S. government employees."

Apparently, doing everything the CPA asked of you still did not guarantee that you would be compensated. Hashim had submitted three different witness testimony papers attesting to the destruction of his home, signed by three people. In addition, he submitted photos, bills, written testimonies, and other certifications of proof and authenticity. Perhaps the real answer was given in the line at the top of the compensation forms, which stated, "The United States Army attempts to repay damages that it may have caused by accident that are not related to combat directly or indirectly."(Thus, U.S. forces are basically exempt from any legal responsibilty in Iraq, and documents such as those given to Hashim, provide the loopholes needed to avoid paying compensation to Iraqis who suffer losses. Calculated choices in both word usage and arrangement, such as how the military would pay for accidents "not related to combat directly or indirectly," illustrate this.)

In Baghdad, I also spoke with an Iraqi journalist, Jasem Hamza al-Jubure. In May 2003, U.S. soldiers had stormed his home. He and his family, clothed only in their nightclothes, were ordered out and held at gunpoint in the garage while soldiers searched through their belongings. One of the soldiers outside quite inexplicably fired his weapon into the house, shattering several windows and damaging the guardrail along the staircase. Before leaving, the soldiers handed him a scrap of paper with a scribbled admission of having damaged his home.

A man of pride, al-Jubure was not going to ask the CPA for money. "I refuse to go and beg the Americans for money for destruction that they caused my home. They embarrassed my wife and daughters by pulling them from their beds, broke my windows. Why should I go to them? They are the ones that should come and apologize to me and pay me. And then they wonder why more Iraqi people want them out of our country."

According to official estimates at the time, the U.S. military had paid up nearly $2 million to Iraqi civilians who had reported wrongful killings of family members to the coalition authorities. The *Guardian* reported that because U.S. forces were immune from prosecution in Iraq courts, "commanders make payments from their discretionary funds, rarely even admitting liability.... Payouts average just a few hundred dollars and in some cases families have been asked to sign forms waiving their right to press for further compensation."[1]

The CPA had an official "human rights" bureau they called the Office of Human Rights and Transitional Justice. It was located behind four heavily fortified military checkpoints, in the basement of the Baghdad Convention Center. Iraqis could go there to file human rights claims, with one provision. In order to qualify for consideration, the abuse had to have occurred between February 1963 and April 2003, during the forty years of Ba'ath Party rule before the U.S. invasion.

◆　◆　◆　◆

My time in Iraq was coming to a close, my funds nearly depleted. I tried to report on as many stories as I could in my last couple of weeks, since I had no intention of returning to Iraq. Public Citizen, a watchdog group based in Washington, D.C., became the catalyst for one of the last stories I covered before leaving Iraq, a report on the progress Bechtel had made on the rehabilitation of various water treatment systems in Iraq. I teamed up with Max Whitaker, a freelance photographer from California. Along with Hamoudi, we ventured south of Baghdad to the areas that the Bechtel contract covered.

San Francisco–based Bechtel Corporation was the largest engineering and construction firm in the United States and also one of the largest in the world, with more than twenty-two thousand projects in 140 nations on all seven continents. Its projects included petroleum and chemical plants, nuclear power and weapons facilities, oil pipelines, mining and metal projects, and water privatization. This politically well-connected corporation, infamously known for extinguishing oil well fires in Kuwait during the 1991 Gulf War, and notorious for its attempts to privatize rainwater in Bolivia, was one of six U.S. companies that were invited by the Bush administration to bid on the first $900 million worth of reconstruction projects in Iraq. On April 17, 2003, Bechtel was awarded a cost-plus-fixed-fee contract worth up to $680 million by USAID for reconstruction projects in Iraq. (By the time Bechtel withdrew from Iraq, the company would be awarded contracts in Iraq worth at least $2.3 billion.[2])

Cost-plus-fixed-fee meant that regardless of its costs (up to a ceiling), Bechtel was ensured a fixed rate of profit above costs, which had been previously agreed to behind closed doors. It also meant that Bechtel had long since been paid in full for their initial contract in Iraq.

One of the main reasons Bechtel fared so well in contractual awards was that former Secretary of State George Shultz was a board member. Shultz was also conveniently the chairman of the Committee for the Liberation of Iraq (CLI), which had close ties to the Bush White House. The CLI billed itself as a nongovernmental organization comprised of a "distinguished group of Americans" who wanted to free Iraq from Saddam Hussein. The group had close links to both the Project for the New American Century and the American Enterprise Institute, both neoconservative groups that were important shapers of the Bush administration's foreign policy. Another helpful factor was that Riley Bechtel, the CEO of Bechtel, was a member of George W. Bush's Export Council, advising Bush on trade issues and the opening of markets with which to trade. In addition, the head of the CPA, Paul Bremer, was a former Bechtel director.

My aim was to visit cities and villages mentioned in the Bechtel contract that were to be served by water-treatment plants. The cities of Hilla, Najaf, and Diwaniyah, among others, were listed as having "short term" needs. Bechtel claimed that their interventions in those places would assure that basic potable water needs and minimal standards regarding effluent sewage discharge were met. While the contract didn't give timelines for completion, it is worth noting that it promised to repair or rehabilitate critical water treatment, pumping, and distribution systems in fifteen urban areas within the first six months. The contract also promised that within twelve months it would supply potable water in all urban centers. Thus, nine months after the contract had been signed, I expected to find at least some progress in these three "short term" areas.

The first city we came upon was Hilla, sixty miles south of Baghdad. We pulled off the paved highway onto a bumpy road. Leaving a growing plume of dust behind us, we slowly approached a crumbling farmhouse situated amid vegetable fields and date palms. An old man with a weathered face that bore the attrition of exhaustion met us in front of his home. His first words to us were a plea for help—for drinking water, for some work, for anything that could ease his struggle.

As we spoke with him, he walked us to a scrappy water pump that sat lifeless near an empty container. A rubber hose cracked from the blistering sun was coiled limply on the dirt, near a hole that he said he tried to fill with water with his pump whenever their two hours of electricity appeared. Essentially, they had no electricity, and what little water they did get was loaded with salt from the region, and left those who used it sick with nausea, diarrhea, kidney stones, cramps, and cholera. Besides apprising us of the desperate water situation, the old man asked us if we could help him find his cousin. "We just want to know if he's dead so we can bury the body."

We drove past Babylon en route to the Hilla water plant. Babylon had been turned into an international military base named Camp Babil. The ancient cradle of civilization was now encircled with spirals of concertina wire, sandbags, guard towers, and three heavily fortified checkpoints.

The water treatment plant and distribution center in Hilla were managed by Salmam Hassan Kadel, who was also the chief engineer of the plant. Kadel informed me that he had received help from UNICEF, the International Committee for the Red Cross (ICRC), and several groups who assisted in some minor reconstruction projects and emergency water deliveries. He said that even during the war there had been running water in every house and, other than the normal problems of needing to replace old pipes and pumps, people had been managing well. At the time of our visit, however, they were supplying only half the water required by the people inside the city of Hilla. The villages had no water at all. The worst thing was that the plant did not have the pipes and equipment that they needed to restore the water supply. There had been no contact either with Bechtel or with any of its subcontractors. I found that vast numbers of people in the area were suffering from cholera, diarrhea, nausea, and kidney stones.

I asked Kadel what he knew of the presence of Bechtel in Iraq and in his city. "Bechtel is painting buildings, but this doesn't give clean water to the people who have died from drinking contaminated water. We ask of them that, instead of painting buildings, they give us one water pump and we'll use it to give water service to more people. We have had no change since the Americans came here."

In a village just outside of Hilla, several men told a similar story. There was no running water to speak of and barely two to four hours of electricity per day, during which they tried to run their feeble pumps to draw contaminated water from a polluted stream for their families to use. An old man named Hussin Hamsa Nagem bemoaned, "We are all sick with stomach problems and kidney stones. Our crops are dying."

Later that afternoon, at another small village between Hilla and Najaf, we found that fifteen hundred people had no other source of drinking water than the dirty stream that trickled by their homes. Most people in the village suffered from dysentery, many had developed kidney stones, and a huge number had cholera.

After spending a night in Najaf, we visited yet another village on the outskirts of the city. Here, the people had taken an initiative and collected funds from each house in order to install new pipes. But in the absence of regular electricity and water from the Najaf center, their initiative could bear no fruit. The villagers had dug a large hole in the ground, where they tapped into already existing pipes to siphon water. At night, when there was a supply of electricity, water from the tapped pipes collected in the dirt hole. The morning of our visit, we watched the operation. Children stood around as women collected what little bit of dirty water remained in the bottom of the hole.

Here, too, waterborne diseases such as dysentery and cholera, plus nausea, diarrhea, and kidney stones were widespread. Women had to walk half a mile down to a stream to collect water for their homes. In the same stream other women had to do their water-related chores, like dishes and laundry. Eight children from the village had been killed when attempting to cross the busy highway on their way to a nearby factory in order to retrieve clean water. Some children had even drowned in this stream while collecting water.

Mr. Mehdi was the engineer and assistant manager at the Najaf water distribution center. With help from the ICRC and the Spanish Army, the center had initiated some of the rebuilding on its own. Mehdi told me Bechtel had begun working on the Arzaga Water Project to help bring water into the city center of Najaf. He said Bechtel had started the previous month, painting buildings, cleaning and repairing storage tanks, and repairing and replacing sand filters.

This was the only project Mehdi knew of that Bechtel had been working on in Najaf. He told us, "Bechtel is repairing some water facilities, but not improving the electricity any, which is also their responsibility. Their work has not produced any more clean water than what we already had. Bechtel has not spoken with us, or promised to help us do anything else." There had been no work on desalinization, which was critical in the area, nor any other purification processes. I asked Mehdi how successful Bechtel had been in restoring electrical service to his water facility. "At least thirty percent of Najaf doesn't have clean water because of lack of electricity," he said. Najaf has a population of roughly six hundred thousand people. Bechtel had claimed it would have the Najaf sewage treatment plant fully restored and functioning by June 2004. (When I was in Iraq from April through June 2004, the treatment plant was still not functioning anywhere near capacity.) In Diwaniyah and each of the five other villages we visited, the same dismal story was repeated.

When we met Salam Fahim Noor, the manager of the Diwaniyah Ministry of Municipalities and Public Works, he told us the town at Diwaniyah was only receiving 55 percent of its potable water requirement and that much of the population was suffering from cholera, diarrhea, kidney stones, and nausea. According to Noor, the water treatment facility only averaged ten hours of electricity per day, and sometimes only six hours, despite Bechtel's contractual obligation to "focus immediate repair activities on restoring or maintaining electric supply to key services such as health facilities and water supply systems," as was written in their contract.

All these people were Shi'ite Muslims, those who had suffered the most under Saddam Hussein, and who the U.S. government had been counting on for unconditional support. These were the people who had been promised the most, and had looked upon the invasion as their only hope for a better life, free of the shadow of Saddam Hussein.

On the way back to Baghdad, we made one last stop at a small village off the highway, about an hour's drive south of Baghdad. We met Hassan Mehdi Mohammed, who lived in a small, two-bedroom mud dwelling with his wife and eight children. He told us that there was 80 percent unemployment in his village. Some of his children and other members of his family joined us for tea. I wanted to know his opinion on how the situation in Iraq would improve. "I think the Americans came here because they want something, not just because they love the Iraqi people. If they really came to help, then they should leave quickly. Now we are waiting for the next six months. The longer we wait, the more we see their promises are not being kept." He took a sip of his tea, thought for a moment and said, "No occupation ever makes things good for the people. All the people in the world must know the Americans are here just to help Bush win his next election. The same people who benefited under Saddam are benefiting more now. And those who suffered under Saddam are suffering even more now."

His brother-in-law, Saduk al-Abid, joined in the discussion. "Iraqi people now have no trust in the Americans or the Iraqi Gov-

erning Council. They have given us one empty promise after another." Both men had been part of the 1991 Shia uprising encouraged
and backed by George H. W. Bush. The rebellion had been crushed
violently when the United States abruptly withdrew support, deciding instead to allow the dictator to continue in power.[3]

In utter contradiction of the initial rhetoric of wishing to bring
speedy "democracy" to Iraq, CPA administrator Paul Bremer fought
to postpone elections for as long as possible. The Iraqi Governing
Council, basically a U.S.-appointed puppet government run by elite
Iraqi exiles, was one part of this delay tactic devised in June 2003 by
Bremer and others in the Bush administration. Bremer's foot-drag-
ging pretexts over the Iraqi elections were absurd. One excuse for
delay was that no electoral lists were available, and would take long to
prepare, though as the revered Shia leader Grand Ayatollah Ali al-
Husseini al-Sistani had pointed out, the food-ration lists established
by the UN during the sanctions regime would suffice.

Bremer's real reason for delaying the elections was to allow suffi-
cient time to install a "stable" pro-American puppet government in
Iraq. This plan, however, was shattered when hundreds of thousands of Shia men, following the call from their seventy-five-year-
old religious leader, Grand Ayatollah Sistani, jammed the streets of
Baghdad to demand elections. It was January 19, a beautiful sunny
day, and Hamoudi and I made our way to the protest as quickly as
possible. (This powerful outpouring of support by Sistani's followers later ensured that the Shia political bloc had the largest representation in the elected Iraqi government, an inconceivable condition
in Saddam Hussein's Iraq, which was ruled by a small, primarily
Sunni, government. Sistani had always advocated Islamic law in
Iraq, and these demonstrations were his first step toward realizing
that goal.)

The demonstration was easy to locate. All we had to do was follow the U.S. military helicopters. Way before we reached the site, we came upon U.S. soldiers logging the size of the demonstration with their cameras and binoculars. It was staggering by any standards. We watched from a pedestrian overpass near al-Mustansariyah University on Palestine Street. The demonstration's clear single demand: democratic elections for Iraq. Masses of protesters marched beneath us, as loudspeakers blasted out the demand and injunctions to followers in the booming voice of one of Sistani's representatives. The street was filled with people as far as the eye could see in either direction. There was a vibrant abundance of colorful flags and banners. People chanted "Yes, yes to unification" and "Yes, yes to voting." Fists were thrust in the air while the crowds echoed the calls from the speakers.

A sign I noticed reinforced the passion of the occasion. It had Sistani's name written on it with drops of blood running from the letters. A middle-aged man grabbed my arm and said, "You are the media? Tell America to give us what they promised! They promised us democracy, so let us have our elections!" Other banners said, "We refuse any constitution that is not elected by the Iraqi people." Another read, "We are all soldiers for Sistani!"

Not coincidentally, on this very same day in New York, Paul Bremer met with UN Secretary-General Kofi Annan to discuss future political plans in Iraq.

Bremer was forced to backtrack via a face-saving UN mediation, and his Washington bosses reluctantly agreed to hold elections by the end of January 2005. A legitimately elected Iraqi government would have demanded an immediate timetable for withdrawal of the occupying forces. It was to avoid this fate that the U.S. government wanted to postpone the elections and to create conditions of bloody sectarian chaos that would irreversibly fragment the country, just as many Iraqis had feared that it would. One of those conditions was to give the sectarian and ethnic-based Iraqi Governing Council more time to deepen the divides upon which it was based. Another condition the United States created and facilitated at length, which appeared before the end of the year, was sectarian-based death squads. (Later, when elections did eventually come to pass, the sectarian and ethnic alignment of the government and which ministries would be controlled by who and by what percentage of votes, was largely engineered by the United States, and guaranteed sectarian strife in Iraq.)

During my last days in Baghdad before leaving at the end of January, I checked the news of the previous week to see what the U.S. military had been saying regarding the situation in al-Anbar province, since there had been so many anti-occupation attacks. A *Washington Post* story from January 23 quoted a "senior military official" as having said, "What we've done in the last sixty days is really taken them [Iraqi resistance] down. We've dismantled the Baghdad piece. We've dismantled the Mosul piece. I'm not saying we've taken down the Fallujah-Ramadi piece, but we've hammered it."[4]

In the same week, a U.S. battalion commander in Tikrit expressed his assessment of the Iraqi resistance (one we have now heard ad nauseam from military officials, George Bush, Dick Cheney, Donald Rumsfeld, and countless other members of the administration.) He stated, "The enemy doesn't have much left. They are desperate and flailing."[5]

Suicide bomber in al-Adhamiya district of Baghdad, the day after Saddam Hussein was captured. December 2003.

CHAPTER 6

GOING "HOME"

After nine weeks in Iraq, I was out of money, emotionally exhausted, and needed to get home. But I knew that I would be returning to Iraq.

I spent my last day, January 28, 2004, saying good-bye to friends. Though I was confident about returning to Iraq, I was fearful I would not find my friends on my return. It was a gray day in Baghdad with brisk, gusty winds as I sat sipping tea with Harb and his brother Ghazwan in my hotel. We had been discussing the Zoman story some more, along with other atrocities I had written about, when I asked them both, "How do you stay here and keep living? How do you not give up hope?"

"Two reasons, Daher. First, this is our home. Second, we are unable to leave. We have no choice." Harb nodded, then lit a cigarette.

Later that evening, Akeel showed up at the hotel with tears in his eyes. He had just found out that one of his friends, who had been freelancing for CNN, had been killed. Akeel's last words to me were simple: "I can tell you'll come back to Iraq, Daher. Just make damned sure you're careful when you do."

(Soon after, Akeel left Iraq to be with his girlfriend in England, only to be kidnapped and nearly killed when he returned to Baghdad later, to visit his family.)

My driver to Amman was a heavyset man in a gray dishdasha. He spoke no English, so aside from the few scant phrases in Arabic he and I were able to exchange, I spent most of the drive out of Iraq sleeping in the back seat of his gray Chevrolet Caprice. We passed through the border without a problem. There wasn't a single U.S. soldier anywhere in sight on either side of the border. A couple of Iraqi policemen stood around smoking cigarettes. When we were inside getting our passports stamped, I ran into Hussein, to my delight, who had driven me into Iraq nine weeks back. With a broad grin, he gave me a giant hug.

By the time we arrived in Amman, it was late afternoon. Cars rolled down the streets in an orderly fashion. The sight of functioning traffic lights, drivers following the directions of traffic police, and streets and sidewalks free of clutter was comforting. Mixed emotions overpowered me as the car drove down the secure streets of Amman. Despite my exhaustion, I experienced immense relief, accompanied by extreme sadness that the people of Iraq could not experience similar relief, and guilt at having the option to leave the occupation behind. At the time, for Iraqis who had the financial means, Jordan and Syria were the only two countries accepting Iraqis. The Iraqi passport permitted far less mobility and freedom now than it did before the invasion.

We pulled up at the al-Monzer hotel, which had been my base camp before entering Iraq. My driver smiled and thanked me when I paid him, and he carried my backpack up the stairs.

Jamil, the young front desk clerk, greeted me enthusiastically and came out for the familiar tea and cigarette ritual. Having realized the integral link between this tea/tobacco combination and Arab culture, I had granted myself permission to smoke for as long as I was in the Middle East. It was a habit that grew difficult to alter as the occupation dragged on. Jamil made my reentry into the relatively normal world outside Iraq both warm and reassuring, "Thank you for staying alive, *habibi*. We read your work and are proud of you for telling the truth on behalf of the Iraqi people." Being of Palestinian descent, like the majority of the Jordanian population, he knew all too well, like others there, what the Iraqi people were enduring.

I went upstairs to my room, sat down to absorb the quietude, and waited for the adjustment inside. What I experienced instead was a feeling of being unsettled, of something being off or not quite right. After unpacking and taking a shower with plenty of hot water—an impossible luxury in Baghdad—I found that the feeling persisted. A loud boom resounded near the hotel when someone closed the metal lid of a garbage dumpster. I was so alarmed, it took me several moments to calm myself down. (In retrospect, it was naive of me not to have anticipated this feeling, which instead of fading only grew stronger over time, particularly after returning to the United States.)

Through discussions with my friend Mike Ferner, whom I had met in Baghdad, I soon learned more about Post Traumatic Stress Disorder. Ferner, a veteran of the war in Vietnam, knew about PTSD all too well. Nevertheless, he had ventured to Baghdad to document life under occupation.

I flew straight back to Anchorage and, once there, minimized the number of trips I took outside of my apartment. Relations with my girlfriend, which were strained already, only worsened with my disinclination to discuss what I had experienced in Baghdad. I couldn't discuss what I'd seen in Iraq with even my closest friends. Listening to people grow excited about a climbing trip, or kayaking, brought feelings of guilt, anger, and tension.

Elementary coordinates of my world—like electricity, hot water, security, and functional telephones—had taken on dimensions other than that of normally assumed comforts. My first week back, I met with some friends for lunch. Listening to them talk was like venturing into an unreal world inhabited by people with pets and cars, who went on hikes and vacations and watered their lawns. This was my life less than three months before, so what had changed that made it impossible to slip back into that existence? Normally, this time of the year, in early February, with spring around the corner, I would be preparing for another climbing season on Mt. McKinley. But coming back from Iraq, the thought of spending money to go traveling or climbing seemed inconceivable, even revolting.

My coping mechanism was to pour myself into completing the stories I had begun in Iraq. My radio calls continued, but my lifeline was the steady email contact with friends in Iraq, particularly with Harb. He and I had truly bonded, although we had only worked together a few times. To keep myself abreast, I monitored the news for hours each day, but it was his emails that actually kept me informed and up-to-date with the ground realities in Iraq.

News "coverage" concerning Iraq in the U.S. corporate media continued along the lines of the preinvasion reportage of weapons of mass destruction and the other lies that had been used to sell the illegal invasion to the public. This invariably infuriated and offended me and served as added motivation to return to Iraq.

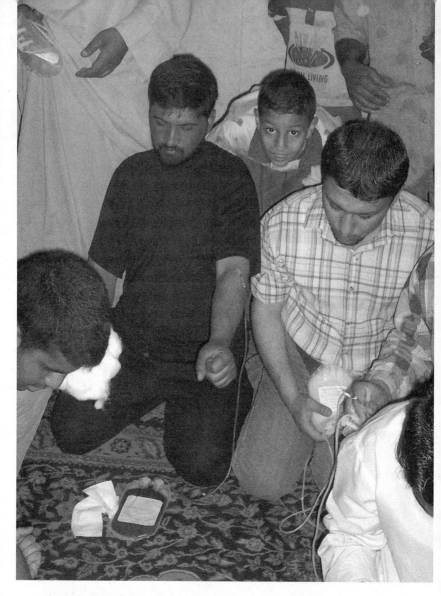

As the April 2004 U.S. assault on Fallujah began, many mosques in Baghdad held food and blood drives to assist the people of Fallujah. In the Abu Hanifa mosque, men eagerly donated blood. April 2004.

CHAPTER 7

REENTERING THE INFERNO

APRIL 2004

Even before I left the United States, I was conscious that my sojourn in Iraq this time was going to be tumultuously different from the previous one. As I waited to depart from JFK Airport, my eyes fell on the cover of the *New York Times* and narrowed in concern at the sight of the charred bodies of the four security contractors killed in Fallujah. I had driven some months back on that very bridge spanning the Euphrates. Blackened limbs and body parts hung from its green crossbars. In the foreground was a small group of young men and boys in what appeared to be a celebratory dance. I knew there were few in my country who would understand the seething anger in those movements.

My first thought was concern over how the Bush administration would use this incident to its advantage. Like its response to 9/11, I feared it would be heavy-handed and blunt. Particularly in light of the fact that the U.S. military had long ago lost control of Fallujah, the killing of the four mercenaries would most likely be used as a green light for another invasion. This was April 2004, a year into the occupation and three months since I had left Baghdad. Iraq was chafing under escalating unemployment, the armed resistance in the country was steadily intensifying, and the hopes for a dictator-free, better future were rapidly fading. I had good reason to steel my nerves en route to the Middle East. Attacks against the occupation forces were increasing. Car bombs and assassinations of government officials had become common in Baghdad, where I was heading.

Ahead of me at customs in Amman were five solemn men in crew cuts and a sixth one who appeared to be their minder. I noticed he had a Turkish passport, and I began to wonder if the group might be employees of one of the many security-contracting companies operating within Iraq. Interestingly, during a layover in Istanbul, as we awaited our flight into Amman, I struck up a conversation with an older man seated beside me, who told me in a thick southern drawl that he was from North Carolina. "We've got a little company working in Iraq, which is having some problems at the moment, so we need to try to get this figured out," he told me. The four men killed in Fallujah were mercenaries employed by Blackwater USA, a security company based in North Carolina.

The action against the bodies of the mercenaries had been vociferously denounced by every religious leader in Fallujah and by Iraqis in general. The grotesque images I had seen at JFK, which were being incessantly broadcast by the U.S. media, had the desired effect of generating rage and hatred toward Iraqis. The vast majority of reports conveniently omitted the Iraqi voices condemning the killings. Nor was there any way to refute the grossly inaccurate representation of the victims as civilian contractors and of the entire population of the city of Fallujah as the culprits.

The very reason I came to Iraq was to try to challenge the distortions of mainstream media reporting on the occupation, yet it startled me how disturbing it was to actually witness facts being used with the obvious intent of manipulating public opinion and at times to create confusion. During my first trip, I had time and again experienced first-hand this disparity between facts and media projections. The Fallujah reportage typified this phenomenon. The first media reports of the incident referred to the four men as "security contractors." The *Associated Press* described them as being "among the most elite commandos working in Iraq." As evidence there was an accompanying photo of young Iraqi men holding the military dog tag of one of the slain men and a Department of Defense badge of another. The story stated that one of the destroyed vehicles contained a cache of captured weapons.[1]

However, soon many mainstream media outlets started referring to the men who were killed as "civilians," "Americans," or as "American civilians." The *New York Times* alone used the term "civilian" twenty-five times in the first three days of April, according to my investigation.

There was little if any mention in the media of simple facts about Blackwater: that it was in the business of providing training to SWAT teams, recruited from among former Special Forces personnel, that it charged its clients, in this case, the U.S. military (and by implication the U.S. taxpayer), as much as one thousand dollars per day per mercenary.[2]

Our establishment media was equally silent on other vital issues. Nowhere did it mention that the residents of Fallujah by this time had been reporting the unscrupulous practices of the Blackwater mercenaries. When I visited Fallujah in December 2003, the city was experiencing collective punishment, a common enough occurrence each time a U.S. patrol was attacked. Long since weary of struggling to survive in their occupied city, the people were additionally forced to put up with the brutality of the private security contractors, who did not come under the purview of military rules of engagement.

Instances of rape, assassination, and pillaging went unregistered and unpunished.

A Human Rights Watch report on Fallujah stated that the organization "did not find overwhelming sympathy for Saddam Hussein" in Fallujah, but instead found many who "considered themselves victims and opponents of his repressive rule."[3] Instead of revealing this fact, most major U.S. news media outlets conveniently presented their readers with an entirely different city, one that was not only "restive" and "lawless," but a "hot spot" and "flashpoint" for violence, ostensibly because it happened to be a "volatile center of support for Saddam Hussein." A little later in April, the *New York Times* parroted the Pentagon by reporting that Saddam Hussein's former officers "are responsible for the majority of attacks today" in Fallujah.[4]

The Eastern European men in Amman, who were clearly mercenaries on their way to Iraq, had their passports quickly stamped at customs following *baqsheesh*, the neat and efficient ritual of bribery between their minder and the customs agent. Downstairs, while waiting for my backpack, I watched the men pull their large locked plastic boxes off the conveyer belt. When their porter briskly loaded them into a white SUV curbside, complete with extra radio antennae, it was clear who these people were.

Waiting in Amman for a colleague, and monitoring the news, I understood that an all-out siege on Fallujah was imminent. The impact of this *shel* (Arabic for lynching) of the four Blackwater mercenaries was soon to be experienced multiplied a hundredfold by Fallujah residents.

◆ ◆ ◆ ◆

On the outskirts of Fallujah, we encountered large concrete blocks and coils of concertina wire across the road. Several U.S. soldiers stood behind these, backed by Humvees and Bradley armored fighting vehicles. Fallujah seemed to be surrounded by the U.S. military, with helicopters rumbling low over groves of date palms in the distance. It was the beginning of Operation Vigilant Resolve. (It surfaced later that the order to lay siege on the city had come from deep within the Bush administration, not via any military channel. In fact, the orders were carried out despite one of the military commanders stationed near Fallujah, who had suggested reconstruction and other projects to win the trust of the people. The pattern was similar to that of the invasion, where high-ranking military officials had had to follow orders against their better judgment.)

We were forced to circumnavigate Fallujah, going farther east along dusty desert roads. Our driver pulled off the bumpy road when we were out of sight of the highway and stuffed a towel in the door in order to cover the window. He then stretched a windshield guard with a red, white, and blue eagle over my window. "This is a good way of not looking American," he added sarcastically with a smile. Our driver then asked me to wrap my keffiyeh around my head, which I gladly did. I had learned from last time that it made me look like a mujahedeen with glasses. It was a tense drive the rest of the way into Baghdad, where we were greeted with news that did our already frayed nerves no good.

I was traveling with Rahul Mahajan, whom I'd met in Baghdad the previous December. His writing about Iraq, which included the events leading up to the economic sanctions and the wars by both Bush administrations, had weighed heavily in my decision to go to Iraq.

An oil pipeline in the south had been torched, and in the last two days at least sixty civilians and twelve U.S. soldiers had been killed across Iraq in uncontrollably spreading violence.

Members of the Mehdi Army militia of Shia cleric Muqtada al-Sadr had taken over a police station in the holy city of Kufa, which is located roughly one hundred miles south of Baghdad, across the Euphrates River from Najaf. The militia's attacks against Iraqi police were in retribution for the American military onslaught against al-Sadr. The head of the CPA, Paul Bremer, had recently declared al-Sadr an "outlaw" and closed down his Baghdad-based newspaper *al-Hawza*, infuriating both al-Sadr and his followers. Bremer claimed that the newspaper was being used to issue edicts and pass information to followers, and was also disseminating anti-CPA propaganda to incite violence. Bremer had accused al-Sadr of having assassinated rival cleric Ayatollah Abdul Majid al-Khoei, widely believed to be a U.S. sympathizer, an allegation that al-Sadr had already disproved.

In demonstrations that followed the closing of the paper, several followers of al-Sadr were fired on by U.S. forces. Instead of isolating the problem and dealing with it, the U.S. military had become embroiled in a multifront war in Iraq now; battling the Mehdi Army in Baghdad and locales across southern Iraq. The crisis was only compounded by the new fierce front opened in Fallujah.

Baghdad felt like a city on the brink. As Iraq bled, the capital city, once referred to as the City of Peace, had been longing, after decades of suffering, for its long-lost greatness. Now it was peopled by Iraqis who were scarred by the ravages of war, dictatorship, sanctions, and a brutal occupation that worsened by the day. It immediately became clear that traveling around Baghdad and other areas outside the capital city was an extremely dangerous proposition, unlike last winter, when taking taxis and walking down the street by oneself was a matter of course. People were stocking up on water and basic foodstuffs. I sensed throughout Baghdad a tangible undercurrent of panic, insecurity, and concern for the future. Most hotels were no longer accepting foreigners, for fear of kidnappings and the threat of car bombs. Outrage had drawn the militant al-Sadr and his millions of followers into the battle against the occupiers.

On April 6, fighting erupted in Sadr City, the predominantly Shia neighborhood of Baghdad. Sadr City is a sprawling slum of impoverished al-Sadr followers and home to roughly three million people. Street fighting in this cramped, sewage-ridden district, which the military referred to as the Black Zone, was a dismal eventuality. The many followers of al-Sadr, enraged at the treatment of their leader by the occupation forces, launched attacks against U.S. patrols in what used to be relatively calm Shia areas.

The chances of a civil war in Iraq were at that point pushed to the back burner, as the heavy-handed tactics of the U.S. military had united the Shia and Sunni in unprecedented ways. Prior to the invasion, there had been an uprising against Saddam Hussein's regime. While some Sunnis had fought alongside Shia at that time, now that had become far more widespread.

The mood on the street was one of disbelief. So many Iraqis I talked with were perplexed at how or why the United States had once again managed to paint itself into a corner with its bravado. If al-Sadr were to be detained, which the military said was its goal, he would be transformed into a martyr. If they failed to detain him, he would end up gaining greater legitimacy and power. As at the time of the invasion, the United States would lose further credibility if, after all the tough talk, it backed down.

In the late morning on our second day in Baghdad, Rahul and I met up with Hamoudi. Smoldering Iraqi tempers and burned U.S. military vehicles accosted us near Sadr City as we headed toward Shuwala, a predominantly Shia neighborhood where fierce clashes had broken out the previous day between the U.S. military and members of the Mehdi Army. According to the residents, it started when U.S. forces opened fire on people assembled for a peaceful demonstration to express their solidarity with their embattled cleric, Muqtada al-Sadr.

We crossed a putrid river of sewage on the edge of the district, driving past a large destroyed U.S. military transport truck, charred black from flames. A small crowd of young boys were gathered about the truck yelling, "No to America! No to Saddam! No to America!" Randomly, one boy picked up a stone and aimed it at whatever remained of the melted windshield of the truck. I could not help recollecting an occasion during my last trip when I had had tea at the same spot with similar young boys. They had happily asked me questions about the United States and been amazed at the stories I told them about Alaska.

We located Sheikh Sa'adoun al-Shemany, a member of al-Sadr's office in Shuwala.

He told us that the soldiers had appeared when the people were holding their demonstration, and had ordered them to disperse. When the crowd did not comply, soldiers began shooting, first in the air and then into the crowd. "People ran for cover, but the soldiers kept shooting at them," al-Shemany continued, "So in some areas residents began returning gunfire to protect themselves."

It was at this point that members of the Mehdi Army arrived and began fighting the soldiers. They killed several U.S. soldiers and then burned two Humvees and the large transport truck we had seen nearby. "We are waiting for the people to respond to this," said al-Shemany. "It is a revolution now. The families of the killed people will avenge this. The Americans attacked unarmed people. All Iraqi people will refuse to accept the occupation now."

According to al-Shemany, one of the main causes for the growing discontent of Iraqis toward the occupation was the appointment of the current members of the Iraqi Governing Council by the U.S. government. "The Americans appointed these leaders here, and they can never become one with the Iraqi people, even if they are the Iraqi Governing Council members, because we did not elect them."

A man named Mundr was sitting with us. He claimed to be an eye-witness and maintained that the violence had been initiated by the occupation forces. "Now we are like one hand, Sunni and Shia, against the Americans," he added sternly. Abbas Ghani, another eyewitness declared, "All Iraqi people will condemn the arrest of Muqtada al-Sadr. If the Americans arrest al-Sadr, they will open the door of hell upon themselves."

Next, we drove back to Sadr City to the office of Muqtada al-Sadr, located in the heart of the sprawling slum. It was a simple, ground-level structure of several rooms surrounding an open courtyard. Prayer mats covered dirt floors in rooms that lay within doorless en-tryways. We found that rooms that were meant for business discus-sions contained simple wooden chairs and a desk at the most. Outside the office, we were met by several young men with pistols hanging in their belts or stuffed in their pockets. Typical of so many al-Sadr followers from impoverished and unprivileged backgrounds, the boys wore sandals or wore no shoes at all.

Al-Sadr spokesman Assad Turkey Suari sat solemnly in a flowing brown robe behind a desk in a cramped but busy office. His piercing eyes overshadowed his large, black beard as he spoke to us. "Now all Iraqi people will attack the Americans because they consider us all terrorists."

As during my first trip, countless Iraqis asked me why the U.S. government continued to refer to those fighting against the occupa-tion forces as terrorists. Earlier that day a man had asked me, "Why are we called terrorists? This is our country. These are foreign army tanks in our streets killing our people. We fight against this and we are called terrorists? They are the terrorists."

There was a nonstop stream of men entering the office obtaining instructions from al-Sadr representatives about their assigned positions for the fighting that was expected to ensue that night. They were given the details of where to procure their guns, or mortars, or IEDs, in preparation for the next U.S. military incursion. Another man in the al-Sadr office, who called himself Ahmed, sat with us as we spoke with Assad. He would periodically run out of the office to deliver a message sent by one of the clerics. When Assad turned to speak with an aide, Ahmed leaned toward my chair and said, "Americans are killing women and children here. Our case is the same as that of the Palestinian people. Of course, when Sheikh Yassin was assassinated, we had joined their cause."

Outside, in the afternoon sun, people were preparing for more bloodshed. Shops did brisk business as residents purchased and stocked up on potatoes, onions, meat, rice, and other staples. We saw a man carrying a mortar tube inside a white, plastic sack toward his car. Dust swirled amid piles of garbage where goats and chicken fed. Back in the car, we slowly made our way out of Sadr City. Several M-1 Abrams tanks were parked in front of some municipal buildings at the entrance to the impoverished area.

Atop one of the tanks, we saw soldiers busily sweeping away broken glass, rocks, and random plastic pieces from the body of the tank. Stones of various sizes dotted the ground around the tank. The mood was tense and quiet. A middle-aged soldier stood smoking beside the tank as we approached, holding out our press passes to identify ourselves.

Private First Class Smith, a soft-spoken member of the crew atop the tank, in his mid-twenties, paused in the middle of brushing off debris with a small hand broom in order to respond to my query about what he made of the violence that had transpired in Sadr City. "Crazy stuff. I think they're testing us because we're new. I've been here three weeks. Some folks wave and smile; others throw rocks and attack us. I'd probably prefer to be home."

I wonder how much of his attitude stemmed from the fact that three soldiers had been killed in the nearby Khadamiyah neighborhood that day and that attacks against occupation forces were occurring in the majority of cities outside of northern Iraq at that stage of the occupation. Ironically, despite the fact that the occupation was supposed to be more acceptable to the Shia, at that point a large section of the Shia population was currently involved in attacks against U.S. soldiers throughout Baghdad and across southern Iraq.

Victor Templer, another member of the tank crew we were interviewing, remained standing in the thin rubble of scattered stones and shards of broken glass. A heap of accessories lay in the dirt. They had been ripped from his tank by a group of what he estimated to be two hundred boys. He looked worried and low and was initially reluctant to speak with us. "They threw stones and bags of feces at us," he said, still in a state of disbelief. I continued with my survey of the tank and found that the small glass portholes had been shattered. Rahul asked him how he felt about being attacked by children. "Made me feel a little uneasy. Little kids, you know? And we're a tank! They are not afraid. The kids stone us during the day, and then the men attack with guns at night."

Compared to what I believed to be a public understanding of events commonplace in occupied Palestine, his surprise left me taken aback. The events Templer experienced might well have occurred in Gaza. While Iraqis, like those I'd just interviewed and so many others, were drawing the direct parallel, U.S. soldiers were missing these connections. The growing hopelessness of the Iraqi people was directly linked to the recklessness being shown by the U.S. military.

Templer was not aware of who al-Sadr was, so we pointed to a nearby painting of Mohammed Bakr Sadr and Mohammed Sadiq Sadr, the esteemed uncle and father of the young cleric. Both had been outspoken critics of the former dictator, and had been assassinated for their words. The painting, common around Sadr City, displayed their long, flowing white beards beneath old, wise, compassionate eyes. It struck both Rahul and me that the soldiers had no clue who the enemy was.

Night was approaching. No more little boys with rocks.

The next day, April 7, I took a trip to Khadamiya, another predominantly Shia area of the capital city, with Hamoudi and Rahul. Usually a bustling, crowded, busy area, today the streets sat eerily empty after three U.S. soldiers and at least one Iraqi had been slain the previous day.

Shortly after entering the area, I found myself sitting with Sheikh Hassam. The gentle, soft-spoken Imam for the al-Ageialap mosque of al-Sadr in the area was more than happy to entertain questions about the recent violence. Sparked by al-Sadr's reaction to the Bremer order to close his *al-Hawza* newspaper, Sheikh Hassam pointed out that the closure of the Kufa mosque by U.S. soldiers was believed to be the handiwork of the Bush administration. This closure, which occurred at nearly the same time as the shutting down of *al-Hawza*, also had a large impact. The Kufa mosque near Najaf could be said to be the brain and heart of the Sadrist movement. Used every Friday by the young al-Sadr to deliver fiery anti-occupation sermons and messages to his millions of followers, it carried tremendous religious and symbolic power.

Administrators in the Najaf provincial government, suspected by al-Sadr to be collaborators with occupation authorities, had ordered the Kufa mosque closed. The official line was that the mosque was being closed for repair and reconstruction. It was perceived by al-Sadr as an act of repression. Not only was the timing suspect, as this move occurred at nearly the same time as the ordered closing of *al-Hawza*, but it perfectly replicated the closing of the same mosque by Saddam Hussein in an attempt to repress al-Sadr's father, Mohammad Sadiq Sadr. As if to intentionally underscore the message, the reason given this time was also the same.

We sat in an office filled with new posters and pictures of the fiery Shia cleric. Outside, in a small courtyard under the date palms, men prayed their allegiance to al-Sadr. Down the street was the huge, ornate al-Khadam shrine. In his mid-thirties, Sheikh Hassam was the leader of the Friday prayers in his area, and used to carry al-Sadr's messages to his followers in Khadamiya. Although the majority of the population in this neighborhood were followers of Grand Ayatollah Ali al-Sistani, al-Sadr still commanded a sizable and loyal group of the Shia population here.

According to Sheikh Hassam, U.S. soldiers had gunned down an Iraqi man there the previous day while other U.S. soldiers had been removing posters of Muqtada al-Sadr from the office walls. The sheikh claims, albeit circumspectly, that it was resistance fighters from outside the area that had attacked the Americans after the soldiers had randomly opened fire on civilians. He went on with greater certainty, "These men who attacked the Americans were not with the Mehdi Army."

The followers of al-Sadr believed the Mehdi militia existed in order to protect the ideas of al-Sadr. The militia had been originally formed to protect the mosques and Imams of the al-Sadr movement. With the invasion and subsequent collapse of the state and ensuing chaos, their duties had been expanded to include providing security in neighborhoods, distributing gasoline and food, providing traffic police, and carrying out other duties necessary for social stability during the tumultuous occupation. Our conversation centered around what the sheikh believed would occur in the calamity of al-Sadr being arrested by occupation authorities, as was their stated objective.

"Our country will be full of blood if al-Sadr is arrested."

Just across the bridge over the Tigris River was the Sunni-dominated area of al-Adhamiya. As we advanced toward the famous Abu Hanifa mosque, we found that throngs of people and vehicles were crowded around its entrance. Small trucks were being loaded with bags of food, boxes of bottled water, and death shrouds for the slain.

"Pull over, Hamoudi," I said, "Let's see what is going on here." We pushed our way past crowds of people who were frantically loading bags of potatoes, rice, flour, and other foodstuffs into trucks bound for Fallujah. Now several days into the siege, the reports emerging from within the city were grim. There had been scores of civilian casualties already.

Omar Khalil, a forty-year-old merchant who lived nearby, was busily loading bags of rice into a small truck. "This is Islam. We give all this aid on our own," he explained to me with great conviction. "We are calling for more trucks, because we already have five lorries full of supplies." Meanwhile the loudspeaker from Abu Hanifa mosque issued instructions as people worked frantically and tirelessly. Each time a truck was filled, an empty one would pull up and begin to take on supplies.

Another man, Salam Khasil, saw me talking with Omar and came up to me. With tears in his determined eyes, he said loudly, "All Muslims have one heart. We help each other no matter what. We want the Americans to leave Iraq. It is the right of a people to be free in their own country. We are all one now—Sunni and Shia! Kerbala, Najaf,

Shuwala, we will help them all." He pointed to what I estimated to be at least a thousand people crowding toward the mosque, and said, "All these people are coming to give blood to help their brothers! We will send it to Sadr City, and to anyone else who needs it!"

People milled around, wanting their voices to be heard. Doctors carrying armfuls of empty blood bags rushed into the courtyard of the mosque as men snatched the plastic bags in order to donate. I was walking into the mosque when a man named Khalil pulled me aside and yelled passionately, "This is the second Halabja! This is worse than what Saddam did in Halabja! Where is the freedom? Saddam did Halabja, but the Americans are doing a greater Halabja now!" He then looked me in the eye and firmly and asked fiercely, "Why are sixty innocent people in Fallujah killed because four Americans were killed there? If the American army wants to stay in Iraq, you must kill all the Iraqi people!"

The sanctuary of the mosque was packed with men yelling "*Allahu Akbar!*" over and over. The powerful chanting echoed throughout the cavernous mosque as fists were raised in the air repeatedly. I held up my small digital camera to film a clip, my hands shaking from the adrenaline coursing through the room. The energy in the place overpowered us. Women were crying and beating their hearts. The men were yelling in solidarity with their embattled countrymen of Fallujah.

I remembered Khalil's last sentence, "If the American army wants to stay in Iraq, you must kill all the Iraqi people," and I believed it at that moment, inside Abu Hanifa mosque, standing in this crowd of shouting men who were repeatedly thrusting their fists into the air.

Over near one of the walls, men pushed their way toward a pile of blood bags. Men sat in small groups while young doctors jabbed needles into their waiting arms. With needles stuck in their arms, the men furiously pumped their hands into fists while their blood flowed into the bags on the ground beside them.

The next day found me, along with several friends, hiding out in an apartment in the Karrada district, as the security situation across Iraq continued to deteriorate. We were all afraid to venture too far from our abode. We had teamed up to rent two apartments across the hall from one another, as most hotels were not accepting Western guests, due to concerns of kidnappings and car bombs. Our landlord informed us that he had posted three armed guards on the roof, and one on the ground floor. The outside lights of the building were left on at night, powered by a generator.

The news streaming in on Arab satellite channels and the BBC was not good. A British contractor in Nasariyah had been missing for several days, six trucks en route to Jordan had been torched and their passengers executed, and three Japanese civilians had been kidnapped in the south. The kidnapped Japanese civilians were being held. Their kidnappers were demanding that the Japanese government withdraw their troops from Iraq within three days. If they failed to comply, their citizens would be burned alive. Video clips of the blindfolded Japanese with RPGs and Kalashnikov-wielding men standing behind were constantly being played on several of the Arab news networks.

Horrible as this information was for us to take in, it only got worse. Seven Korean Christian aid workers were kidnapped while traveling from Amman into Baghdad, and two Arab men who lived in Jerusalem had been kidnapped. (The disturbing trend of kidnapping had begun and would only increase with time.)

Meanwhile, the U.S. military assault on Fallujah continued—the city remained powerless and without water. That day, a mosque was bombed and forty people had been killed inside. Graphic images of dead women and children were continuously being shown on the Arab satellite channels. In the last week alone, 459 Iraqis had been killed by the U.S. military, 280 of them in Fallujah alone. There were reports that several trucks delivering aid supplies to Fallujah had been shot by the U.S. military. Refugees reported that the military was dropping cluster bombs within the city. At least thirty-five U.S. soldiers had died in the operation thus far.

An Iraqi friend, Ra'id, who was dating a woman from Australia who lived in one of our apartments, looked at me as we sat watching the news and said, "They kill 280 Iraqis in Fallujah because four American mercenaries were killed? This is the justice? This is fair?" Any illusion of the United States having any control of the situation at that point was just that. Any media that reported otherwise was simply not reporting the truth. All of us were frightened, fearing for the worst, and just waiting. This was by far the most tense it had ever felt in Baghdad, even compared to my last trip, when there were several large bombings around the time of Saddam's capture which had triggered widespread attacks against the occupation forces.

Meanwhile, we had received live broadcasts of General Sanchez announcing how things were under control in Iraq, and George Bush was vacationing at his ranch in Crawford, Texas.

Al-Sadr's militia had taken full control of the holy cities of Najaf and Kut, and the U.S. military, at least for the moment on this first anniversary of the fall of Baghdad, would not dare enter Najaf to arrest him for fear of worsening the situation. The military had attacked al-Sadr's office in Sadr City where I had recently interviewed Sheikh Hassam. Images of the small compound, with huge holes blasted through bullet-pockmarked walls, flashed across our television. The next day, it would be completely rebuilt by the people in the area in one day, from the ground up. This was the determination of the people in Sadr City to resist the onslaught from the occupation forces.

These attacks, coupled with Fallujah, were serving to unite much of the Shia and Sunni populations of Iraq against the occupiers. In what was perhaps an ominous foreboding of things to come for the United States in Iraq, a huge demonstration of Shia and Sunni people broke through a U.S. military checkpoint on the perimeter of Fallujah, chanting vehemently, "Sunni, Shia, we are united against Americans and fight for our country together!"

Fallujah had been under siege by the United States since Monday. There had been more than three hundred Iraqis killed in Fallujah since fighting began, and well over five hundred wounded. We were receiving reports of bodies literally rotting in the streets.

Of the sixty trucks full of relief supplies that had arrived at the outskirts of Fallujah, only three had been allowed into the besieged city.

It had been three days of intense fighting. Soldiers were comparing the situation to that in Vietnam in the past and felt that it was worse than during the invasion a year ago. U.S. Marines had managed to push one mile into Fallujah, all the while incurring heavy losses. There had been at least forty U.S. troops killed in Iraq within the past week. Marines who fought against Saddam's Republican Guard said the fighting in Fallujah had been far worse.

Fighting raged on in the south as Kut had been bombed heavily by U.S. warplanes. Occupation forces managed to retake the city after being forced out, but only after hitting the city more heavily than when it was attacked during the invasion of Iraq.

I stood atop the roof of our apartment, looking down the street through the ink-black night toward Firdos Square, where the statue of Saddam Hussein was pulled down by U.S. forces. Now this square, which was supposed to symbolize freedom for the Iraqi people from a brutal dictator, was encircled with concertina wire three coils deep and Bradley armored fighting vehicles were parked around the area. The square had been closed and a new curfew imposed by the military due to heavy, widespread fighting, and possibly because the nearby Sheraton Hotel, full of U.S. contractors, had been hit by yet another rocket.

Meanwhile, over in Sadr City, the United States had withdrawn from the town hall and all the police stations it was occupying, after five days of fighting.

Random firing of machine guns echoed across Baghdad. Otherwise, aside from the occasional popping of small arms fire, only the sound of generators filled the tense air of the weary capital city.

The next day, I was in conflict with myself as the horrific news from Fallujah continued to pour in. The intensity of the news and widespread threat of kidnapping had part of me wanting to hide under a bed, another part of me wondering if I shouldn't try to book a flight out of Baghdad International, and a larger part of me wanting to stay and report what was happening.

A colleague and his friend had just returned from inside Fallujah and said that, along with one correspondent for Al-Jazeera, they had been the only two reporters inside the city.

He claimed that most of what he'd been witnessing wasn't making the news, such as the heavy U.S. casualties along the road between Baghdad and Fallujah, as well as inside Fallujah. He informed us that the military had ordered families to leave the city, and commenced bombing them while they made their attempt to exit.

He told unbelievable stories, making the U.S. onslaught sound more like a Mongol invasion of barbaric proportions, complete with pregnant women being sliced open by U.S. Marines, deliberate targeting of children and elderly, and bombings of ambulances.

Unfortunately, within the next forty-eight hours, I got all the proof that was necessary when I found myself at a clinic inside Fallujah and witnessed most of these atrocities with my own eyes.

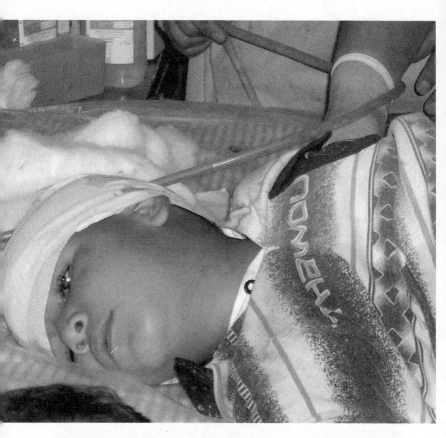

A young boy shot by U.S. snipers in Fallujah. He later died from his wounds. According to Fallujah General Hospital, 736 Iraqis were killed in Fallujah during the April 2004 U.S. attack on the city. More than 60 percent of those killed were women, children, and elderly. April 2004.

CHAPTER 8

SARAJEVO ON THE EUPHRATES

War is for itself, only. Wars of freedom against tyranny, warrior codes of chivalry and courageous self-sacrifice . . . these are human derivates, accidental results of war's basic inhumanity, not war's own intentions, because war is in essence sui generis, autonomous, inhuman.

—James Hillman, A Terrible Love of War

On Friday April 9, 2004, Paul Bremer told reporters, "As of noon today coalition forces have initiated a unilateral suspension of offensive operations in Fallujah."[1] Typifying the ongoing disconnect between the pronouncements of civilian and military officials in the Bush administration, the ever-pliant military spokesman Brigadier General Mark Kimmitt denied there was any report of a cease-fire.[2] Agence France-Presse reported, "Men, women, and children were fleeing on foot through back streets and paths that cut through fields, carrying small bags, food, and medicines."[3] The repugnant part of this report is that the civilians were seeking safety in a village that was already under attack by the United States.

At this point, three hundred Iraqis had already been killed in Fallujah and more than five hundred wounded since the Monday before Bremer's lie. In other words, the U.S. military managed to kill three hundred Iraqis and wound five hundred others in the first four days of the siege.

The general impression was that the current situation was far worse than the invasion a year back. The marines had incurred heavy losses and by way of progress had pushed a single mile into the city. Marines who had earlier fought against Saddam Hussein's Republican Guard said the fighting in Fallujah was much more intense. It was many of the same men who the marines were fighting in Fallujah, but this time around the battle was for themselves and not for a dictator. Sixty-three U.S. troops had been killed since the U.S. assault on Fallujah began five days earlier, according to the U.S. Department of Defense.[4]

While the U.S. continued to proclaim to the world and to itself that the invasion and occupation of Iraq were about freedom and democracy, Iraqis and most others in the Middle East experienced it as the devastation of Mesopotamia. They also experienced the ignorant brutality of the occupation forces. The official military line maintained that Fallujah was being liberated, but few in the Middle East bought the propaganda because they witnessed directly and via Arab media the bombing of civilians before, during, and after the siege.

In this landscape of lies and death, Fallujah soon became a symbol not just of resistance to the occupation but to U.S. hegemony. By and large, Fallujah began to be seen as an island of proud resistance backed by strong tribal and religious affiliations. History was poised to repeat itself in Fallujah, eighty-four years after the rebellion against the British.

Much of southern Iraq convulsed with violence. Kut had been "retaken" by the U.S. military and bombed into submission as heavily as at the time of the invasion. Six more Iranian pilgrims were shot dead at a Polish military checkpoint near Kerbala.

In Baquba, a city with a mixed Shia and Sunni population to the northeast of Baghdad, demonstrators marching in support of Muqtada al-Sadr after their prayers were fired on by American soldiers. The fighting that ensued engaged U.S. forces in heavy combat, and there were reports that the government building that housed the U.S. forces had been damaged badly. Explosions had also been heard near the U.S. base in the area.

In Baghdad, the U.S. imposed another curfew on the area surrounding the Sheraton Hotel, since it had been struck by another mortar round. Strands of concertina wire three coils deep blocked the streets. Bradley fighting vehicles were parked throughout the area.

The night before we ventured to Fallujah, I was on the roof of our apartment taking a radio call, and in the background, from central Baghdad, came the sound of firing machine guns.

The crossroad city of Fallujah, which lies on the banks of the Euphrates River, was home to roughly three hundred and fifty thousand Iraqis. It is situated in a conservative region with strong tribal ties and a prosperous agricultural economy. The surrounding countryside is full of lush vegetation—date palm orchards and vegetable fields—and irrigation ditches. Although many officers of Saddam Hussein's army had settled here, the population was perceived as one opposed to the dictatorial regime and one that had been victimized. As a result, remarkably large number of mosques had conferred upon Fallujah the name "city of mosques," but for the locals it soon became known as the "city of heroes."

For thousands of years, Arabs had traveled up and down the north-south desert passageway near the city, which used to serve as a port in the desert where people from Jordan, Syria, Saudi Arabia, and Iraq met, a place held together by longstanding ties of marriage, family, and tribe.

It was in Fallujah that the first rebellion against the British occupation broke out in 1920, prompting T. E. Lawrence to declare: "Things have been far worse than we have been told, our administration more bloody and inefficient than the public knows....We are today not far from a disaster."[5]

To quell the resistance as it gained momentum, the British had sent Lieutenant Colonel Gerald Leachman, who had experience in putting down uprisings against the British empire. Leachman was killed in Fallujah by Sheikh Dhari, a local leader, whose grandson, Harith al-Dhari, was the most prominent Sunni cleric in Iraq and head of the Association of Muslim Scholars. Al-Dhari was instrumental in brokering the deal that ended the April 2004 siege.[6]

Now, in the same city, the death of Sheikh Yassin in Gaza at the hands of the Israeli military on March 22, 2004, and the U.S. response to the deaths of four Blackwater mercenaries in Fallujah on March 31, led to the deaths of thousands of Iraqis and hundreds of occupation soldiers.[7]

"The Americans are committing the most heinous war crimes imaginable in Fallujah," said a deeply affected Lee Gordon, who had just returned from the city on the evening of April 9. The British freelance journalist was begging his friend Jo and the rest of us to go to Fallujah to help collect bodies and document what was occurring. "There is no medicine and the Americans are shooting ambulances. The only way the Yanks will let sick and injured people out is if we take them ourselves." Gordon then added, "American soldiers are going to people's homes and telling them if they don't leave by dusk, they will be killed. We took out children who had their limbs blown off, and the Americans are turning people back at checkpoints or making them wait." After many questions and some arguing, several of us decided to go the next day in order to document what was occurring, bring medical aid, and transport out as many of the wounded as we could.

Any informed discussion of the April 2004 siege of Fallujah has to take into account its recent history and experience. The residents of the city had good reason to feel strongly against the U.S. forces. During the 1991 Gulf War, British warplanes had bombed a bridge in Fallujah, killing 130 civilians. When friends and relatives ran to the scene to assist the injured, the war planes returned to bomb them, as well.[8]

In the spring of 2003, the city was spared the ground assault of the U.S. invasion, but it was bombed from the air, generating scores of casualties. However, no attacks were launched against the U.S. forces when they first rolled into Fallujah because most people in the city supported the removal of Saddam Hussein by the United States. Tribal leaders were quick to cooperate and to appoint a pro-U.S. sheikh to work with the CPA.

Problems arose, however, on April 28, 2003, when soldiers occupying the al-Kaahd school opened fire on a crowd protesting how the 82nd Airborne had converted a school into a military post, thus barring children from using it for their classes. According to Iraqis at the scene, seventeen were killed and seventy-five wounded. Not a single shot had been fired at the U.S. soldiers.

Two days later, on April 30, a demonstration against the occupation and the murders committed by the U.S. troops took place, with similar results. According to the mayor of Fallujah, two people were killed (another died later from gunshot wounds) and sixteen wounded when a crowd of one thousand protestors stopped in front of the former office of Saddam Hussein's Ba'ath Party, which had been turned into the American battalion headquarters. A U.S. military convoy en route from Ramadi to Baghdad passed the demonstrators when some of the demonstrators threw their footwear at the building—an act considered highly insulting in Iraqi culture. The convoy opened fire on the protesters after a young boy threw his sandals at a Humvee. U.S. troops killed three more citizens this time, and injured another sixteen. Again, the military claimed U.S. troops had taken fire from the crowd, a statement refuted by journalists at the scene, as well as Iraqi officials in the city.

Photos of the incident taken by Julian Andrews, which were published in the *Daily Mirror* in the U.K., clearly show unarmed demonstraters fleeing a large caliber machine gun being fired from atop a U.S. Humvee as it sped down the main street in Fallujah. Chris Hughes, in an article for the *Mirror*, wrote of the incident, "I watched in horror as American troops opened fire on a crowd of one thousand unarmed people here yesterday. Many, including children, were cut down by a twenty-second burst of automatic gunfire during a demonstration against the killing of thirteen protesters at the Al-Kaahd school on Monday."[9]

From this point on, attacks against the U.S. military in Fallujah became a near daily occurrence. Within a few months, the military was unable to run patrols into the city without encountering fierce attacks.

A Human Rights Watch report entitled "Violent Response: The U.S. Army in al-Falluja" thoroughly documented these events by interviewing soldiers, officers, townspeople, and other witnesses. It included an investigation of ballistic evidence found at the scene of the two attacks. No bullet holes were found in the school that the soldiers occupied, directly refuting the bogus military claim that they had come under fire. The report added that U.S. troops had responded in both instances, causing "disproportionate harm" and added that, "U.S. authorities should conduct a full, independent, and impartial investigation into the April 28 and April 30 violent incidents in al-Falluja to determine the circumstances that led to the shootings, and to hold accountable anyone found to have committed violations of international humanitarian law."[10]

According to the Geneva Conventions, under international humanitarian law, the United States, as the occupier in Iraq, is obliged to ensure public order and safety and, when engaged in law-enforcement activities such as crowd control, should use lethal force only "when strictly unavoidable in order to protect life."[11] At these times, as well as all others, they are obliged to act with restraint and in proportion to the seriousness of the threat posed. Yet, again and again, the U.S. military did just the opposite in Fallujah. On September 17, 2003, U.S. soldiers fired on a wedding party in the city, killing a fourteen-year-old boy and wounding several others. That same month, U.S. soldiers killed eight Iraqi policemen, supposedly mistaken for bandits, despite being in uniform and driving in clearly marked vehicles. The policemen had reportedly begged and screamed over their radios for the firing to stop. U.S. military officials were unable to explain to reporters why their soldiers had opened fire on the policemen as they passed in front of a U.S. military base in two clearly marked Iraqi police cars with sirens flashing on top. (Wounded police officers who survived the U.S. attack later described to reporters how they had pleaded with the soldiers to stop firing as their colleagues fell dying around them.) A security guard from Jordan at a Jordanian-funded hospital opposite the U.S. base was also killed in the attack. Inside the hospital, four other guards were injured by the heavy firing.

The morning of April 10 found us at the "Italian House," a nice home in central Baghdad, not far from our apartment, out of which the Italian organization A Bridge to Baghdad operated. Jo, David Martinez (an independent filmmaker from California), Rahul, Helen (an Australian activist) and her boyfriend Ra'id, two female

Iraqi journalists, Nuha and Ahrar, Lee Gordon, Ghreeb, and I had teamed up for the trip, accompanied by Hannah, our trusted translator and fixer.

A large bus had been hired to ferry us in, along with medical supplies donated by the INTERSOS NGO for a clinic in the city that we knew was operating with next to nothing. Under a bright sun, all of us worked briskly to load bundles of blankets and boxes of gauze, rubber gloves, and various medications onto the back of the bus. Simona Torretta and Simona Pari, two Italian activists who had worked in Iraq for many years, had been instrumental in arranging our transportation, as well as the supplies. ("The Two Simonas," as they came to be known, were later kidnapped on September 7 in broad daylight from the same house, as were Iraqi aid workers Raad Ali Abdul Aziz and Mahnouz Bassam. Later they were released unharmed.)

The mood was anxious as we quickly took our seats on the bus. I knew that we were going into a city that was being heavily attacked by the most powerful military on the planet, but I felt obliged to do what I could to bear witness to the atrocities being carried out against the people of Fallujah by the U.S. military, especially because the U.S. forces had gone to such great lengths to keep reporters out of the city. With only two Al-Jazeera journalists there, I felt compelled to go.

Rahul, sitting in front of me, turned around with a small smile as the bus began to pull away from the Italian House, following the car with the sheikh's nephew. "Too late now," he said.

Leaving Baghdad now was extremely dangerous. The military continued to seal off Fallujah, and the main highway between the capital city and Jordan was shut down. The highway, even close to Baghdad, was desolate, and littered with the smoldering carcasses of destroyed fuel-tanker trucks. We rolled past a large, still burning, M-

1 tank that had just been hit by the resistance. Flames licked toward the sky from the turret as the smoking body of the tank sat useless under an overpass.

Still within the outer reaches of Baghdad, we approached a long line of vehicles waiting at the first and last U.S. checkpoint. Once we had inched our way toward the soldiers, we were ordered off the bus and searched. The anxious young soldier searching me told me they had been at the checkpoint for thirty hours straight. He was exhausted and scared. We learned that no men under the age of forty-five were being allowed to leave Fallujah, but our guess that having Westerners aboard the bus would enable us passage through the U.S. checkpoint proved true. They waved us ahead.

Our bus headed off the highway along bumpy dirt roads, winding through parts of the town of Abu Ghraib, slowly but steadily progressing toward the besieged city. As we passed a small home in Abu Ghraib, a small child yelled at the bus, "We will be mujahedeen until we die!"

Of the sixty trucks full of relief supplies that had arrived at the outskirts of Fallujah, only three had been allowed into the besieged city. Meanwhile, Lieutenant General Ricardo Sanchez, commander of coalition forces in Iraq, had been insisting that the U.S. military was in no way impeding the delivery of relief supplies to the residents of Fallujah. Other relief trucks had been shot at by U.S. forces. The only reason we were able to proceed toward the city is because we had used back roads. Slowly, we worked our way back onto the highway, which was a wasteland of torched military hardware and exploded fuel trucks. A large semi-tractor trailer that had been hit was being looted by people from a nearby village. This scene of men running to and from the highway carrying away large boxes against a backdrop of pure devastation, with barely any other moving vehicle other than ours on the road, was surreal.

We turned off the highway into territory completely controlled by the Iraqi resistance. Our bus wound its way through farm roads, and each time we passed someone they yelled, "God bless you for going to Fallujah!" Everyone we passed in the sprawling green fields that border the crystal blue waters of the Euphrates gave us the victory sign, waves, or gave a thumbs-up.

As we neared Fallujah, groups of children on the side of the road handed out water and bread to people coming into the city. They began throwing stacks of flat bread into the bus as they cheered us, the floppy warm bread spun through our windows. Groups speckled the road, cheering us and handing cups of water through the windows.

As we approached the outskirts of Fallujah, a huge billowing plume of smoke caused by a large U.S. bomb rose from the city. We saw several warplanes roaring nearby, and found attack helicopters strafing certain areas of the city. Meanwhile, the corporate media was busy obediently reporting on the so-called cease-fire. The annoying mosquito-like buzz of remote control military surveillance drones was ever-present. The closer we got to the city, the more numerous grew the number of resistance checkpoints we encountered. At one, men with keffiyehs around their faces and holding Kalashnikovs began shooting their guns in the air, proudly displaying their eagerness to fight.

Fallujah seemed devoid of all people other than groups of mujahedeen who stood on every other street corner. Most residents had either evacuated or chosen to hide in their homes. The marines had occupied the northeastern edge of Fallujah, but most of the town was occupied by local Sunni as well as Shi'ite members of Muqtada al-Sadr's Mehdi Army, who had come in from Baghdad and the south. There seemed to be separate groups of mujahadeen in charge of different parts of the city and the various roads in and out of it.

Between the clearly marked territories of the mujahedeen and the marines was a no-man's-land. Sounds of sporadic gunfire, warplanes, and bombs were punctuated by an electrically charged silence, a push-pull of frenetic deadly action followed by more of the dreadful, anticipatory silence.

We rolled toward the one small clinic where we were to deliver our medical supplies. The small clinic was managed by Maki al-Nazzal, who was hired just four days ago. He was not a doctor. The other makeshift clinic in Fallujah was in a mechanic's garage. He had barely slept in the past week, nor had any of the doctors at the small clinic. Originally, the clinic had just three doctors, but since the U.S. military bombed one of the hospitals and were currently sniping at people as they attempted to enter or exit the main hospital, effectively, there were only these two small clinics treating the entire city.

The boxes of medical supplies we brought into the clinic were torn open immediately by the desperate doctors. A woman entered, slapping her chest and face, and wailing as her husband carried in the dying body of her little boy. Blood was trickling off one of his arms, which dangled out of his father's arms. Thus began my witnessing of an endless stream of women and children who had been shot by the U.S. soldiers and were now being raced into the dirty clinic, the cars speeding over the curb out front, and weeping family members carrying in their wounded. One eighteen-year-old girl had been shot through the neck. She was making breathy gurgling noises as the doctors frantically worked on her amid her muffled moaning. Flies dodged the working hands of doctors to return to the patches of her vomit that stained her black *abaya*.

Her younger brother, a small child of ten with a gunshot wound in his head from a marine sniper, his eyes glazed and staring into space, continually vomited as the doctors raced to save his life while family members cried behind me. "The Americans cut our electricity days ago, so we cannot vacuum the vomit from his throat," a furious doctor tells me. They were both loaded into an ambulance and rushed toward Baghdad, only to die en route.

Another small child lay on a blood-spattered bed, also shot by a sniper. The boy's grandmother lay nearby, shot as she was attempting to carry children from their home and flee the city. She lay on a bed dying, still clutching a bloodied white surrender flag. Hundreds of families were trapped in their homes, terrorized by U.S. snipers shooting from rooftops and the minarets of mosques whenever they saw someone move past a window.

Blood bags were being kept in a food refrigerator, warmed under running water before being given to patients. There were no anesthetics. The lights went out as the generator ran dry of fuel, so the doctors, who had been working for days on end, worked by light provided by men holding up cigarette lighters or flashlights as the sun set. Needless to say, there was no air-conditioning inside the steamy "clinic."

One victim of the U.S. military aggression after another was brought into the clinic, nearly all of them women and children, carried by weeping family members. Those who had not been hit by bombs from warplanes had been shot by U.S. snipers. The one functioning ambulance left at this clinic sat outside with bullet holes in the sides and a small group of shots right on the driver side of the windshield. The driver, his head bandaged from being grazed by the bullet of a sniper, refused to go collect any more of the dead and wounded.

Standing near the ambulance in frustration, Maki told us, "They [U.S. soldiers] shot the ambulance and they shot the driver *after* they checked his car, inspected his car, and knew that he was carrying nothing. Then they shot him. And then they shot the ambulance. And now I have no ambulance to evacuate more than twenty wounded people. I don't know who is doing this and why he is doing this. This is terrible. This has never happened before. And I don't know who to call because it seems that nobody is listening."

The stream of patients slowed to a sporadic influx as night fell. Maki sat with me as we shared cigarettes in a small office in the rear of the clinic. "For all my life, I believed in American democracy," he told me with an exhausted voice. "For forty-seven years, I had accepted the illusion of Europe and the United States being good for the world, the carriers of democracy and freedom. Now I see that it took me forty-seven years to wake up to the horrible truth. They are not here to bring anything like democracy or freedom.

"Now I see it has all been lies. The Americans don't give a damn about democracy or human rights. They are worse than even Saddam." I asked him if he minded if I quoted him with his name. "What are they going to do to me that they haven't already done here," he said.

Another car skipped over the curb outside, and a man who was burned from head to toe was carried in on a stretcher. He surely died shortly, as there was no way this clinic could treat massive burns. Maki, frustrated and in shock, said, "They say there is a cease-fire. They said twelve o'clock, so people went out to do some shopping. Everybody who went out was shot and this place was full, and half of them were dead."

More than twenty dead bodies had been brought to this clinic during the last twenty-four hours of the "cease-fire." Shortly after this, another car skidded to a stop, and a man hit with cluster bombs was unloaded. "The Americans have been using cluster bombs often here," Maki tells me somberly. "And of course they love their D.U. [depleted uranium]"

We heard bombs sporadically exploding around the city, along with intermittent gunfire, as we were taken to the home of Yasser nearby. Luckily, it was close enough to walk. Any car in the street would have been shot immediately by snipers. As we walked through the empty streets toward the house, a plane flew over us, dropping several flares. We ran, panicked, for a nearby wall, and ducked behind it, afraid it was dropping cluster bombs. Two of the last victims that had arrived at the clinic were reported by the locals to have been hit by cluster bombs. They were horribly burned and their bodies were shredded with the usual pockmarks, a trademark wound from these munitions.

It was a long night and I barely slept. Each time I began to slip into sleep, a jet roared overhead, a bomb exploded in the distance, helicopter blades chomped the air, or guns rattled in the distance, forcing me to wonder when the full-scale bombing would commence. Military drones buzzed constantly. Also, drinking much of the local, untreated water made me violently ill through the night.

The next morning, we walked back to the clinic to find a group of extremely edgy mujahedeen in the vicinity. They were expecting the invasion at any time and were taking up positions to fight. Jo and the others went out on two ambulance runs to collect two bodies. She said that a marine she encountered had told them to leave, because the military was about to use air support to begin "clearing the city." One of the bodies they brought to the clinic was that of a fifty-five-year-old man shot in the back by a sniper outside his home while his wife and children huddled wailing inside. The family could not retrieve his body for fear of being shot. His stiff corpse was carried into the clinic, flies swarming above it. One of his arms was half-raised by rigor mortis.

I intermittently walked over to the side of the clinic to vomit, still reeling from the water I'd ingested the previous night. While doing so, I looked up to find one of the weary doctors from the clinic offering me some pills to treat my nausea. "*Shukran jazeelan*," (thank you very much) I muttered humbly, incredulous that he had taken the vital moment away from his work to help a Westerner.

The already insane situation continued to degrade, and by the time the wounded from the clinic were loaded onto our bus and we prepared to leave, everyone felt the invasion was imminent. U.S. bombs continued to fall near us, and sporadic gunfire continued.

We slowly drove out, past loads of mujahedeen at their posts along the streets. In a long line of vehicles loaded with families, we slowly crept out of the embattled city, passing several military vehicles on the city's outskirts. We took a wrong turn at one point, attempted to go down a road controlled by a different group of mujahedeen, and were promptly surrounded by angry men cocking their weapons and aiming them at us. The doctors and patients on board explained to them we were coming from Fallujah and on a humanitarian aid mission, so they let us go, unlike the U.S. military, that continued to turn back families trying to flee Fallujah.

With no end in sight for the fighting that raged in Fallujah, I sat on the floor of the bus, holding my head in my hands, wondering how the thousands of civilians trapped in the city would survive.

An ambulance in Fallujah shot by U.S. snipers. It is common for the Iraqi medical infrastructure to be attacked by U.S. forces during large-scale military operations. April 2004.

CHAPTER 9

RAIDING MOSQUES, TORTURING IRAQIS

Having survived the hell of Fallujah, I returned to Baghdad to find that most of the remaining NGOs in Iraq were either pulling out completely or leaving behind a skeleton crew. There was even talk of a UN airlift to fly remaining members of international development organizations out of Iraq if necessary. Others spoke of the possibility of the Baghdad airport being closed down for security reasons.

All of us were appalled when we found CNN on the satellite TV channels declaring that the cease-fire in Fallujah was "holding." Other corporate media outlets like National Public Radio and the *New York Times* had their reporters happily embedded with the troops, obediently regurgitating the military press releases for U.S. audiences.

In my gut, I was beginning to experience a feeling of being trapped. Conditions, particularly those related to mobility, were growing increasingly restrictive. Planes entering and exiting Iraq had to use corkscrew descent and ascent. The road to Amman was virtually impassable for any Westerner because of the threat of kidnapping. It was fear of being kidnapped that forced me to consider abandoning my mission and leaving Iraq. Most of us had decided to take it a day at a time. Our strategy was to stock up on provisions and sit tight in our apartment in the Karrada district of Baghdad.

Many of our Iraqi friends and interpreters had received death threats for working with us, more and more Iraqis were staying at home, and all of us were afraid.

That night, from the roof of our apartment, I watched soldiers and Humvees seal Firdos Square. In "liberated Iraq," U.S. soldiers announced on loudspeakers, from behind coils of concertina wire, that anyone approaching the square would be shot on sight.

◆ ◆ ◆ ◆

In an April 13 prime-time press conference addressing the ongoing violence in Iraq, George W. Bush told reporters, "America's armed forces are performing brilliantly, with all the skill and honor we expect of them."[1] He went on to say that he knew what the United States was doing in Iraq was right. When I read this in Baghdad, I wondered if Bush included the massacre of unarmed women, children, and elderly in Fallujah? When he said he believed the soldiers in Iraq were performing brilliantly "with all the skill and honor…" did this include the snipers shooting ambulances with blaring sirens and flashing lights? Did this include dragging an entire country into a bloody chaos that was worsening by the hour?

My sources from inside Fallujah, many of whom were doctors, said that by now more than six hundred bodies had been counted at area emergency facilities, although the local medical authorities in the city believed that a significant number of victims had been buried without any possibility of receiving care at a clinic or hospital. Mass funerals were conducted during brief lulls in the fighting. One of the two soccer fields in the town had been converted into a mass martyr cemetery. I tried hard to imagine a soccer field back in the United States being turned into a graveyard—headstones above ground and buried shrapnel-shredded bodies underneath, populating a dry field where children once laughed, ran, and kicked soccer balls—but my imagination failed me.

Alber was seething. "On April 11, at 3:30 a.m., U.S. troops raided the mosque by using tanks to crash through the gate adjoining the food storage area that was being stocked for the besieged people of Fallujah. Another tank smashed through the gate next to the student dormitory and the martyrs' cemetery." The spokesman for the Abu Hanifa mosque in the neighborhood of Adhamiyah, in Baghdad, slowly recounted the recent U.S. raid on his mosque. Rahul, Harb, and I sat listening in disbelief in a visiting room inside the mosque. Near us lay tattered plastic bags containing three tons of food meant as relief for Fallujah, now rendered useless by the crushing wheels of a Humvee. This and other aid material lay wasted inside a metal gate that had first been demolished by the same vehicle.

"Forty soldiers entered the mosque while about sixty were guarding it from the outside," continued Alber as tea was served to us. "Those inside went first into the main area of the mosque where all of us were praying. Some Red Crescent volunteers from Kirkuk were also resting there before setting out with the supplies for the people of Fallujah." The soldiers had entered with their weapons and with their footwear, strictly forbidden in a mosque, and then ordered everyone at gunpoint to lie on the ground. There was anger in his voice as he told us, "I speak good English. I pleaded with the Americans to let us open all the doors for them to avoid further damage to our mosque. I was afraid of how the people would react when they found out. But the Iraqi translator accompanying them yelled at me, 'Silence! Shut your mouth!'" While some soldiers held all the people at gunpoint, their colleagues broke in every locked and closed door in the mosque and some that were not even locked.

Later, walking around the Imam Adham Islamic College attached to the mosque, I had found door after door smashed in and random bullet holes spotting the walls and ceilings. Students' papers lay strewn about an instructor's desk, the U.S. soldiers having rifled through them—looking for what?

"After two hours of holding us with our faces to the ground and with their booted feet on our backs, which we consider a highly insulting gesture, the soldiers did not find a single bullet. Then they simply left. A year ago they would have apologized for such actions. Now they don't even bother. Now they apologize by stomping on our necks."

This was the third time Abu Hanifa had been raided. The first time was last December. I had covered the story during my last trip and had taken photos of shots fired into the outer walls and the clock tower of the mosque. After talking with Alber, we were walking to the other side of the mosque when a woman from Fallujah arrived, weeping, with her son. She explained to the men at the mosque that she had no ID card. The U.S. soldiers had taken it away. She had come begging for aid. Residents of Adhamiyah had begun housing the refugees of Fallujah by the hundreds, if not thousands. One family was said to have taken in eight entire families and would not allow anyone to remove any of them.

Around the other side of the mosque, we were introduced to Kassem, a fifty-four-year-old grandfather, blind in one eye and with a disabled leg. He worked as a guard at the mosque, and lived within the compound with his family, which included grandchildren. I noticed a bloody bandage on his forehead. We were told he had tried to stand up when the U.S. soldiers had crashed the door of his quarters and barged in on his family. Then, one of the soldiers had smashed Kassem's head with the butt of his M-16, knocking him to the ground. Kassem pointed to his leg and said, "When I fell to the ground they kicked me. They came to humiliate the people of Islam. Why else? We have no guns here, no mujahedeen. They want to destroy the Islamic religion."

We were taken to the martyrs' cemetery in the mosque courtyard. There I saw the fresh graves of the ten-year-old boy and his older sister who I had watched dying in the clinic in Fallujah. Earlier, Alber had told us, "I was against Saddam. I was jailed by his regime in 1996 for making pastries because at the time sugar was being rationed due to the sanctions. But the U.S. policy now in Iraq will fail 100 percent. No people here support them now."

"The managers of the U.S. policy here are not clever people," he calmly added, "When you come by terrorism, you create terrorism."

Later, Harb took Rahul and me to interview Professor Adnan Mohammed Salman al-Dulaimi. Dulaimi was the director of the board that is in charge of all the Sunnis in Iraq, with more than ten thousand Imams under his control (and was to become a leading political figure in the upcoming elections.) A teacher for fifty-one years, his first words to us were, "Our situation is bad. We are struggling now." He went on to tell us how in the past few days three mosques in Baghdad had been attacked by U.S. soldiers—Abu Hanifa, which I had reported, and two others on Palestine Street. The two issues he held responsible for most of the current problems were the high rate of unemployment and the dissolving of the Iraqi Army by Paul Bremer. Both were direct results of the occupation and needed to be addressed immediately if Iraq was to become stable.

"Bush declared Iraq will be an example of democracy for the Middle East," he said. "What has happened here does not give that impression."

In Baghdad, chaos, uncertainty, fear, and anxiety reigned more than ever. Everyone awaited with apprehension the outcomes of Fallujah and Najaf. People I spoke with felt that if the United States launched a larger attack on either city, the already critical situation would explode in a way no one wanted to contemplate. (It took less than seven months for people's worst fears to materialize.)

The morning of April 17, a thundering explosion rocked my bed at just before 8:00. Many of us ran to the roof of our apartment building. The cracking of light weapons' fire echoed across the city, but we were unable to spot the location of the attack. This was often the case when bombs exploded in Baghdad. Life continued to be on edge as everyone awaited the outcome of the Najaf standoff between U.S. troops and Muqtada al-Sadr and his men. There was understandable concern about the eventuality of a U.S. strike at the sacred Imam Ali Shrine, one of the most revered Shia shrines in Iraq.

I attended a press conference at the Ministry of Health, led by the Iraqi Minister of Health himself. It was held basically to stave off criticism that the administration was doing little to nothing to provide medical assistance to the residents of besieged Fallujah and other areas in the south that had seen conflict.

What was stunning, however, was that the minister acknowledged that the U.S. military was intentionally targeting ambulances in Fallujah. He expressed outrage and stated that he had personally pressed the Interim Governing Council and Bremer for explanations about why these human rights violations and violations of the Geneva Conventions were occurring. The Ministry of Health is housed near the Medical City, and on our way out I sadly watched a man with one leg and one of his hands heavily bandaged riding out of the hospital on a donkey. All the time, my face was slammed up against the acute level of poverty and struggle that many in Baghdad endured on a daily basis. In nearly every traffic jam, I looked out the window at women and children begging. Sometimes I gave some dinars, sometimes I stared at my feet and just stomached the sadness.

The daily flights leaving the Baghdad airport continued to depart full. Those of us who chose to remain continued to watch Najaf and Fallujah with great concern. I found tempers boiling everywhere I turned. The previous evening, an old Shi'ite man in his shop in Karrada had told me, "The situation here is worse than I can ever remember. I still can't understand their policy here. Where is the freedom they promised?"

We had news that some of our friends who had attempted to reenter Fallujah had been detained by mujahedeen for a night, so we decided to cover the siege by visiting hospitals in Baghdad, rather than risking another trip. Whenever they could manage to do so, doctors from Fallujah were carting wounded people to the capital.

At the large, centrally located Yarmouk Hospital, we had a discussion on the situation in Fallujah with the lead doctor. He said that during the first days of the U.S. siege of Fallujah, many of the wounded had been brought to his hospital. "The Americans came here to question my patients, even though we tried to refer our patients to other hospitals to prevent them from being detained." He sounded outraged by what he referred to as a massacre. "The Americans shot at some of our doctors who were traveling to Fallujah to provide aid. One of our doctors was injured when a missile struck his vehicle. I have also been told by my doctors in Fallujah that the Americans are targeting ambulances there, and at the main hospital. I have reports that the Americans are using cluster bombs. Patients we have treated from there are reporting the same." Using cluster bombs in civilian areas is a violation of the Geneva Conventions. He continued, "One of my doctors in Fallujah asked the Americans there if he could remove a wounded patient from the city. The soldier did not allow him to move the victim, and apparently said, 'We have dead soldiers here, too. This is a war zone.' The wounded man died. So many doctors and ambulances have been turned back from checkpoints there."

At al-Numan Hospital in Adhamiya, I spoke to a doctor who said, "We are treating an average of one gunshot wound per day, which is something we never saw before the occupation. This is due to the absence of law enforcement in Baghdad. The Iraqi police have weak weapons and nobody respects their authority." He told me when U.S. soldiers came to the hospital asking for information about resistance fighters, "My policy is not to give my patients to the Americans, or to provide them any information. I deny information to the Americans for the sake of the patient. I don't care what my patients have done outside the walls of the hospital. I do my job and then let the patient go. Ten days ago, the Americans raided our hospital looking for people. It has been occurring since people started coming in from Fallujah, even though most of them are children, women, and the elderly."

When I asked if he had heard that the U.S. military was bombing civilians in Fallujah, he said, "Of course the Americans are bombing civilians, along with the revolutionaries. One year ago there was no revolution in Fallujah. But they began searching homes and humiliating people, and this upset people. The people became angry and demonstrated, then the Americans shot the demonstrators, and this started the revolution in Fallujah. It is the same in Sadr City." He grew angrier as he continued. "Aggression against civilians has caused all of this. Nothing happened for the first two months of the occupation. People were happy to have Saddam gone. And now, we hope for the mercy of God if the Americans invade Najaf."

Another doctor who wanted to remain anonymous stated that he saw the U.S. military dropping cluster bombs on the al-Dora area last December. "I've seen it all with my own eyes." He told me that, based

on reports from field doctors presently working there, and statements taken from wounded civilians, it was obvious that cluster
bombs were being used in Fallujah. He also said many of the Fallujan
victims he treated had been shot with dum-dum bullets, which are
hollow-point bullets designed to inflict maximum internal damage.
These are also referred to as "expanding bullets."

Harb and I decided to drive over to the al-Karam Hospital, where
a doctor, who agreed to speak on condition of anonymity, informed
us that one of the doctors from his hospital had just returned from
the al-Sadr Teaching Hospital in Najaf because she was unable to
work there. She reported to her hospital that Spanish military forces
were currently occupying the hospital in Najaf because it was close
to their base. The roof of the hospital overlooked their base, so soldiers had taken it over for strategic purposes. He was seething as he
said, "The Americans don't care what happens to Iraqis."

◆   ◆   ◆   ◆

One day, as we neared the end of April, Harb drove me to the
other side of his neighborhood of Adhamiya. The setting sun was
bathing the nearby groves of date palms in a dark orange when we
pulled in front of the old but elegant home of Dr. Womidh Omar
Nadhme, on the banks of the Tigris River, directly across from the
sprawling Green Zone. We were escorted into his sitting room by
one of his sons, before Dr. Nadhme entered. The old stately professor greeted us formally, then immediately lit a cigarette and engaged
Harb in some small talk in Arabic before getting to my questions. An
outspoken critic of the former regime, Dr. Nadhme was truly a na-
tionalist and had always worked for the Iraqi people, rather than any
particular sect or political party. It quickly became apparent to me
that he had no qualms about criticizing U.S. policy. "Once you abide

by the policy of the U.S.A. you are not a terrorist anymore. In 1991 Syria was not a terrorist because they supported the war against Iraq. Syria opposed the recent invasion, so now they are a terrorist state," he explained. When I asked what he thought about the Bush administration's claim that Iraq was the front line of the "war on terror," he replied, "Here, one would have to distinguish between terrorism and resistance. Terror was unseen here before the invasion. In Fallujah, it is not terrorism, it is resistance."

We spoke of U.S. policy throughout the Middle East. When I asked the professor about Palestine, he said, "The crimes against humanity in Palestine are shown daily on the television. This does not indicate that the current U.S. administration is committed to democracy or human rights. How can the United States, a war criminal in Palestine, be accepted as a state-builder in Iraq?"

We had a lengthy discussion on the reality in Iraq, where more and more Iraqis had long since woken up to the fact that the true U.S. agenda was not for their liberation or benefit but for the oil, and its own geostrategic military position. "The American's war against Iraq is over," he told me, "Now we have the war of Iraq against America. It is a war of Iraqis fighting for their country, their homes, their money, and their lives."

The next evening, I interviewed a resistance fighter in Baghdad. I was taken to a preset location in advance and waited for him to arrive. I was nervously sipping tea with Harb when a tall, hulking man wearing a blue ski mask entered. He chose to be called "Ahmed." In a deep, coarse voice, he greeted us with "*Salam Aleikum*" and bade us be seated.

"The media concentrates on the Americans, and does not care about Iraqis," he began. "This is not a rebellion, this is a resistance against the occupation." The twenty-six-year-old member of the growing Iraqi resistance used to work as a portrait photographer, and maintained his trade even as a member of the Iraqi Army, where he was a guard at the presidential palace. He insisted he was opposed to Saddam Hussein, and rejoiced when the U.S. military managed to topple his brutal regime. In fact, he didn't even fight in the war against the U.S. military during the invasion. But he grew weary of watching his fellow countrymen humiliated, mistreated, and killed by the aggression of the occupiers and, like so many others, he subsequently took up arms to fight against them.

"We were under great stress during the time of Saddam," he told me. "He put me in prison. We were never loyal to Saddam, but now he is our representative, one of us because he is a native of Iraq, he is Muslim, and he is Iraqi."

Ahmed was a member of a group of twenty fighters who carried out attacks. His group had a "narrow" relationship with other groups in the resistance, he said. "We meet on the day we have a job, then after we complete the job, we don't know each other until it is time for another job." His last job had been the day before we met. He claimed his group had carried out 250 attacks so far and he personally had participated in 70 of them.

How did he know when it was time to meet with his group? "When a house or city is attacked by the Americans, we meet and decide what job to do." His group used RPGs, IEDs, grenades, and Kalashnikovs. "We have all the arms," he said gruffly, "that we need to do our jobs." When asked who comprised the resistance, he held his hands out and replied, "There are Shia, Ba'athists, Sufis, tribalists, and Arab fighters." He added pointedly, "I have been fighting for a year now, and I have not seen one Al-Qaeda fighter, nor have I heard of one fighting in the resistance." He said that around half of the Iraqi police were members of the resistance, and the resistance was growing rapidly. That very week, five more men had joined his group. He leaned forward and said, "As more Iraqis are provoked, more are joining the resistance. Even children who have had their parents killed by the soldiers are joining." Ahmed also told us that nobody in his group was paid, and many held regular jobs.

"The Americans are the terrorists," he continued. "Their military has killed millions of people all around the world. Is killing people like this acceptable? I will stop fighting when the last American soldier leaves Iraq."

The very next day, April 28, the CBS program *60 Minutes II* aired photos of Iraqi detainees being tortured by U.S. soldiers inside Abu Ghraib prison. The visual confirmation of all the stories and testimonies I'd been hearing and documenting for months spread like wildfire across not just Iraq, but the entire Middle East.

It is important to note that the CBS program had been sitting on the story for a significant period of time, and only aired the photos when they did because journalist Seymour Hersh would have scooped them with an article on Abu Ghraib in the *New Yorker* if they didn't air their show. In fact, a reporter for the Internet magazine *Salon* published a story about torture and the inhuman conditions in Abu Ghraib in early March. I had also made futile attempts back in January to feed U.S. newspapers a story on torture.

What few shreds of credibility the United States may have had left in Iraq were completely erased by the photos, which resulted in an outrage that manifested itself in shock, anger, and increased violence. Once again, U.S. actions in Iraq were serving as the greatest recruitment tool for the Iraqi resistance.

I could feel the security situation deteriorating. By this time, my friend Dave Enders and I decided it would be safer to find a low-key hotel to set up shop in, as most people in the area where we had the apartment were well aware that several Westerners were staying there. Not far away, still in central Baghdad, we found a room in the Arasat Hotel. We hoped the fact that it was owned and managed by a man from Samarra would provide at least a hint of protection from being kidnapped. Samarra being predominantly Sunni, his affiliation would, in theory, dissuade members of the Sunni resistance from visiting his hotel in order to collect guests.

◆ ◆ ◆ ◆

At roughly 7:30 a.m. on May 6, we were awakened by a huge explosion that rocked the hotel building. This one I felt through the floor.

Dave and I quickly gathered our cameras, note pads, and press credentials, and caught a cab to follow the huge plume of black smoke billowing from the direction of the Green Zone.

We arrived at the checkpoint near the Fourteenth of July suspension bridge that spans the Tigris. Huge flames reached into the morning sky from what was left of a car smoldering between the two large concrete walls that led to the checkpoint. It was roughly forty-five feet away from the entrance to the Green Zone, and many cars behind it were crushed by the blast. Soldiers angrily barked at the crowd to stay back from the concertina wire they had pulled across the streets in front of their Humvees. A fire truck feebly sprayed water onto the incinerated vehicle, but the flames always reignited, and smoke spewed out the sides of the wrecked car.

Glass in all the surrounding buildings had been blown out, as well as windows of most cars along the street. A leg was found six hundred feet from the blast site. Broken glass covered the grass near the line of blasted cars. We quickly scaled the stairs of a nearby apartment building to get a better view of the scene as the area rocked with another small explosion, perhaps a gas tank going off from another car in the line behind the burned vehicle. Iraqis crowded near the concertina wire reflexively moved backward, fearing another bomb. Ambulance sirens blared, as soldiers yelled at people who got too close.

Word was that as a soldier approached the car, the bomber detonated the explosives, killing himself and the soldier, and injuring many others. At least two other Iraqis who were in cars in line for the checkpoint were killed. We caught a cab back to our hotel and the driver angrily declared, "Before with Saddam, we had no bombs like this."

Meanwhile, intense U.S. military operations had occurred very close to the sacred Imam Ali Shia Shrine in Najaf, as the coalition forces attempted to take advantage of growing anger toward Muqtada al-Sadr from more moderate Shi'ite clerics in the region. At least one U.S. soldier and fifteen Iraqis had died in the fighting thus far. However, simultaneously, followers of al-Sadr were marching together in early May with Sunni resistance fighters in the streets in the predominantly Sunni al-Adhamiya district of Baghdad, publicly showing their solidarity in battling against the U.S. military.

The Bush administration scrambled for damage control from the stream of photographs documenting the atrocities from Abu Ghraib prison. Bush, appearing on the U.S.-funded Al-Hurra television network, chose not to apologize to the Arab community, leaving this for his aides at a later date. Instead, by saying things such as "it's also important for the people of Iraq to know that in a democracy, everything is not perfect, that mistakes are made," Bush infuriated and insulted most Iraqis.[2] Almost all the Iraqis I spoke with about his speech said they had noticed that he didn't even apologize and instead opted to talk down to the Iraqi people.

"This shows he doesn't care about Iraqis," one of my Iraqi friends told me. "All he cares about is himself and the image of America. What is the image? That America has brought us freedom and democracy? Does he think we are stupid and blind?"

According to residents and doctors in Fallujah, U.S. military snipers were killing so many people and shooting so often that residents were forced to turn a soccer field into a martyr cemetery. Attacks occurred so often that Fallujans often buried their loved ones in gardens, then transferred the bodies to this stadium when the fighting subsided. May 2004.

CHAPTER 10

THE AFTERMATH IN FALLUJAH

The U.S. siege of Fallujah was in its last phase at the end of April 2004, by which time stories of atrocities committed by U.S. soldiers in Fallujah were rampant. Refugees, wounded civilians, and doctors from the town who experienced the horrors had by then flooded the hospitals and neighborhoods of the capital city.

On our way to meet a family in Adhamiya that had taken in three refugee families, we phoned the Islamic Party spokesperson in Fallujah who was trying to distribute relief aid. "Many families remain trapped in their homes and the stench of dead bodies here is overpowering," said Khaled Abu Mujahed over the phone, as we passed a patrol of three Bradley fighting vehicles rumbling down the street. "Some relief is getting in, but it never seems to be enough. So many people are lacking water, electricity, and medical services, and most of the time nobody can get in or out of Fallujah." He informed us that the previous day the U.S. military had violated the cease-fire by launching an attack on the Julan neighborhood and the industrial section of the city. "This is a disaster! Only a few people can get to the main hospital because the Americans are controlling it. Snipers are firing into Julan and killing so many civilians."

He reported that areas all around Iraq were donating supplies to

Fallujah, and that they had even received aid shipments from follow-ers of Muqtada al-Sadr. He was heartened by the unity the fighting had brought about among different sects and the displays of gen-erosity he was witnessing.

"Women are bringing their gold from Baquba. A man in a wheel-chair from Kirkuk brought his wheelchair in to donate, then used crutches to leave, and supplies are coming from Mosul, Adhamiya, Tikrit, Nasariyah, Baquba, everywhere in Iraq you can think of," he said. He went on to say that many refugees were reporting that they had nowhere suitable to stay outside of Fallujah. "We have at least seven hundred dead from the fighting," he said. After a long pause he added, "So many of them are children and women."

When we arrived at the house, we met Abu Muher. The wrinkled, kind-eyed gentleman, carrying a cane, dressed in his traditional dishdasha, was the elderly patriarch of one of the families that had fled their embattled city just a few days earlier. "We were nearly bombed by the Americans when we tried to leave on Friday," he told me, his eyes sparkling despite the tragedy of their situation. "Bombs fell in front and behind us, so we had to turn back. The next day we were lucky to escape."

By then at least sixty thousand Fallujans had fled and were either camping in the desert outside of their city or staying with people in Baghdad. Abu Muher said that U.S. warplanes were bombing the city heavily just before he left and that marine snipers continued to shoot at the countless civilians who were trapped in the city. "There were so many snipers, anyone leaving their house was certain to be killed," he said grimly.

He and two men from the other families at the home revealed that warplanes had dropped cluster bombs on a road behind their homes in Fallujah. One of these men, speaking to me on condition of anonymity, said, "My neighbors saw the bomblets and heard the horrible sound that only the cluster bombs make when they are dropped on us. My home was hit by their shrapnel. I was too afraid to leave my home and check it out myself because of the snipers."

I had noticed how uncommon it was in Iraq, particularly for men from al-Anbar province, to speak of their fears to other men, especially a stranger. That men now admitted fear showed how truly desperate the situation had become.

Abdul Aziz, the fifteen-year-old son of Abu Muher who was standing with us said, "I saw two of my neighbors shot by American snipers once when I went outside. I also saw on the ground some of the small cluster bombs that were dropped by the warplanes of the Americans. Most times, we were too afraid even to look out our windows." A man, obviously from one of the sheltered families who refused to give his name, spoke up angrily, "This is the way the Americans are freeing Iraq? America's freedom is killing Iraqis. Fallujah is becoming another Palestine! How long will we have to live like this?"

As we drank tea, all of them told us that their city remained without electricity and the stench of decaying bodies filled the air. They also told us what we had been hearing from doctors coming out of the city, that for fear of the snipers, families were often forced to bury the bodies of their loved ones in their gardens.

Another refugee in the house, Abdel Salam, said that medical relief was being delayed and sometimes altogether prevented from reaching the people inside Fallujah. "Sunday, when we left the city, we saw an ambulance from the United Arab Emirates being turned around from the main checkpoint by the Americans. Why are they not allowing ambulances into Fallujah?"

Later that day, I made my way to the CPA press center that had been set up to handle inquiries directed to the Iraqi Ministry of Health. I spoke with Christy Clemmons, the CPA spokesperson who in effect was representing the U.S. military. She assured me that the U.S. military was cooperating with Iraqi medical workers by escorting ambulances into Fallujah. She told me, "The U.S. military is escorting the ambulances, since in the past they have been commandeered by insurgents and used to attack U.S. soldiers." Yet when I spoke with Faris Hamed, Secretary General of the Iraqi Red Crescent, he said that no Red Crescent ambulances had been allowed into Fallujah since April 13.

In his usual five o'clock follies manner, which I had witnessed at staged press conferences in the Green Zone, coalition spokesman Brigadier General Mark Kimmitt announced that U.S. marines were continuing to engage in "aggressive patrols and offensive operations," in Fallujah, "as well as providing humanitarian assistance to the citizens of Fallujah." Not one refugee or doctor from Fallujah that I met endorsed the statement that U.S. soldiers were providing humanitarian assistance.

The assault on Fallujah came to an end when an agreement was reached between the U.S. forces, tribal leaders, and a people's body from the city to end U.S. patrols inside the city. Security was "handed" over to Iraqi forces within the city. Former Republican Guard commander General Jassim Muhamad Saleh was appointed to establish the Fallujah Brigade and the Fallujah Protection Army by locals in the city. In essence, responsibility for the security of the city was handed back to the people of Fallujah and local mujahedeen.

On May 7, Harb and I decided to go and see for ourselves what had happened. We connected with Hannah, hired a driver, and ventured into Fallujah under an air of nervous anxiety. We bypassed the main checkpoint into Fallujah and drove through side roads into the city. Once in, we met our local contact, who took us to one of the soccer fields that had been converted into a martyrs' cemetery. The marine snipers had surrounded the main cemetery, making it impossible for the people to bring their dead there.

An older Iraqi man was wailing near the grave of a loved one in the dusty heat of the converted soccer field, one side of which was enclosed by ten rows of concrete benches. Between wails, he raised his fist and yelled, "*Allahu Akbar!*" We waited outside until he slowly exited the new cemetery with his brothers holding him. Rows and rows of fresh graves filled the soccer stadium. Many of them were smaller than others. As we walked down the rows of the dead, Hannah read the gravestones to me: "This one is a little girl." We took another step. "And this one is her sister. Next to them is their mother." We walked under the scorching sun, along the dusty rows of humble makeshift rock headstones. She continued reading them aloud to me. "Old man wearing jacket with black dishdasha, near industrial center. He has a key in his hand." Many of the bodies were buried before they could be identified. Tears welled up in my eyes as she quietly read. "Man wearing red track suit." She pointed to another row. "Three women killed in car by American missile while leaving city."

Iraqi doctors I met later at the local hospital estimated that over half of the dead are women, children, and elderly. There were nearly five hundred graves, and mourning families brought in more bodies while we were there. As we walked back to the car, the loudspeaker of a nearby mosque magnified the words of an Imam. "We have two reasons to be happy this month. One is the birthday of our prophet. The second is our victory over the Americans!"

At a large mosque near the city center, under the constant buzzing of unmanned military surveillance drones, we found the mood to be defiant. Prayers ended and men congregated around us in the mosque courtyard. A rumor was going around that the marines would resume patrolling the streets on the approaching

Monday, along with Iraqi police and the Iraqi Civil Defense Corps (ICDC). Because this rumor was being widely circulated by both the police and ICDC, I wondered if it was misinformation passed on to them from the U.S. military to keep them on edge.

One of the men, Abdul Mohammed, told me, "When the Americans start patrolling on Monday, even more people will fight them this time because there are many who seek revenge now."

This discussion took place in the rubble beneath a minaret that had been blasted by either an air-missile or tank, and from where we stood, a gaping hole was visible just below the top. Two men joined me and we climbed as high as we could on the damaged spiral staircase to look out over the city that resembled more of a ghost town. I saw much more destruction than when I was there a few weeks ago. One of the men who was conversant in English said, "I saw American snipers shoot a woman while she was putting out the wash to dry on the roof. This was during their cease-fire."

Carefully, I picked my way back down the rubble-covered steps and we drove to the Julan area of Fallujah, which was very heavily bombed during the fighting. The narrow streets and numerous alleys of Julan were mostly empty as we passed through two mujahedeen checkpoints. In this area, entire blocks of homes were now reduced to piles of broken, jagged concrete. Broken tables and splintered chairs poked out of small open spaces in the piles of concrete blocks. Sometimes, an edge of a mattress or a shoe was visible in the wreckage. Many, many homes were bombed, others riddled with bullets, date palms were torn down, and the air was thick with the putrid stench of the rotting bodies buried under the rubble.

There was a huge crater, at least eight feet deep and three times that wide in front of a small mosque with a green dome. The hole was partially filled with water from a leaking pipe below. People sat inside the mosque listening to their Imam. I began to take photos as several men gathered around. One of them said, "I hope the Americans come back on Monday. They killed my cousin and burned my house. God gave us the victory, and He will give us another when they come back!"

One of the other stories going around Fallujah was that marines were using mosque minarets as a vantage point from which to shoot people. Every group that I spoke with at each location had repeated this. These beliefs, cemented by the recent photos coming out of Abu Ghraib, had fueled Iraqis' distrust of the occupiers.

Driving a little farther into Julan, we passed a scorched ambulance on the side of the road. At yet another mosque, I was shown a copy of the Holy Qur'an that had two bullet holes through it. Another man brought me casings of a tank shell from a minaret that had been completely demolished. Aziz Hussein, who was in the city for much of the fighting, told me about the horrific bombings by U.S. war planes. He was convinced that all of Fallujah stood united in supporting the mujahedeen. "When someone lost one of their family or their home, they didn't blame the mujahedeen. Most of the people killed by bombings were civilians. Americans said the civilians were killed by mujahedeen, but this is just not true." He too told the story of marines shooting people from minarets. "When we tried to go to our mosque, the snipers shot at us."

◆ ◆ ◆ ◆

The first week of May, the IGC came up with another brilliant idea. The council was comprised primarily of expatriate Iraqis and people of the likes of Ahmed Chalabi, who was known to have embezzled a quarter of a billion dollars from the Petra Bank of Jordan and to have fed false intelligence to members of the Bush administration in order to justify the war. It proposed, or more likely received orders from above to propose, a new "flag idea" for Iraq.

The new "flag idea," a pale blue crescent on a white background, with a yellow stripe supposedly representing the Kurdish population, set between two lines of blue at the bottom that represent the Tigris and Euphrates rivers, came to public attention in late April. The flag was created by an artist in London who just happened to be the brother of Nassir al-Chaderchi, the chairman of the IGC committee in charge of selecting a new flag for Iraq. By early May, the IGC had evidently decided to try some test runs in various locations. During a visit to my friend Sheikh Adnan in Baquba, I was told that a few days before my arrival the office of the Patriotic Union of Kurdistan (PUK) had decided to fly the new "flag." He was annoyed, since the IGC had no authority to adopt a new national flag or pass any other law. Its attempt to change Iraq's flag was therefore patently illegal. It is, in fact, a violation of the Geneva Conventions for an occupying power to change the existing laws of the country it occupies.

There was nothing in the "flag" to represent the majority Arab population of Iraq. For every Iraqi I spoke to, the colors of the new flag were distressingly similar to those of the Israeli flag.

The flying of the new flag in front of the PUK building of Baquba did not go too well. Within twenty-four hours of its unfurling, a car bomb destroyed much of the building, and, of course, the flag. I had not yet seen the new flag anywhere, apart from seeing it torched in Fallujah. Anywhere it was hoisted, it was promptly torn down. Nobody dared display one in their car windows.

The residents of Adhamiya responded to the flag by hanging countless original green, black, red, and white Iraqi flags all over their neighborhood. A huge version, over sixty feet long, was put up near Abu Hanifa mosque. Smaller versions of the flag fluttered atop buildings and homes. Tiny paper versions adorned car dashboards. The U.S. military responded to this show of defiance by coming to the area and tearing down as many of them as possible. One was rolled over by a tank. As usual, dissent in occupied Iraq was dealt with by tanks and guns. And of course the people of Adhamiya responded by putting up even more flags.

The spokesman for the IGC, Hamid al-Kafaei, said, "This is a new era. We cannot continue with Saddam's flag."[1] This move showed yet again how out of touch with Iraqi opinion the exiles of the IGC truly were.

We came across several demonstrations against the new flag around Baghdad. At one, in the primarily Shia neighborhood of Khadamiya, thirty-two-year-old merchant Adel Hassan told me what he and so many Iraqis felt about the flag. "Our flag is not Saddam's, it is that of Iraqis!" The push by the IGC for the new flag ended shortly thereafter.

◆   ◆   ◆

On May 10, Harb and I decided to return to Fallujah. I felt there was much more about the siege that remained undocumented, and I was able to contact more doctors who had worked inside the city at the time and were willing to talk to me directly about their experiences.

Our timing was perfect. We quickly learned that part of the recent truce allowed the marines to run one last symbolic patrol into the city that very day. Iraqi police and the ICDC were milling about every intersection on the main street. The street was blocked off, and many people were watching in anticipation and apprehension from storefronts and windows as we parked the car down a side street and walked toward the mayor's office.

Marines from the 1st Marine Division began to roll a convoy of Humvees and Stryker vehicles into the charged atmosphere, in a laughable attempt to show cooperation with the police and ICDC who were supposed to take over patrolling the city for them. A press release about the exercise later stated, "Marines from the 1st Marine Division traveled into Fallujah today to exercise freedom of movement and meet with city officials."[2]

The Iraqi police and ICDC who I spoke with along the street all said the deal was for the marines to have an hour-long visit with the mayor inside the heavily blockaded tribal council building. The small convoy rolled behind the eight-foot-high concrete barriers that surrounded the building, leaving the accompanying police and ICDC who had been surrounding them on all sides. One policeman turned to me and said, "The Americans are not good people. We are here to take care of you." His words echoed around in my mind as I pondered the way the U.S. soldiers were using Iraqis as human shields, and had left them outside the guarded compound without any qualms.

As we stood about outside the building, Abdul Rahman, a captain in the ICDC, said to me, "There were negotiations between the people of Fallujah and the occupation forces. The plan is for the Americans to pull all their troops out of the city after they get this one patrol." After a pause, during which he looked significantly at the military vehicles inside the concrete barrier surrounding the tribal council building, he added, "We want them out of our country."

Nervous residents of the city watched silently from sidewalks as the armored vehicles sat inside the tribal council building. This patrol had traveled a daunting two miles from the highway bridge to this building, with full Iraqi escort. Was this a show of force or an attempt to save face? I read it as an attempt to save face, a futile effort to show the people of Fallujah that the U.S. military still had something resembling control of the city, which was clearly untrue.

"We brought the Americans from the bridge into the city. They couldn't even come in here alone," says Alla Hamdalide, another member of the ICDC, "The victory for Fallujah remains." After only half an hour inside the building, with scores of Iraqi police and ICDC once again riding in pickup trucks surrounding the vehicles of the marines, the patrol slowly made its way back out of the city.

Harb, who was aware of the truce, assured me there will be no fighting unless the marines started it. Nevertheless, I looked around for something to hide behind or duck under if it became necessary. The normally busy street was eerily quiet, and had the tangible air of expectancy for bloodshed that the people of Fallujah had come to know so well.

A few people waved at the Iraqis who were accompanying the patrol, who tentatively waved back to them. I spotted a couple of soldiers who, thinking the waving was for them, waved back. The "embeds," as usual, had no idea what the Iraqis in the city thought about all this. They never talked with any of the Iraqi doctors, medical workers, or families of the victims. Clustered together in the back of a Stryker vehicle, peering out from under their black helmets, the embedded reporters saw the scene only from the perspective of the U.S. soldiers they relied on for their safety. Thus, they could not see what I was about to witness after they departed with the soldiers.

As the patrol receded, spontaneous celebrations erupted, and crowds of residents flew into the street. Iraqi flags appeared everywhere. People began chanting and waved the flags wildly. Members of both the Iraqi police and ICDC joined in the celebration, waving their guns in the air and giving the victory sign. A parade was quickly formed. Trucks with boys and men riding in the backs lined up, their horns blaring. Policemen who were there to guard the marines promptly turned into parade escorts, as well as participants.

The ruckus began to inch down the street. An old Fallujan man riding in the back of a truck waving a tattered Iraqi flag yelled, "Today is the first day of the war against the Americans! This is a victory for us over the Americans!" Mujahedeen brandishing RPGs, Kalashnikovs, and hand grenades were paraded on trucks as thousands of residents began to move up and down the main street in the victory parade. Loud music blared from the minarets of mosques.

Ahmed Saadoun Jassin, an Iraqi policeman, smiling from ear to ear, said, "I can't describe to you the happiness I feel right now. This is a victory for Islam." Many of the policemen and ICDC were holding their weapons in the air with one hand while giving the victory sign with the other. When I asked about their having cooperated with the marines, Jassin said, "This was the deal that was negotiated. They couldn't stay in Fallujah for over one hour, which they didn't."

I was pulled up into the back of a pickup truck. We were all being pelted by handfuls of candy thrown by shopowners at the crowds who pass. Many of the revelers were waving Iraqi flags. Some held up the Qur'an. Vehicles carrying armed mujahedeen and rejoicing residents rolled up and down the main street of the city. Iraqi police and ICDC members, along with the mujahedeen, were firing their guns into the air. Men held up children in the air, their small fingers spread in the "V" sign, a fistful of candy in the other hand.

An RPG-wielding fighter riding on the roof of our truck told me, "They [marines] just made the people of the world laugh at them. But I think they will come back, because they don't keep their word." The celebrations continued throughout the day. After several hours the parade dispersed but small groups of honking cars full of triumphant flag-waving Iraqis continued to buzz around the streets. Children ran around carrying flowers toward mosques. People planned more celebrations for the evening. Boys set up water and juice checkpoints, giving cups of juice to cars that slowly passed through the street. I watched more children waving flowers about as they played in the sun that had now come out. Despite tremendous loss during the fighting, the will of Fallujan residents apparently had been galvanized.

The press release from the 1st Marine Division about the patrol stated that freedom of movement in Fallujah was crucial to the city's rebuilding and revitalization efforts. The officials added, "Team-work . . . serves notice to those who violently oppose stability in Iraq; they are nothing more than unwanted barriers on the road to a truly free Iraq."[3]

We still had a few hours before sunset as the parade began to wind down, so we headed over to the general hospital to interview some of the doctors I had met previously.

Dr. Abdul Jabbar, an orthopedic surgeon, said it was difficult to keep track of the number of people they treated, as well as the number of dead, since there was no facility for documentation. This was primarily because the main hospital, which was located across the Euphrates from the city, was sealed off by U.S. Marines for the greater part of April. "We treated at least eight hundred to nine hundred people, but since we couldn't use this hospital, we were using smaller clinics inside the city. We didn't have access to our computers because the troops had sealed the hospital where our offices are."

According to Dr. Jabbar, the frequent shortages of medical supplies and medications were periodically staved off by donations from relief groups such as the Red Crescent and the odd NGO, which sporadically managed to get them into the besieged city. In addition, he estimated that at least seven hundred people were killed in Fallujah during April.

The doctor also talked of the use of cluster bombs by U.S. war-planes. "Many people were injured and killed by cluster bombs." I myself had heard cluster bombs when I was there during the fighting. The munitions make a drawn-out roaring sound when they first explode, then the hundreds of bomblets explode like countless giant firecrackers afterward.

Speaking of the medical crisis that his hospital had to deal with, another orthopedic surgeon, Dr. Rashid, said that during the first ten days of fighting, the U.S. military had not allowed any evacuations at all. "Even transferring patients within the city had been impossible. You can see our ambulances outside. Snipers even shot into the main doors of one of our centers." Several ambulances were parked in the parking lot of the hospital. Two of them had bullet holes in the windshields; one of these was riddled with bullet holes, and the tires had been shot, as well. The siding of the vehicles had holes pushing the metal into blooming flowers inside the van, and most of the glass was shattered.

"I remember once we sent an ambulance to evacuate a family that had been bombed by an aircraft," Dr. Jabbar recalled. "The ambulance was sniped while returning with the wounded. One of the family died, and three were injured by the firing." He estimated that 20 to 30 percent of the patients they treated were victims of snipers. "It is always one or two wounds, never more. The shape of the wound also shows that it was a sniper round. The [more the] fighting continued, the more they used them." Both doctors told us they had not been contacted by the U.S. military, nor was any aid material delivered to them by the military. "They send only bombs, not medicine," Dr. Rashid explained.

Pensively, we left Fallujah, viewing one destroyed home after another on our way out of the now liberated city. Children played on many street corners and we were handed some juice at one of their celebratory checkpoints. We passed several more houses with walls riddled with gunfire and tank rounds. None of us knew that all that we had seen would pale in comparison to what would happen here in a few months.

A victory parade in Fallujah after local resistance fighters thwarted the U.S. attack on the city. From May to November 2004, Fallujah remained the only city in Iraq not occupied by foreign occupation forces. May 2004.

CHAPTER 11

SHATTERED DREAMS

It was May 15, 2004. U.S. soldiers had once again sealed off the Abu Hanifa mosque in Adhamiya, which I was just approaching. Holding my press badge up in the air, from about fifty feet away, in loud, clear English, I yelled to a soldier sitting on a Bradley behind a machine gun, "I am press! May I please get a comment from one of you about what the goal of your operation here is?" Before I completed my sentence, a soldier standing near the armored vehicle pulled his M-16 to his shoulder and held me in his sights. Feeling a rush of adrenaline, I repeat, "I am press! I just want to get a comment from someone!" Two soldiers shook their heads no, while another waved me away. All the while, the first soldier kept his gun trained on me.

Freedom of the press in the "New Iraq."

I turned around and walked back to a crowd of Iraqis who were shaking their heads in disbelief.

Three days earlier I had interviewed Ismail Zayer, the editor of a U.S.-funded Iraqi newspaper, who had recently resigned in protest of the U.S. censorship of his newspaper, the *Al-Sabah* daily. "I wanted to help build a good, democratic, and free media in Iraq. I wanted to create a paper that was 100 percent independent, with no conditions, no censorship, and one that we Iraqis are the bosses of," he told me in the new office of his new paper in Baghdad, which he had decided to call *Al-Sabah Al-Jadeed* (The New Morning).

Zayer and his colleagues had made headlines when they walked away from *Al-Sabah*, which was seen by most Iraqis as the mouthpiece of the occupation authorities.

"Earlier, a lot of Iraqis thought we were pro-American, but not anymore," he told us, as Harb and I sat sipping tea in his office. "Everyone is willing to talk to us now."

Al-Sabah, along with Al-Iraqiya television and a number of radio stations, were at the time being run by Harris Corporation, a Florida-based firm, through a $96 million Pentagon contract. "A U.S. company called Science Applications International Corporation (SAIC), which had funding from the Pentagon, was in charge of overseeing *Al-Sabah*," he said. "But then SAIC was replaced by Harris Corporation, which had no experience with the media and was in no way qualified to oversee us. Harris Corporation told us we did not have the right to be independent, under CPA Order 66, which stipulates that *Al-Sabah* has to be part of a new media group. They did this without our knowledge, and we rejected the move." He said this action would have linked the newspaper to Harris Corporation and the Pentagon for the next two years and also would have authorized the Pentagon to run it. The Pentagon did not want the paper to publish the names of U.S. soldiers who had been killed in Iraq, Zayer recalled, and a U.S. general had come to the offices of his paper to talk to the staff and pressure them. Zayer accused the corporation of having interfered with the paper by using the U.S. military to push a pro-U.S. agenda, attempt to block its advertising, and try to corrupt its reporters.

"I told them I would leave if I was not allowed to function independently, and most of my staff would leave with me," Zayer told me. As he prepared to quit, Harris Corporation raised the salaries of his employees by 40 percent in an attempt to keep them at *Al-Sabah*. "It did not work. When I left to start my own independent paper, *Al-Sabah Al-Jadeed*, nearly 100 percent of the staff came with me." Before he left *Al-Sabah*, the paper had a circulation of seventy-five thousand. This dropped to forty-one thousand when it changed hands.

Zayer, as a senior Iraqi editor, had in his paper thanked the people of the United States for toppling the dictator Saddam Hussein. However, he said, "Everything following this has been different. I will not give them the right to confiscate my right." Perhaps a model of hope for Iraqi businesses who wish to be independent, *Al-Sabah Al-Jadeed* was off to a running start in its new office completely free of U.S. and Pentagon control. "We are on our land, in our country, and this contractor will tell me how to be independent? No," he exclaimed. "We left. We got out. They can keep their money. We'll be independent the way we want."

A few days later, on May 31, my friend Salam stopped by my hotel, obviously shaken. "There was an assassination attempt on Ismail Zayer," he told me. "A group of men in four cars, one of them an Iraqi police car, showed up at his office claiming that the minister of interior had requested that he accompany them to his office. Zayer was suspicious. On the pretext of changing clothes, he went inside to call the minister, whom he knew personally, and verify their claim. The minister told him he did not order this, and said he knew nothing about it."

When Zayer was on the phone, his driver and bodyguard were taken away by the men. Later that evening, their bodies were found with gunshots in their heads. As Salam narrated, I recalled the friendly large guard with a ponytail whom I had met when I had gone to interview Zayer. Even though he wasn't a friend, merely someone I had met, it was difficult to believe he was gone.

Having delivered the horrible news, Salam muttered, "It is getting worse by the day here." After a pause, he added, "Today is better than tomorrow."

◆ ◆ ◆ ◆

In May, we also traveled to Ramadi, in order to interview the governor of al-Anbar province. Roughly sixty miles west of Baghdad, at first glance Ramadi appeared to be much more stable than nearby Fallujah, where the U.S. military no longer dared enter the city after the failed siege of April. In Ramadi, U.S. military patrols still roamed the streets, resistance attacks seemed to be down, and some of the damaged and destroyed water-treatment facilities, schools, irrigation systems, and bridges were reportedly receiving the necessary attention.

Under a hot, late-morning sun, Harb parked our car outside the heavily fortified compound in the middle of the city that housed the governor of the province, Ezzedin Abdul Kareem. Just as we closed the doors to the car and started to walk toward the security checkpoint, we heard screeching tires and saw a truck with several Kalashnikovs and RPG-wielding mujahedeen in the back careening around a nearby street corner, racing in a direction away from us. Iraqi police and ICDC posted at the governor's building looked on, with apparent unconcern. Inside, Governor Kareem was upbeat about the situation, despite having survived three assassination attempts in the last year. "Both Ramadi and Fallujah are extremely tribal," he said. "But Ramadi is closer to Baghdad, and the terrorists have less control over this region. Moreover, the people of Ramadi are predisposed toward their religious leaders and their injunctions."

(The pro-occupation governor was incorrect on both counts, and the fact that he referred to the Iraqi resistance as "terrorists" came back to haunt him during the next siege of Fallujah, when resistance members kidnapped two of his sons and demanded his resignation. After Kareem resigned, his sons were returned unharmed.)

Seated in his plush office the governor maintained that relations between the CPA and the administrative structures within Ramadi were good. Apart from the $500 million that the CPA had allocated for rebuilding in Ramadi, he claimed, an additional $70 million had been earmarked for Ramadi and Fallujah. His hopeful attitude belied the fact that the money had not been delivered. "Unemployment remains around 30 percent in Ramadi," he said, thumbing his prayer beads in the vast, air-conditioned office. "This causes many problems and affects people very much."

Kareem was justifiably pleased at the undisrupted and effective formation of the councils in cities and villages throughout al-Anbar in January. Even though the caucuses had been set up by the CPA, people by and large felt a fair degree of autonomy, given that it was their own tribal leaders selecting their governor and other council members. In sum, the governor believed, "The people asked me to be in this position."

Unlike in fragmented Baghdad, the tribal system in Ramadi remained intact. The preservation of that traditional power structure within the administrative power structure enabled leaders to exercise greater control than elsewhere in Iraq. This differed greatly from the appointment of IGC members by the CPA. I had yet to find any Iraqis who supported the IGC.

There was another important reason for Ramadi being calmer. When members of the Ba'ath Party were removed from their government positions here, they had been promised their jobs back under the new dispensation, along with their lost wages. Many of them had already returned to their positions. Ramadi was perhaps a rough but functional model of how the CPA could have functioned better in

Iraq. Certainly what the governor was doing here was a better alternative to Paul Bremer's ill-advised de-Ba'athification program, which when implemented had generated hundreds of thousands of unemployed and bitter government and military personnel. Unemployment and lack of reconstruction were the two key factors responsible for the popularity of the growing Iraqi resistance.

We thanked the governor for the interview and then immediately met with Jaadman Ahmed al-Awany, the commander of the Iraqi police of al-Anbar province, who was in charge of 10,850 police in the region. He agreed with the governor that the sheikhs and religious leaders had helped to calm the volatile situation in Ramadi. "There have been fewer attacks on police here the last few months because so many of them come from this area, and are better equipped than before." Nevertheless, two policemen had been killed in Ramadi just before our interview. Calm was always a relative term in occupied Iraq.

The day we were at the governor's building happened to be the day when all Iraqi police commanders of the province were slated to meet. Sitting with us in al-Awany's office. Colonel Sabar Fahdil, the commander of the police in Fallujah, openly expressed his anger about the April siege. "The Americans used the execution of the four American contractors there as an excuse to surround and attack Fallujah," he said. He lamented over how helicopters and warplanes had been used to bomb civilians and their homes. "They killed over twelve thousand Fallujans," he continued. "I was there negotiating with the Americans, but they broke the cease-fire so many times."

Out on the street, the mood was anything but calm. One shop owner, named Sfook, told us, "It is not safe here, for Iraqis or for Americans. The Americans attack our homes so much, whether there is a reason or not. The problem is the American presence here. We will never accept the occupiers." I asked him what would happen in Ramadi if the military attempted to do what it did in Fallujah. "This would be worse than Fallujah. Even now, the Americans are hit three to four times each day. We are honored to have the resistance here."

Just then, news of the car-bomb assassination of the current president of the IGC, Ezzedin Salim, flashed across the television screen of the shop we were in. I was taken aback by the spontaneous celebration that the news provoked. I asked Sfook what this was about, and he replied, "They are not the Iraqi Governing Council. They are the Prostitution Council. They are not Iraqi. They were not here suffering during Saddam's time like we were. They are only puppets of the Americans."

On the main street of Ramadi, we saw countless cars honking their horns in celebration of the bombing. Groups of men on the sidewalks danced about, thrusting their fists in the air, a gesture common to many public display of emotions. The assassination of Salim underscored the instability of the U.S.-led occupation and the burning anger most Iraqis felt toward the U.S.-appointed council. Salim was killed by a car bomb while waiting to enter the Green Zone in central Baghdad. But he was not the first IGC member to be assassinated: Akila Hashimi was killed in September 2003.

It is important to note that Regulation 6, section 2 of the CPA Orders, known in Iraq as the Bremer Orders, read: "In accordance with Resolution 1483, the Governing Council and the CPA shall consult and coordinate on all matters involving temporary governance of Iraq, including the authorities of the Governing Council."[1] This meant that essentially the IGC could not do anything without first consulting the CPA. In addition, the CPA retained veto power over any decision the IGC took, effectively usurping what little authority the IGC may have had.

Bremer claimed the IGC "will have real power and real responsibilities."[2] But the document he signed that created the IGC on July 13, 2003, made it very clear that the council would have little, if any, real power or autonomy, as most Iraqis knew.

The IGC had appointed many ministers, but had limited powers. The council members could not agree on a president, so they had adopted a rotating system that installed a new member at the helm every thirty days. In setting up the council, U.S. officials had evinced greater concern about ethnic and religious representation than about the adequacy or effectiveness of the nominees. The selection, made strictly along sectarian and ethnic lines to reflect the populations of these groups in Iraq, comprised thirteen Shias, five Kurds, five Sunnis, a Christian, and a Turkoman. This deliberate U.S trend of highlighting and encouraging ethnic and sectarian divides was to increase in the run-up to the coming Iraqi elections, and eventually lead Iraq into a sectarian-based civil war of militias.

Allegations of indecision, corruption, and controversy hovered over many of the IGC members. Many were accused of awarding contracts to friends and family members. They were also charged with outright self-aggrandizement through their newfound privilege. Nepotism was rife in the council. The oil minister happened to be the son of a council member. Most IGC members were exiles during the days of the past regime, and Iraqis resented their return not as ordinary citizens but as occupiers of seats of power in the U.S.-installed government.

We returned to Baghdad and to the astounding news that Abu Hanifa mosque has been raided yet again by U.S. military forces, further provoking already widespread anti-occupation sentiment.

◆   ◆   ◆   ◆

Seventeen-year-old Amir was crying during much of the interview. "We were coming home from work, and were shot so many times," he said with deep anguish and frustration. "Walid told me to leave the car because he was hurt and needed help."

Walid Mohammed Abrahim was a carpenter, and Amir worked as his apprentice. On May 13, U.S. troops occupying an Iraqi police station in the al-Adhamiya district of Baghdad gunned down their small car as they traveled home after a long day of work.

"I still can't believe Walid is killed," whimpered Amir, crying inside the home of Abrahim's brother. "He is like my brother, he was so decent and honest. So many people are killed because of their crazy, haphazard shooting." U.S. troops riddled the car with more than twenty-five bullets. While they were driving past an Iraqi police station, a resistance fighter fired upon the station from a building on nearly the opposite end of the station from their car. But, being the closest moving object, Walid and Amir were the most convenient suspected targets.

Abrahim's brother, Khalid Mohammed Abrahim, was beside himself with grief. "All my brother was doing was coming home from work." He explained that his brother was a kind man, with no involvement in the resistance, and did not even own a weapon. "Why has my brother been killed? They searched his car and knew he was innocent. All we seek is for God to give us patience to deal with such conditions."

Later that afternoon, I went to the home of an Iraqi policeman who had been at the station that night and who agreed to confirm the incident on condition of anonymity. He said Mr. Abrahim had passed the police station on his way home to Adhamiya at 2:00 a.m. Due to much celebratory gunfire earlier in the night, following the Iraqi soccer team's victory over Saudi Arabia, which earned them a trip to the Olympics, U.S. soldiers had occupied the police station in the district. The police report of the incident stated that Abrahim's car was shot twenty-nine times, with Abrahim suffering two gunshots in the head and five in the chest. Another policeman who was at the station when the incident occurred, also speaking on condition of anonymity, said that when several men attempted to pull Abrahim from the car, U.S. troops opened fire on them. "This is the usual policy of the Americans. They always shoot first, because there is nobody to punish them for their mistakes."

"It was the Americans who shot Mr. Abrahim, and not Iraqi police, because none of us were even allowed on the roof," he stated firmly, before adding that he personally had between 150 to 200 files of incidents in which U.S. occupation forces had killed innocent Iraqis, and that several other Iraqi policemen at his station had a similar number.

Continuing his account of the atrocity, the policeman said, "When I reached the scene I saw people trying to pull him out of the car, but the Americans began shooting at them so they ran away." When he was finally able to reach Abrahim, he had died of his wounds. He then attempted to take the body to a nearby hospital, along with Amir and two other witnesses at the scene, "But several Humvees appeared and shot at us, even though we were in a police car." After the troops stopped firing, he told them they were carrying a body, but was told by U.S. soldiers at the scene to take another route to the hospital.

Events like this had become commonplace in occupied Iraq. Driving in Baghdad on any given day, funeral announcements on black banners hung everywhere from buildings, homes, and fences. Yet these announcements of untimely Iraqi deaths never made it into the Western media, or even into most Arab media outlets.

◆ ◆ ◆ ◆

On May 23, I was on the street with Harb. Over tea, we were discussing with some Iraqi men the recent court-martial trial of one of the soldiers complicit in the widespread torture at Abu Ghraib. Their attitude toward the recent news was contempt and anger. The newest promise made by the U.S. military to improve treatment of detained Iraqis had come and gone. Iraqis understood it as just more empty words. One recently released detainee I had interviewed told me, "The Americans brought electricity to my ass before they brought it to my house."

A day earlier, I had been to Abu Ghraib and talked with distraught family members waiting without hope in the dusty, dismal, concertina wire–fenced waiting area outside the prison. In the pervasive air of despair and futility that hung over the heavily guarded area, I discovered one horror story after another from melancholy family members who hoped against hope to be granted the permission to visit their relatives being held inside the awful compound. Men, women, and crying children congregated every day on the patch of barren earth, expressing bewilderment and outrage at their continuing inability to visit or gain information about loved ones. Behind us stood the high, tan-colored outer walls of the prison. Armed guards manned camouflaged posts near the entry gate and the corners of the prison. The wall was so high, it was impossible to see beyond it. This entry area, strictly controlled by the U.S. soldiers who periodically barked orders in English at Iraqis trying to find out when they could visit their loved ones inside, was as close as one could get to the prison, roughly thirty yards from the massive wall.

Sitting on the hard-packed dirt in his white dishdasha, his head scarf languidly flapping in the dry, hot wind, Lilu Hammed stared at the high walls of the nearby prison, as if trying to see his thirty-two-year-old son Abbas through the tan concrete. He sat alone, his tired eyes unwaveringly gazing upon the heavily guarded prison. When Harb asked him if he would speak with us, several seconds passed before Lilu slowly turned his head to look up at us. "I am sitting here on the ground now, waiting for God's help."

His son had been in Abu Ghraib for six months following a raid on his home that had produced no weapons. The young man had never been charged with anything. Lilu held a crumpled visitation permission slip in his hand that he had just obtained. It allowed for a reunion with his son, but not until August 18. Lilu, along with every other person I interviewed there, had not found consolation either in the recent court-martial or the recent release of a few hundred prisoners. "This court-martial is nonsense. They said that Iraqis could come to the trial, but they could not. It was a false trial." As for the recent release of several hundred prisoners from Abu Ghraib, he added, "I know someone who was captured for counterfeiting money, and he was released. So the thieves are released, and my innocent son is still inside."

Another man told us of his brother, Jabbar Atia, who was detained by the U.S. military without any reason. "I don't know why he is here!" he cried in despair, "Even my brother does not know why he is here. Please tell me why! I am always coming here waiting for him to be released, but it never happens."

According to the mother of another prisoner, Jilal Samir, her son Habib was walking down the street when he was mugged by thieves. Habib found some U.S. soldiers to ask for help, and was detained immediately. "He has been in jail for ten months now, and what did he do to be here? Where is the justice?" With tears in her eyes, she spoke of her attempt to gain access into the penitentiary by reasoning with a soldier. She asked him if he would feel sad if he had a mother and were unable to see her, and the soldier had dismissed her plea smugly with a "no." Holding her hands in the air, she asked, "Do the Americans have no feelings? They may not feel, but we do."

A convoy of Humvees full of soldiers with their guns pointing out the small windows rumbled out of the front gate of the penal complex.

The huge dust cloud they produced engulfed all of us waiting at the checkpoint. "We hope the whole world can see the position we are in now," said Samir, waving away the clouds of dust that framed her face.

Meanwhile, a May 21 CPA press release stated for the record, "The Coalition Provisional Authority has recently given out hundreds of soccer balls to Iraqi children in Ramadi, Karbala, and Hilla. Iraqi women from Hilla sewed the soccer balls, which are emblazoned with the phrase All of Us Participate in a New Iraq."[3]

I met Nihad Munir in a small coffee shop in Baghdad. "I want to talk to an American general or judge," he said. "I will give them my guarantee that my son is innocent. I will tell them that if he is not, then they can take me."

His son, Ayad Nihad Ahmed Munir, had been taken from their home during a U.S. military raid in the middle of the night. Ayad remained in Abu Ghraib, and his father had not been allowed to visit him, despite having tried everything he could think of to do so. As in most other instances Ayad, married with three children, had not been charged with anything.

Munir carried his small brown satchel which held copies of paperwork, the fruits of months of futile attempts to break down the illusive barrier that barred him from seeing his son. Here is a translation of his written account of what occurred:

On late night September 27/28, 2003, my own house/son's house has been attacked in a very bad and severely disrespectful manner by the American Military Occupation Forces with utter disregard for our Islamic and traditional safety and security manners. Claiming that they had received information about strangers hiding in the area who were in touch with the recent explosives accidents that occured near the main highway connecting Abu Kharib Amiriaa/Shouala close to our house. They put us outside our main gate entrance (me and my sick wife of over seventy years, my son Ayad's wife and three children taken from bed in deep sleep). Our two houses were both thoroughly and repeatedly inspected for three and a half hours. Finally they took my son away with them without explaining the main accusation or charge. This incident resulted in: Losing cash money (son had $1,500 U.S.), three women's and men's watches. My son's ID card, his passport, No. 459835 issued March 5, 2001, valid until February 5, 2005, and food stuff form No. 863553.

Munir had visited the United States and his dream was to return there again someday. "I'm a sixty-five-year-old man, do you think I'm too much a dreamer?" he said with a wistful smile.

"I had a brother in Michigan who I so wanted to visit in the 1970s, but he died," he continued. He pulled out a copy of his son's passport to show me a photo of the handsome detainee. "I visited America. I know Americans are very friendly people." While distraught with the actions and behavior of the U.S. military in his country, he still separated this from the populace of the country that caused his grief. Smiling, he added, "See my hope? I still want to go to America."

He pulled another paper out of his bag and showed me a form he had filled out from the Islamic Party, another useless document to help gain contact with his son. Next, he showed me the letter he had written last January, which was signed by tribal sheikhs. The CPA was granting the release of some prisoners on condition that their tribes swore to be responsible for any crimes the freed detainees might commit. This plea too had been useless.

A car bomb at one of the entrances to the Green Zone. June 2004.

CHAPTER 12

"NOBODY HERE LIKES THE OCCUPIERS"

On June 2, 2004, Harb and I decided to venture one more time to Fallujah to interview the new security forces in the city. We knew they were made up mostly of locals, and rather than going on hearsay, we wanted to interview them face to face.

Coming to the city prior to the April assault had felt like driving into any other city in Iraq. One could move about town freely, children often played on the side of the streets, and food and cigarette vendors were active. This time, the highway to Fallujah was busy with cars. The burned-out military vehicles that we found littered along the highway during my last trip to the city were missing. After a short wait at the main checkpoint, we were searched and waved through by members of the ICDC. A few U.S. marines stood around in the background, as they had before. A short drive into the city brought us to the mayor's headquarters, which was where we had stood watching the victory parade on May 10.

Once inside, Ali Abed, a twenty-five-year-old member of the ICDC, told us, "Fallujah is secure now, and you can stay out late because it is safe." He and several other ICDCers sat relaxed inside their headquarters, drinking soda, and laughing from time to time. "As long as the Americans stay out, it is calm here."

Things had certainly changed in Fallujah. Journalists were now required to go to the al-Hadrah al-Mohamudia mosque in the city in order to obtain a press pass. Shortly after Ali told us this, four mujahedeen entered the compound. Their faces were wrapped in keffiyehs and they carried brand-new Russian-made compact RPG units. One of them ordered some of the ICDC to escort us to the mosque in order to be cleared. A jolt of fear stirred me. Harb caught my eye and nodded. He moved his hand in a slow downward gesture that I read to mean "wait." We were loaded into a brand-new green GMC. As Harb and I slid into the middle of the backseat, with a soldier on either side of us, Harb caught me giving him another anxious look and said, "Don't worry, *habibi*, we'll be all right."

After the four mujahedeen got into a car in front of us and three more ICDC sat down in the front seat of our vehicle, we slowly drove to the mosque. The ICDC who drove us to the mosque said they were worried for me, but it was obviously not the mujahedeen that they perceived as a threat. It was the combination of the marine presence on the outskirts of the town and the seething anger of its residents that made any Westerner a likely target of the desire for revenge that fueled residents of Fallujah at the time. "My cousin works for Al-Arabiya television and his camera was smashed just yesterday," said one of the ICDC. "Yesterday two German journalists were beaten up because the people here are very angry with Westerners."

We arrived at the mosque and followed the *muj* inside the office of Khassem Mohammed Abdel Satar, the vice chairman for the city council. I was made to stand with two armed ICDC on either side of me as he described to me the anger in the city. Nearly every family in Fallujah had lost one or more member during the April siege. "In some cases, entire families were killed," he said somberly. He issued me a press pass, but told me I would have to conduct my interviews with the

ICDC in his office and then leave the city. The reason I was given a pass without much ado was that one of the mujahedeen recognized me from my first trip to Fallujah, when I had been at the clinic.

Satar referred to the U.S. soldiers as "invasion troops" and told me that Fallujah was much better off without them in the city. "We have Fallujah completely under control now with the Iraqi police and the ICDC," he said. "The security in Fallujah hasn't been this good since the fall of Baghdad." He asserted with justifiable pride that Fallujah was the first city in Iraq that the U.S. military had left because of the resistance rather than through negotiations. "We hope all cities in Iraq become as liberated as Fallujah is," he said.

According to Satar, the new clampdown on the press in Fallujah was intended as a security measure for journalists and would be coupled with plans to give the media better access inside the city. I saw no indications of this, however.

Dhasin Jassim Hamadi, a major in the ICDC, told me that the Iraqi Civil Defense were fully independent and had nothing to do with occupation forces inside the city. "During April the Americans bombed our headquarters and killed three men," he said angrily, "but now we work under the supervision of the mayor and conduct joint patrols with the police. We demanded independence from the Americans, and we got it."

ICDC members felt that their credibility had gone up with the residents ever since the U.S. military had left Fallujah. "It is obviously better here without them, so of course the people respect us more," said Amin, a twenty-eight-year-old member of the ICDC. Amin questioned the legitimacy of foreign fighters and the labeling of Iraqis who fought against occupation forces as "terrorists." "They are fighting to protect their city. Why don't the Americans refer to soldiers from Honduras who are here as terrorists?" he asked, referring to the few hundred soldiers from Honduras who were part of the so-called coalition of the willing. "They are fighting Iraqis . . . but they are not called terrorists? What is the difference?"

Later that day, I read an Associated Press story that referred to the city as "the guerrilla stronghold of Fallujah,"[1] while the CPA went to great lengths to establish that the U.S. military was working in conjunction with the ICDC and mayor of Fallujah to ensure security—a complete lie. But then, according to the official U.S. line, the military operations in Fallujah during April were said to have been carried out with the goal of "pacifying" the city, a city that at that time the mayor and ICDC claimed was the calmest and most secure it had ever been. Despite the extreme violence perpetrated by the U.S. military on the city and its residents, including entire city blocks being bombed into piles of rubble, people in Fallujah were already beginning to put their lives back in order. Bulldozers were clearing the rubble of homes and removing burned cars from the streets, the hospitals were resupplying, and each day hundreds of families were returning to the city. While bodies pulled from under the rubble continued to be carried to the soccer field for burial, people began to rebuild their houses and put their lives back together.

By mid-June, I was beyond the point of burnout. I hadn't slept well in weeks. Increasing anxiety about car bombs made my rest fitful and the slightest noise outside my window would wake me. The morning of June 14, I shuffled past Dave, who was typing on his computer in our sitting room, and on my way to the kitchen to make some coffee, when there was a thundering explosion somewhere down the street near Tharir Square. Our daily car bomb had viciously greeted another day of the wretched occupation of Iraq.

When I visited the site of the explosion later, I found that at least thirteen people had died. The targets were white SUVs used by contractors and mercenaries. Five of the foreigners were killed in what was apparently a carefully planned and orchestrated attack. In the aftermath of the blood and chaos of the blast that tore off the front of a nearby building, many Iraqis began dancing in front of the charred vehicles, holding pieces of twisted metal from the vehicles over their heads and chanting, "Down, down America," and "America is the enemy of God!" The vehicles were then set ablaze. As the crowd grew in size and furor, U.S. tanks with soldiers in riot gear arrived to seal the area. Anxious soldiers kept their guns aimed at the angry crowd as investigators attempted to collect evidence from the scene of devastation. The investigators, some from the military, others apparently either plainclothed CIA or contractors, searched for dog tags of the victims.

The next morning, in the supply room at Yarmouk Hospital, Harb and I met Dr. Aisha Abdulla at her desk. "This is just like Afghanistan," she said. "We lack everything here." Referring to the occupation authorities, she added, "They've destroyed the foundations of Iraq—what do you think we can do without foundations?"

"Even if the Americans stay here for fifteen years, there will be no security. The West knows what is happening here but nobody can stand up to the superpower America. Look at this hospital! Anything they do or build is superficial, not fundamental. Abu Ghraib attacked the dignity of the Iraqi people. Did America not become barbarians from killing Indians, Vietnamese, Central Americans, Afghanis, and bombing us and our young children, who now have psychological scars? If these did not reveal the true barbarian nature of America, then Abu Ghraib certainly did. I never liked Saddam, nor did I support him, but at least under the dictator there was order and some basic services," she continued. "Now, there is no order, no electricity, no fundamental stability.

"So many Iraqis believed that the Americans would treat them better than Saddam, but when they saw them stealing and killing, the Iraqis started to think differently about Americans. The ugly facet of the Americans has been exposed to Iraqis now, and this is what we are seeing. My husband and I used to want to go to America. Now ... never."

Later that same afternoon, Hamid, an interpreter who had good connections in Sadr City, offered to take me and Christian Parenti, who had recently returned to Baghdad, to that area. Hamid had been introduced to us through one of our regular interpreters. We went to interview doctors at Chuwader General Hospital, the largest in Sadr City, which served an average of three thousand people every day. Dr. Qasim al-Nuwesri, the hospital director, told us his hospital often received upwards of 125 dead and wounded Iraqis whenever fighting broke out between the Mehdi Army and U.S. soldiers in the area.

"Whenever large groups like this are brought in, we know it is because of the Americans," said al-Nuwesri. He was quick to enumerate the setbacks his hospital was facing under the occupation. "We are short of every medicine," he said, something that had not previously been as severe, even under the economic sanctions. "It is forbidden, but sometimes we have to reuse IVs, even the needles. We have no choice." When he finished speaking, his eyes held mine. I couldn't look away or start to write. Not until he looked at one of his colleagues in the room, who I found was also staring at me. Another major problem that all the doctors mentioned was lack of potable water. "Of course we have typhoid, cholera, kidney stones ... but we now even have the very rare Hepatitis Type-E ... and it has become common in our area." Hepatitis Type-E is transmitted primarily via ingestion of feces-contaminated drinking water. I had been in people's homes where they had run the tap to show me the brown water that gurgled out. Water the color of a wet, dirty sock that smelled of gasoline.

Inside the hospital, we saw open sewage in the bathroom and crowds of people waiting for medical treatment. The hospital seemed to embody the bleakest peak of poverty and suffering of Sadr City.

Young and middle-aged adults were affected the most by Hep-E, along with women in their second or third trimester of pregnancy. Miscarriages had grown more common, and the best way to prevent infection was to avoid potentially contaminated water and food. Dr. Qasim al-Nuwesri told us that his hospital had only 15 percent of the clean water it needed to operate hygienically.

On the upper floors of the hospital, the younger doctors were even more forthcoming with information. A twenty-five-year-old resident doctor said that U.S. soldiers periodically stormed the hospital looking for wounded resistance fighters. "They come here asking for patients, and are very rough, because they shout, curse, and aim their guns at people."

Driving out of the garbage-strewn streets of Sadr City, we passed a wall with the words "Vietnam Street" spray painted on it. Below it read, "We will make your graves in this place." Shortly after we shot a photograph of the graffiti from the car window, we had to pull over when two men in a beat-up car waved us down. One of them, his hand on a pistol under his dishdasha, fired questions at us, wanting to know what we were doing, who we were, and why we were taking pictures. I held my breath while Hamid explained that we were Canadian journalists writing a story about the situation of the hospital. The self-proclaimed member of the Mehdi Army said, "Excuse us, sirs, but we are defending our city. We are at war with the Americans here, and we are responsible for patrolling this area."

◆ ◆ ◆ ◆

The next day, Christian, Harb, and I went to the Baghdad morgue to talk with the manager, Dr. Faiq Amin. He told us their freezers could hold a maximum of ninety bodies. But in the five months since January 2004, an average of more than six hundred bodies had been brought here each month. Of these, at least half were deaths caused by gunshots or explosions. Dr. Amin pointed out that these numbers did not include the areas of Fallujah and Najaf, which had seen heavy fighting. He added, "We deal only with suspicious deaths, not deaths from natural causes. And so many bodies are being buried that never go to any morgue anywhere." According to Dr. Amin, the current rate of bodies brought to the Baghdad morgue was three to four times greater than it ever was during the regime of Saddam Hussein. "I am sure not all of the bodies that should come here do," he said. Then he added tactfully, "Because our legal system has some problems right now." Before the invasion, there was a coordinated system between Baghdad and the other governorates that allowed his morgue to track deaths throughout the country, but this too had been smashed, along with the rest of the infrastructure of his country.

Outside of the morgue, we met Jassim, who was mourning the loss of his five-year-old daughter Najala. The kind, obese man wearing a blue button-down shirt, smoking as he spoke with us, described how he and his family had been driving when a Humvee had abruptly pulled in front of their car, causing him to lose control. His car had flipped over, and Najala was crushed. He was told he would have to wait yet another day to pick up her body.

Shortly thereafter, Harb and I visited the headquarters of the Iraqi police of Baghdad. We obtained permission to visit one police station from Brigadier General Amer Ali, the assistant commander of the police for the capital. "Now everything is smashed," he told us, "We are in a collapsed country."

"The Americans invaded our country," explained Major Said, the information officer for the Baghdad police. "They are the invaders, so of course Iraqis don't like to work with them." He spoke of the ongoing problem of U.S. soldiers occupying police stations. "As long as the Americans are in our stations, nobody comes to us for help because they are afraid of them. This is interfering both with our men doing their job and with Iraqis getting assistance. We didn't want this 'democracy' to come. This is not democracy here. I can say this as a civilian, if not as a police officer. I really feel it would be better if the Americans let us do our work and stayed out of our stations. The Americans are turning the police into targets."

Baghdad was growing more tense by the day as the scheduled date for the so-called transfer of sovereignty, June 30, approached. The day I went to pick up my ticket at an airline office in Baghdad, I learned that the airport road, which by then had been nicknamed "RPG Alley," would be closed on June 30, and all civilian flights out cancelled that day, underscoring the tenuousness of the grip that the occupation forces had on the situation. Flights in and out of Baghdad were using corkscrew descents and ascents, as they had done in Vietnam, because occupation forces had no control over the area outside the perimeter of the airport. Several planes had already been hit with either gunfire or rockets as they left the airport. The airport and the road from it leading into Baghdad were two of the most important areas for the U.S. military to control in Iraq. It spoke volumes that more than a year into the occupation, the military still failed to control either.

One evening, in my hotel, I watched a BBC clip that showed U.S. soldiers handing out Frisbees to residents of a village near Fallujah. The story opened with a marine saying, "What happened on 9/11 really affected me, so our duty now is to export violence to the four corners of the globe so that that doesn't happen again."[2] I listened in disbelief, amazed at the fact that he, like so many other soldiers in Iraq, still believed the propaganda that Iraq had anything whatsoever to do with the events of 9/11. (Stunningly, results of a Zogby International poll released on February 28, 2006, found that 85 percent of the soldiers in Iraq said the U.S. mission was "to retaliate for Saddam's role in the 9/11 attacks," while 77 percent said they believed the main or a major reason for the war was "to stop Saddam from protecting al Qaeda in Iraq."[3] Never underestimate the power of propaganda.)

Christian, Harb, and I had made plans to visit my friend Sheikh Adnan in Baquba on June 24. We went to the small city just northeast of Baghdad on the day that would see a widespread offensive launched by the Iraqi resistance across several cities of Iraq, claiming the lives of more than one hundred people.

On our way out of Baghdad, we stopped at the Ministry of Health to interview the deputy minister about the decrepit state of the country's health care system. He complained of the lack of assistance from the CPA and alluded to Western corruption, as his aides quietly filed in and out of his office. Acknowledging that a possible uprising was occurring, he revealed that at least 1,250 Iraqis had been killed between May 4 and June 17, and more than 4,300 had been wounded. Most of these deaths, he said, "are generated by the Americans."

After talking with the deputy minister, we ventured downstairs to the office of the U.S. adviser. Every Iraqi ministry had one such adviser installed by the CPA. The adviser was out of the office, but we were fortunate to catch an assistant liaison for the CPA, Ken Backus, who, sidearm in tow, adjusted his bulletproof vest and informed us, "We are in the midst of a national emergency." Huge attacks were occurring in Baghdad, Ramadi, Fallujah, Mahawil, Baquba, and Mosul.

I asked him what he knew of the situation in Baquba and he told us that the administrator of the General Hospital there and his assistant had been assassinated during that morning's fighting.

"Let us go see this intifada for ourselves," said Harb, as we walked briskly to his car. Once inside, we listened to the radio as he translated the news. "All of the great revolutions in Iraq happen in June," said Harb. "This occurring now, six days before the so-called transfer of sovereignty to the bastard [Iyad] Allawi, is proof that he cannot exist without the invaders' troops." If the goal of the offensive was to generate chaos in the days leading up to June 30, it had already been successful. Several police stations had been seized by rebels, and in Mosul alone four car bombs killed sixty-two people, including a U.S. soldier, and wounded more than 220. At the end of the day, 104 Iraqis were dead, 321 wounded, and three U.S. troops killed.

Released from the traffic of Baghdad, we swiftly covered the thirty miles northeast to Baquba only to find a traffic jam near the main entrance to the city. We sat in the car, surrounded on all sides by transport trucks and other cars, in the middle of the large, wide road that led into the city. "The Americans have sealed the city while they drop bombs on people," said an angry truck driver, when Harb asked him what was happening. "There is no way in through the main road. You will be killed if you go there."

We pulled off the road, drove around the parked vehicles, and followed three cars down a nearby dirt road. While meandering through date palm orchards and vegetable fields, at 12:15 p.m. we saw two Apache attack helicopters strafing part of the city, their dive-bomb flight patterns bobbing above the date palms, then swooping back out of sight, as they trailed smoke behind their blazing guns and rocket tubes. Their dance of death was repeated several times as we neared the city. This contradicted what Brigadier General Mark Kimmitt, the ever pliant and obedient spokesperson for the military, and deputy director of operations for the U.S. Army in Iraq, had told reporters about the fighting having subsided by noon.

As we slowed down to make a turn on the road, to the right we saw some Humvees and Bradleys across a vegetable field. Almost at the instant that Christian said, "Those soldiers are sighting in on us," the pops of bullets generating tiny sonic booms began exploding around our car. "Those are bullets flying near us," yelled Harb, as he hunched down into his seat and stomped on the gas pedal. The cracking of the gunfire whizzing over our car continued. I looked back to see Christian lying on the floorboards with his arms over his head.

As we drove away, the shooting and the bullets stopped. I took a long drag off my cigarette and looked out at the farmlands. My survival instincts were not functioning. I felt no fear, no concern, nothing. I didn't care if I lived or died.

◆ ◆ ◆ ◆

Baquba was a ghost town when we arrived. The main roads were sealed by the military. The constant, high-pitched buzz of remote control military drones admonished the residents with the threat that more air strikes were only a matter of time. Early morning attacks on a U.S. patrol by resistance fighters had killed two soldiers and wounded seven others. At 9:00 a.m., the U.S. military retaliated by dropping three 500-pound bombs in the city, near the soccer stadium. The strikes destroyed three buildings that the military claimed were used by resistance fighters for launching attacks, though locals said they were civilian homes. The Health Ministry reported thirteen civilians killed and fifteen wounded by U.S. military bombing raids and the attacks by resistance fighters.

We drove through the city looking for someone who could tell us how to get to the home of Sheikh Adnan. All the shops were closed. Bits of plastic bags and garbage blew around the streets in the dry, hot wind. Torn Iraqi flags fluttered, and dogs ran about randomly, as gunfire popped in the distance. Two cars full of armed men passed us, eyeing us suspiciously. Finally, we found an old man outside a mosque who told Harb where the sheikh lived. The man, Abdel Human, told us, "There was so much fighting here this morning. The freedom fighters took control of everything here, and kicked the Americans out of the city."

After a short drive, we were relieved to find the place. When we knocked on his gate we were greeted by our friend. He welcomed us in, shocked that we had actually come this day, as planned. "You could have called and rescheduled your visit, *habibi*," he chided me with a smile and a hug. As we sat for tea with him, his brother, and many of their friends, his children played in an adjoining room. Just before lunch, several loud bombs exploded nearby. Christian and I looked at each other while the sheikh, his brother, Harb, and an older man, who is a hajji, began to laugh. "This is normal. Even my children laugh at the bombs now," said Sheikh Adnan. "God will take us when it is time. People are killed in their homes by warplanes, yes. But people in the middle of fighting remain unharmed. It is up to God. We are a people of faith."

Shortly after the attack on the U.S. patrol that morning, fighters had taken control of the western district of al-Mufraq in the city, and the occupation forces had retreated from the area after being ambushed. "This morning, the mujahedeen defeated the occupying forces in al-Mufraq," said Amer Alwhan, the sheikh's twenty-nine-year-old brother, who lived near the area. He also said that early in the morning, resistance fighters had distributed leaflets throughout the city, instructing residents to stay in their homes because of impending attacks against U.S. forces in the city. In another offensive that occurred nearly simultaneously with the patrol ambush, at least thirty resistance fighters attacked the police station in central Baquba with small arms and RPGs. Our friends said that twenty-one Iraqi policemen were killed during the attack, and that Iraqi fighters subsequently took control of the station. At the same time, resistance fighters attacked the Blue Dome government building in central Baquba with mortars, RPGs, and automatic weapons, then proceeded to occupy the building, which continued to be under their control.

Hajji Faisal, the old man who was a member of a very large family in the area, told us, "The mujahedeen are fighting for their country against the Americans, who are the occupiers. We all accept this resistance." Qahtan Mahmoud, one of the sheikh's neighbors, nodded and said, "We do not like the occupiers. Nobody here likes the occupiers."

On the television, General Walid Khalid, the police chief of Diyala province, in which Baquba is located, told Al-Jazeera that the situation in the city would soon be under control, though it was no secret that resistance fighters had torched his home just before the interview.[4] We decided we should try to get back to Baghdad, so we thanked the sheikh and his friends for meeting with us and serving us lunch. He hugged each of us and said, "*Fim'Allah*" (go with God) and advised us that the best route to take would be the main road.

Surveillance drones buzzed overhead as we cautiously drove down the main road out of the city. A car riddled with bullets and scorched black with soot sat on the median of the main road, with a pile of empty bullet casings glistening gold under the hot sun. The lifeless body of the car's driver lay beside the vehicle, draped in a black mourning flag, his feet uncovered. The scene had all the famil-

iar, classic signs of an Iraqi who attempted to turn around on noticing a checkpoint and was indiscriminately killed.

A bit shaken, we slowly continued on and saw several Humvees
and soldiers blocking our exit further down the road. We pulled the
car over, and while Harb waited, Christian and I grabbed our press
credentials and slowly walked the quarter mile toward the soldiers.
"We are unarmed journalists," we took turns yelling, while holding
our press cards in the air. "Please do not shoot! We just want to leave
the city!" The walk felt like it took hours. Halfway there, I saw three
soldiers, who knelt down and kept us in the sights of their guns. I felt
naked in the middle of the street with guns aimed at my head and
heart. I looked behind us to see a string of cars in what was apparently a wedding party approaching. The timing could not possibly
be worse. I walked toward the side of the road, but Christian wisely
suggested we stay in the middle and keep walking. Our pace quick-
ened, and our shouts grew louder. Thankfully, the wedding party
turned around.

Needless to say, the soldiers were anxious about cars that approached them in those days, as Iraq had averaged more than one
suicide car bomb per day that month. The troops understood our
situation when we approached them and asked to be allowed to
leave. I stayed to talk with them while Christian went back to get
Harb and bring the car through. I spoke with a Sergeant Johnson
who was smoking a cigarette and squinting toward the city nervously. "After seeing that bullet-riddled car and the corpse back
there," I said, "we thought it would be better to approach you guys
on foot." He told me that the car had rammed a tank, so they had to
shoot it. "Crazy motherfucker," he added. I recalled that, aside from
being completely riddled with bullets, the car was intact, particularly the front end of it, but kept my mouth shut. Two embedded

photographers were standing off to the side with the soldiers. One of them asked me, "Did you see any bad guys in there?" I replied, "No, I did not see any 'bad guys' inside the city. Perhaps you should have gone in to see for yourself."

It was around this time that General Kimmitt told reporters in Baghdad about Baquba, "Coalition forces feel confident with the situation."[5] Meanwhile, I stood at the checkpoint with nervous soldiers who told me that no U.S. military remained in the city, which was "full of resistance fighters."

Harb and Christian pulled up, and just before I walked toward the car I asked Sergeant Johnson if he thought the worst was over. He looked at me and said, "This is just getting warmed up."

A man in a village in southern Iraq, where Bechtel was responsible for water treatment reconstruction. Because most Western corporations failed to fulfill their contractual obligations, Iraqis throughout most of the country suffered a lack of potable water, resulting in kidney stones, waterborne diseases, diarrhea, and nausea. January 2004.

CHAPTER 13

LEAVING THE VOLCANO
FOR THE EYE OF THE HURRICANE

Not wanting to risk an indefinite closure of the airport, I decided to leave Iraq on June 27, just before the "transfer of sovereignty."

Harb picked me up at my hotel and we were off through the uncharacteristically empty streets of central Baghdad en route to the airport. It was early enough for us to drive with the windows down. The warm breeze carried the sounds of shop owners sweeping the sidewalks in front of their stores, of palm fronds rustling in the wind, and of the growling treads of passing Bradley fighting vehicles.

Neither of us spoke much. Our good-byes had been said the day before. We had spent three months together under the constant threat of random death, a circumstance bound to create strong bonds.

Three checkpoints later, we arrived at the final drop-off area for the airport. Harb was not allowed to go to the airport simply because he was Iraqi and did not have a plane ticket.

"You can't go farther," a gruff soldier said in a thick, southern accent to Harb after glancing at my passport. "Pull the car over there." We pulled onto the gravel and reluctantly got out of the car together. "We will stay in touch," he said to me as we hugged good-bye. "*Insh'Allah,* we will stay in touch until you return. You are a friend of the Iraqi people." I was awkward and tongue-tied with emotions and, in parting, told my dear friend, "Take good care of yourself and your family, *habibi*. I'll see you in September, *insh'Allah*."

Slowly I walked up to the road to another car that would take me the rest of the way to the airport. I looked back and saw Harb standing by his car watching me. I waved and smiled, before getting into the car. From the rear window, I saw him watching me drive away.

How can I reconcile myself with the privilege I have of being able to leave here? We all knew it was going to get so much worse.

I was driven the remaining distance to the airport by two Iraqi police. We passed a huge row of concrete suicide barriers topped with concertina wire. The once finely landscaped area was brown with dead vegetation and strewn with garbage. "This used to be green and beautiful," said the police captain as he drove, waving his hand across the area, "but now it is all dead." After a pause, he added, "Our situation is like this now."

Inside the airport, there were large crowds of people waiting to get out of Iraq. Royal Jordanian had added an extra flight, so there were three now, all of them fully booked. Folks weren't sticking around for the "celebrations" of the handover.

After a while, I boarded the plane. The engines of the fourteen-seat twin-prop whined with power. We raced down the runway for a quick takeoff and buzzed along just sixty-five feet above the runway to gain speed. Just as we approached the end of the runway, we were all lying in our seats as the plane promptly jerked upward into what felt like a fifty-degree climb. Shortly thereafter it banked hard to the right. We climbed in a corkscrew up to an elevation from where war-torn, occupied Baghdad took on the appearance of the sprawling, proud capital it once was. The green waters surrounding Saddam Hussein's old palace near the airport sparkled in the sun.

Once we were above the range of rockets, we finally straightened out and headed toward Jordan. After Baghdad faded out of sight, I drifted into a deep sleep. A transport plane that departed Baghdad a few hours after mine was shot up with small arms fire, killing a contractor inside.

The next day, in Amman, I watched the news. The U.S.-led coalition had granted full "sovereignty" to the U.S.-appointed Iraqi Interim Government two days in advance of the announced date, in a bid to avoid the large-scale attacks expected on June 30. The fact that Bremer was forced to hold a private ceremony to anoint the new head puppet Iyad Allawi, a CIA asset, was evidence that the Iraqi resistance had begun to control events (a trend that was to grow as the occupation continued).

Allawi had said that his first move would be to take actions to insure the security of the Iraqi people, including possibly imposing martial law. Not only were the occupation forces and new interim government of Iraq operating out of the old palaces and military bases of the regime of Saddam Hussein, but they were now issuing threats and using heavy-handed tactics reminiscent of the old dictatorship the Iraqi people recognized all too well.

◆ ◆ ◆

The differences thrust in my face on returning home to America were glaring.

There were no checkpoints in the United States. People didn't have to stop their cars, have guns aimed at them and their children, get out to be searched, and have their vehicles searched. No military vehicles roamed the streets, carrying soldiers who aimed their weapons at powerless civilians who watched them pass. There was mail service and the phones worked on the first try. You could order takeout and have it delivered to your door. There were employees of the city who cleaned the streets, watered the trees and grass, and kept the parks clean.

I didn't have to worry about my friends here being detained simply because of their nationality. In Iraq, any Iraqi at any time could have been detained by the U.S. military without charges being made and held indefinitely. Iraq was a place where the U.S. military had all the power and no accountability. (This is why more than fourteen thousand Iraqis languish in detention centers in their own country, with no recourse. Iraq is a place where the mightiest military on earth is the judge, jury, and often the executioner.)

The front lines of American imperialism were so frightening. In Iraq, there was no hiding the raw, ugly face of corporations profiting from the blood and suffering caused by the brutal occupation of Iraq. Yet, back in the United States—the country that launched the invasion and now supported the occupation—people were going about their daily lives, to my amazement. If the news got too intense, these people were able to simply turn it off and take a walk. Or go to a movie. Or call a friend. The words of a friend in Baghdad played in my mind. I had asked him how he coped under such horrible circumstances, and he said, "We just live day by day. It is only up to God whether I die because of a car bomb or am run over by a tank today. I just try to make it through each day. What else can we do?"

From July through October, I spent much of my time making presentations to the American public—showing photos and telling people what I had seen and learned. It became apparent to me that I had a relatively large readership and group of supporters; the crowds coming to attend my presentations were several times larger than those prior to my last trip to Iraq. The growing audience was an indication that support for the war in Iraq was decreasing. Steadily, as it became clear to many in the United States that the invasion and occupation were an abysmal failure, and the situation was worsening over time rather than improving, the crowds at my talks and presentations swelled.

Occasionally during presentations, I struggled to hold back tears, but I pushed myself to speak, driven by the compulsion to get out the information about the real situation in Iraq. The information from Baghdad kept reaching me through Harb and my other friends there. At night, I often slept fitfully. I was once again inhabiting two worlds simultaneously.

Small incidents would send me into a fury. My blood boiled when reading what members of the Republican Party were saying. During a speech in May 2004, Bush said, "We did not seek this war."[1] Although it had grown clearer than ever that the invasion and occupation of Iraq were based on lies and misinformation, the Bush administration was well on its way to using its rhetoric of fear to spearhead its 2004 campaign for "reelection."

My fury motivated me to do everything in my power to return to Iraq. I already knew that permanent military bases were under construction and the occupation would last indefinitely. Reporting on it was more critical than ever, since the misinformation by the corporate media persisted. By the time fall 2004 rolled around, Jeff Pflueger had my website up and running. I uploaded hundreds of photos and blogs and news stories I had written. Jeff set up a dispatch list by which I could more effectively disseminate my reports, and I raised enough money to return to Iraq.

The November assault on Fallujah by the U.S. military appeared imminent. I wanted to get back into Iraq before that happened. It was clear as U.S. forces began their buildup around the city that it was poised to be launched just after the presidential election in the United States.

Many of my colleagues thought I was crazy to go back at that time, but I felt more impelled to do so than ever before. Harb thought we could work, although we would have to dramatically alter the way we traveled around Baghdad. I bought an airplane ticket for November 2, 2004. The fact that I would soon be leaving the United States, which felt more like Disneyland than a real country, to return to Iraq, which for me was undeniably real, relieved me.

A gasoline shortage began during the early days of the occupation and worsened as it progressed. In Baghdad, a man pushed his car in a gas line in order to save what was left of his precious fuel. December 2003.

CHAPTER 14

SPIRALING INTO OCCUPIED IRAQ

On the evening of the U.S. presidential election, I flew back to the Middle East. I wanted to be in Baghdad in time for the impending attack on Fallujah. The television monitors in JFK Airport in New York City were showing a neck and neck race between Bush and Kerry, which—knowing what had happened in Florida in 2000—left me little hope during the flight across the Atlantic. Shortly after landing in Amman, as I waited to catch a bus into the city, I heard a Jordanian woman talking with her father in English.

"Are you serious?" she said into her phone with a despondent look. "So Bush won, then?" She saw me watching her, hung up, and said, "How can Americans be such idiots?" Everyone I spoke with that evening and the following day seemed to be in a somber mood, not surprising, considering that roughly 70 percent of Jordan's population is Palestinian. The unbridled support that the Sharon government received from the Bush administration at the time was a source of major concern.

NOVEMBER 5, 2004

The flight felt normal, until we arrived over Baghdad International Airport. The nose of the plane dipped, the left wing dropped and the downward spiral began, dropping us four thousand feet per minute into the inferno that was occupied Iraq. Instead of an in-flight magazine, a lonely card in the seat pocket was the only available reading material. It began with: "For those of you who have not traveled with us before, you need to be aware that, for your security and safety, and not for your comfort, we do a spiral descent into Baghdad. This is carried out to avoid any risk from anti-aircraft missiles or small arms fire."

The airport was filled with nearly as many foreign security guards from the private security contractor company Global Risk Strategies as actual passengers. A large influx of Third Country Nationals (TCNs) who had just arrived on another flight, and appeared to be either Sri Lankan or Indian, was rounded up onto the Kellogg Brown & Root bus to go work at jobs that could well be done by Iraqis.

I nervously waited until another small bus arrived to take me to the front checkpoint. En route, I passed signs alerting soldiers to have their weapons ready and flak jackets on as they enter the "unsecured area," which was virtually all of Iraq that lay outside of the U.S. camps. The atmosphere was tense as I unloaded my backpack from the bus at the front checkpoint of the airport. A huge car bomb detonated here just a few days earlier, killing nine people. One of the security guards approached me and said, "You don't want to be here long. There are bad things going on here, very bad things." I noticed a line of cars being searched as they attempted to enter the pickup area and sensed deep relief at seeing Harb. He waved at me with a big smile as he walked up to be searched.

We hugged and exchanged cheek kisses per Arab custom. Despite the extremely tense atmosphere at the checkpoint, we were unable to contain our joy. This entire trip was worth it just to see my dear friend. We loaded my luggage into his car and as we drove out, some men in a BMW, the favored vehicle of criminal gangs, asked if I just flew in. Harb told them he had come to pick up a friend, and asked me for a pen and paper to note down their license plate numbers. "They could be kidnappers. There is no other flight after yours. I will watch to see if they follow us." As we drove past three burned car frames, detritus from the recent suicide bomber, Harb told me, "Everyone is being kidnapped now. It is a booming business here since there are no jobs. You must be extremely careful, Daher."

It was Ramadan and the deep red sun peered through the pollution as the time to break the daily fast approached. We went to a few stores to pick up supplies. Harb cautioned me not to speak English in public anymore. Iraq had transformed into a different country. A year ago, other journalists and I had been able to ride around together and walk the streets, sometimes even at night. We had shared the same hotel without fear of kidnapping or car bombings. Six months earlier, at the time of my last trip, conditions had changed somewhat and we functioned in units of one Westerner with one interpreter, very rarely in any other formation. A rogue band of us had stayed in an off-the-map dive of a hotel and kept our heads down. We hardly traveled around Baghdad without an interpreter. Car bombings had become the norm, and the mood of Iraqis had grown sullen and bitter.

Now, Iraq was yet another country. I typed my stories from within the guarded compound of my hotel, the constant rattle of gun battles with automatic weapons on the street in the background. Fallujah had once again been sealed in preparation of the imminent attack, and the mood in Baghdad was gloomy and tense with expectation. People were stressed and angry. Chaos reigned and nobody was safe.

In the backdrop was the prospect of another four years with George W. Bush and his junta.

◆ ◆ ◆ ◆

Shortly after I arrived back in Baghdad, Salam Talib, who had worked before as my translator, began developing radio dispatches with me. Requests for radio interviews were pouring in; when I was not out on the street collecting stories, I was in my hotel room writing up news stories or taking radio calls from around the globe.

At night, I would wake up to find myself grinding my teeth. Whenever I was on my own, without Harb or Salam, I fought fear by keeping myself intensely busy. The three of us were working on a story about the Iraqi economy, with a particular focus on unemployment. Nearly twenty months into the occupation, countless numbers of Iraqis were struggling merely to survive. George W. Bush had said in a speech at the U.S. Army War College on May 24, 2004, that the United States wanted "freedom and independence, security, and prosperity for the Iraqi people."[1] Prosperity currently looked like over 50 percent unemployment. A recent study revealed that if the food ration program set up by Saddam Hussein's regime during the U.S.-led sanctions was disbanded, more than 25 percent of Iraqis could starve to death.[2]

Bush, in his speech, had also commended "a growing private economy" in Iraq, after the former governing council had approved a new law "that opens the country to foreign investment for the first time in decades."[3] But my friend and colleague Antonia Juhasz, project director at the International Forum on Globalization based in San Francisco at that time, had evidence that measures enacted by the disbanded CPA would allow the economy of Iraq to be sold off to the detriment of the Iraqis.

In her paper "The Hand-Over That Wasn't: Illegal Orders Give the U.S. a Lock on Iraq's Economy," she wrote that Bremer Order No. 39 allowed for "(a) privatization of Iraq's 200 state-owned enterprises; (b) 100% foreign ownership of Iraqi businesses; (c) 'national treatment'—which meant no preferences for local over foreign businesses; (d) unrestricted, tax-free remittance of all profits and other funds; and (e) 40-year ownership licenses." Iraqi companies that had already been working on the infrastructure were therefore not given any preference in reconstruction efforts in their own country. Foreign corporations such as Halliburton and Bechtel had been allowed "to buy up Iraqi businesses, do all of the work and send all of their money home," Juhasz wrote. "They cannot be required to hire Iraqis or to reinvest their money in the Iraqi economy. They can take out their investments at any time and in any amount."[4]

I was witness to the consequence of those decisions and the impact they had on Iraqi households. Ahmed al-Hadithi, forty, sold vegetables in the Adhamiya district of Baghdad. "The economic situation is very bad now," he told me as he stood selling some cucumbers. "The costs of gas and food are going up so high. Even if we make more now, everything costs more." The vegetables he sold were imported. "I make less profit now. I have nine people to take care of, and it has made my life very difficult." This was a direct result of Order No. 12 of the Bremer Orders, named after former U.S. administrator in Iraq L. Paul Bremer. The order suspended "all tariffs, customs duties, import taxes, licensing fees and similar surcharges for goods entering or leaving Iraq."[5] According to Juhasz, this led to "an immediate and dramatic inflow of cheap foreign consumer products—devastating local producers and sellers who were thoroughly unprepared to meet the challenge of their mammoth global competitors."[6]

I was witness to another horrible reality, which was the complete absence of reconstruction work. Anthony Cordesman, from the Center for Strategic and International Studies in Washington, had written as of June 25, 2004, "the Program Management Office (PMO) data show . . . out of 18.4 billion dollars in aid, 11 billion dollars has been apportioned, 7.6 billion dollars has been committed, 4.8 billion dollars has been obligated, and all of 333 million dollars has actually been spent."[7] Electricity had now dropped to barely six hours per day, and there were water shortages in neighborhoods even within the capital city.

Fifty-year-old Abu Gouda, whom I interviewed, as well as countless others, had personal experience of what these facts and figures meant. The ex-factory worker was now selling vegetables in an Ad-hamiya market. "I make between eight and ten thousand dinars [five to seven dollars] a day, and this is just enough to feed my family of seven," he said at his vegetable stall. "Things have become so difficult, this is what I have to do to take care of my family."

Sabah Ahmed, an unemployed former city council member from the same neighborhood, told me, "The gasoline, transportation, everything is going up so much. People are in a critical situation because of the increase in prices."

◆ ◆ ◆ ◆

"The enemy has got a face. He's called Satan. He's in Fallujah, and we're going to destroy him," proclaimed U.S. Marine Colonel Gary Brandl, a battalion commander, describing the impending attack on Fallujah, unscrupulously demonizing the Iraqis, as reported by the Associated Press on November 6.[8]

The military doctors at the U.S base near Fallujah reported that casualties had already been averaging twenty per day. By November 6, the combat hospital at the closest U.S. base to Fallujah had set up a morgue and doubled the medical staff in anticipation of large numbers of U.S. military casualties.

In this short period leading up to the official beginning of the siege of Fallujah, fighting had broken out across most of Iraq. Near Kirkuk, a gas pipeline was blown up, snapping the supply of electricity to homes and businesses. In Baquba, attacks from resistance fighters claimed the lives of two civilians when a mortar landed on their house near a police station.

Samarra, supposedly under U.S. military control since the beginning of October, saw four car bomb explosions, killing forty people, ten of whom were Iraqi policemen, and wounding at least sixty-two. An Iraqi health official reported that twenty-three people, including nine policemen, were killed and forty wounded in that city, in the first of three bomb explosions against Iraqi police all on the same day. A second car bomb detonated while rescue workers were assisting victims of the first blast. A third bomb then struck a U.S. patrol while it was attempting to reach the scene of the first two blasts. The fourth blast occurred at 12:30 p.m., when a suicide bomber rammed his car into a police station that, according to Iraqi police, killed several policemen and wounded five others. Witnesses claimed that American troops had fired sporadically in the city center after they were attacked, injuring civilians and destroying cars. Resistance fighters had handed out leaflets pledging solidarity with their brothers in Fallujah.

Meanwhile, the U.S. and British governments, along with the U.S.-installed Iraqi interim government, had rejected an appeal made by Kofi Annan, the then secretary-general of the United Nations, who warned the authorities against attacking Fallujah. Ignoring his warning, U.S. warplanes, AC-130 gun ships, and artillery continued to pound Fallujah over the weekend. One of the targets razed to the ground was Nazzal Emergency Hospital in the city center.

Over in Ramadi, twenty U.S. soldiers were injured in an attack on their convoy and a suicide car bomb detonated outside a U.S. military base in the al-Fujariyah district near the entrance of the city. The lifeless bodies of Iraqis caught in the attack were scattered about on the road outside the base.

And in Haditha, two hundred resistance fighters using RPGs and mortars stormed a police station, killing twenty-three policemen execution style. The fighters took the policemen out of the station with their hands tied behind their backs and shot them. There were three simultaneous attacks on police stations there and in Haqlaniyah.

Meanwhile, back in Baghdad, a car bomber on the airport road killed an Iraqi civilian and wounded three U.S. soldiers. Near constant gunfire was part of the daily reality as sporadic fighting simmered around the capital. From Friday night until Saturday of the last weekend before the siege, the sound of U.S. war planes roaring over the capital en route to Fallujah was ever present.

By Sunday, November 7, 2004, fifty people had already been killed across the country since the start of the month. Amid all the bloodshed, the Iraqi government imposed martial law throughout Iraq, excluding Kurdistan, for two months. The night this announcement was broadcast, Harb called me. He was unable to leave his neighborhood because it had been sealed by the military. Humvees were in the main square and roaming the streets. "I cannot reach you tonight, Daher. We are under martial law," he told me over the phone.

Salam, who was with me when Harb called, observed, "This won't give the government any power. They were already powerless. Let them put on any law they want, it doesn't matter."

Later that night, Harb managed to slip out of his neighborhood, and came to my hotel. He was distraught. Before coming over, he had driven around the city to observe the conditions. "There is no electricity all over the city. It is Ramadan, so all shops should be open now, but none are open."

We decided to go out and have a look. There were traffic snarls everywhere. Three quarters of the homes, shops, and traffic lights were without electricity, and the other quarter were being run by generators. Near the National Theater, only three shops were open.

The lines at the petrol stations were miles long. Many of the stations were closed because of martial law.

Whenever I went out, I wrapped my keffiyeh up around my bearded face, to disguise myself and blend in with Iraqis. Prior to this trip, I had cut off my ponytail, a leftover from my mountain-guide days, after Harb told me, "You should get a haircut so you do not get a head cut." I was taking every precaution possible. I had never imagined the situation in Iraq would have degraded so quickly. It was barely four months since my last trip, but I found everything to be far worse than before, from security and infrastructure to the spirit of the Iraqis. The overwhelming tension in the lead-up to the second siege of Fallujah (named by the U.S. military Operation Phantom Fury) made matters worse.

Less than forty-eight hours before the siege was launched, Iraqi Secretary of Defense Hassim al-Sha'alan announced on Al-Arabiya television that the Iraqi resistance was well-organized and that the fighting in Fallujah would not end when the U.S. military took the city. Everything was on hold as we waited for the siege to begin. We knew in advance that retaliation attacks would ripple out to cities like Baghdad, Baquba, Latifiya, Ramadi, Samarra, Khaldiya, Kirkuk, Balad, and elsewhere. The siege was opposed even by Iraqis who were members of the puppet interim government.

There was a feeling of deep apprehension and concern across Baghdad as thousands of U.S. troops massed around Fallujah and sealed it off in preparation for the attack. Already, in Baghdad, the fighting was so widespread that Salam was unable to return home and had to spend the night on the couch in my hotel room.

For several weeks leading up to November 8, the bombing of Fallujah by U.S. war planes had been on the increase—as had negotiations between city council members from Fallujah, tribal representatives, and members of the Iraqi interim government, including Iyad Allawi. Until hours before the invasion of the city, the people of Fallujah held out hope that a compromise could be reached that would avert the attack.

Just before the last meeting that had been planned between the city council members and interim Prime Minister Iyad Allawi, however, the council members stared in horror at their television screens as Allawi came on to announce that he had given the "green light" for the siege of Fallujah to begin on the evening of November 8.

After this day, the United States could have no chance of containing the Iraqi resistance and popular support for it. Since the April siege, Fallujah had come to be known as a city of both actual and symbolic resistance to the U.S. empire throughout the Middle East. The display of brute force that the U.S. military unleashed on the people of Fallujah underscored how the guerrillas had Goliath both frustrated and angry. As the occupation forces rushed headlong into this trap, the message was clear to all Iraqis: their well-being was of little or no interest to the occupiers who had come to "liberate" them.

Fallujan refugees at a mosque on Baghdad University campus told of the white phosphorous, cluster bombs, and other weapons used by the U.S. military in their city. November 2004.

CHAPTER 15

OPERATION PHANTOM FURY

These events of war were performed not by atavistic savages following the code of archaic rituals, but usually by trained troops from societies boasting civilized values, humane laws, moral education, and aesthetic culture. Nor were these acts specific to one nation—typically Japanese, typically American, or German or Serbian. . . . Nor were they confined to exceptional psychopathic criminals among the troops. No: this is what wars do, what battles are; conventions of rampage on both a monstrous collective and monstrous individual scale, implacable archetypal behaviors, behaviors of an archetype, governed by, possessed by, commanded by Mars.

—*James Hillman,* A Terrible Love of War

On the same day martial law was declared, U.S. tanks began rolling into the outskirts of Fallujah, while warplanes continued to pound the city with as many as fifty thousand residents still inside. Allawi laid out the six steps for implementing his "security law." These entailed a 6:00 p.m. curfew in Fallujah, the blocking of all highways except for emergencies and for government vehicles, the closure of all city and government services, a ban on all weapons in Fallujah, the closure of Iraq's borders with Syria and Jordan (except to allow passage to food trucks and vehicles carrying other necessary goods), and the closure of Baghdad International Airport for forty-eight hours.

Meanwhile, in the United States, most corporate media outlets were busy spreading the misinformation that Fallujah had fallen under the control of the Jordanian terrorist Abu Musab al-Zarqawi. There was no available evidence that Zarqawi had ever set foot inside the city. It was amply evident that the resistance in the city was composed primarily of people from Fallujah itself. However, that did not deter the establishment media, which portrayed the assault on the city as a hostage intervention situation.[1]

As they had done during the April siege, the military raided and occupied Fallujah General Hospital, cutting it off from the rest of the city. On November 8, the *New York Times* reported, "The assault against Falluja began here Sunday night as American Special Forces and Iraqi troops burst into Falluja General Hospital and seized it within an hour." Of course, this information was immediately followed by the usual parroting of U.S. military propaganda, "At 10:00 p.m., Iraqi troops clambered off seven-ton trucks, sprinting with American Special Forces soldiers around the side of the main building of the hospital, considered a refuge for insurgents and a center of propaganda against allied forces, entering the complex to bewildered looks from patients and employees."[2]

Harb arrived at my hotel the next morning in a somber mood. "How can we live like this, we are trapped in our own country. You know Daher, everyone is praying for God to take revenge on the Americans. Everyone!" He said even in their private prayers people were praying for God to take vengeance on the Americans for what they were doing in Fallujah. "Everyone I've talked to the last couple of nights, eighty or ninety people, have admitted that they are doing this," he said as I collected my camera and notepad to prepare to leave.

Out on the streets of Baghdad, the anxiety was palpable. The threat of being kidnapped or car bombed, or simply robbed, relentlessly played on our minds as Harb and I went about conducting interviews that had been prearranged. We tried to minimize our time on the streets by returning to my hotel immediately on completing interviews. The security situation, already horrible, was deteriorating further with each passing day.

That night, when Salam arrived at my hotel to work on a radio dispatch with me, he had a wild look in his eyes and sweat beads on his forehead. "My friend has just been killed, and he was one of my best friends," he said staring out my window. Salam went on to tell me that a relative of another of his friends had been missing for six days. "This morning, his body was brought to his family by someone who found it on the road. The body had been shot twice in the chest and twice in the head. There were visible signs of torture, and the four bullet shells that were used to kill him had been placed in his trouser pockets. This news has driven me crazy, Daher. The number of people killed here is growing so fast every day," he said, his hands raised in that familiar gesture of despair. "When I was a child, it was common to have some family member who was killed in the war with Iran. But now, it feels as though everyone is dying every day."

Not yet one full week into the latest assault on Fallujah, the flames of resistance had engulfed much of Baghdad and other areas in Iraq. In Baghdad alone, neighborhoods like Amiriyah, Abu Ghraib, Adhamiya, and al-Dora had fallen mostly under the control of the resistance. In these areas, and much of the rest of Baghdad, U.S. patrols were few and far between, since they were being attacked so often.

People we interviewed showed no surprise at fighting having rapidly spread across other cities. It was expected, because the general belief was that the resistance had fled Fallujah prior to the siege.

Most of the fighters had melted away to other areas to choose effective methods to strike the enemy. Fighting had thus spread across much of Baghdad, Baquba, Latafiya, Ramadi, Samarra, Mosul, Khaldiya, and Kirkuk just days into Operation Phantom Fury.

Over near the Imam Adham mosque, a huge demonstration erupted. It was organized by the Islamic Party, which had just withdrawn from the interim government and had called for a boycott of the upcoming January 30, 2005 elections. The demonstration was comprised of many more than five thousand enraged people denouncing Iyad Allawi, demanding his resignation, and calling for jihad against him. The demonstration was a defiant declaration that people were unafraid of the U.S. military.

One week into the siege, violence around Baghdad continued unabated. If the U.S. plan was to dampen the resistance by destroying a city sympathetic to it, clearly the plan was a dismal failure. Like clockwork, each night at around 9:00 p.m. the Green Zone would take mortars, sometimes in a sustained barrage.

Iraq's borders with Syria and Jordan remained closed, in accordance with Allawi having declared a state of national emergency. Baghdad International Airport remained closed for the same reason. To be in Baghdad at the time felt eerily like being entrapped. Theoretically, we had a few options for escaping if the need arose. Driving around the city had also become more difficult, as the petrol lines snarled traffic and raised tempers.

In Baquba, another police station was attacked, and five police vehicles were torched, along with several Iraqi National Guard trucks. The U.S. base in the city was mortared during the fighting.

The humanitarian disaster in Fallujah worsened as the U.S. military continued to refuse entry to the Iraqi Red Crescent (IRC) convoys of relief supplies. I was told at the Red Crescent headquarters in Baghdad that they had appealed to the UN to intervene, but once again the UN proved its impotence in all matters. While there, I also heard that Iraqi Army members, under U.S. control, engaged in the supervised looting of Fallujah General Hospital during the first week of the siege.

Inside Fallujah, the U.S. military allowed some bodies to be buried by residents, but others were being eaten by dogs and cats in the streets, as reported both by refugees coming out of the city and residents still trapped there. The military claimed that there was no need for the IRC to deliver aid to people inside Fallujah, since there were no more civilians inside the city. (Later, officials acknowledged that thirty thousand to fifty thousand residents had remained in the city.) "There is no need to bring [Red Crescent] supplies in because we have supplies of our own for the people," explained marine Colonel Mike Shupp.[3] But IRC spokesperson Firdu al-Ubadi told me, "We know of at least 157 families inside Fallujah who need our help."

Media repression during the second siege of Fallujah was intense. The "100 Orders" penned by former U.S. administrator Bremer included Order 65, passed on March 20, 2004, which established an Iraqi communications and media commission. This commission had powers to control the media because it had complete control over licensing and regulating telecommunications, broadcasting, information services, and media establishments. On June 28, when the United States handed over power to a "sovereign" Iraqi interim government, Bremer simply passed on his authority to Iyad Allawi, the U.S.-installed interim prime minister, who had longstanding ties with the British intelligence service MI6 and the CIA. The media commission sent out an order just after the assault on Fallujah commenced ordering news organizations to "stick to the government line on the U.S.-led offensive in Fallujah or face legal action."[4] The warning was circulated on Allawi's letterhead.

The letter also asked the media in Iraq to "set aside space in your news coverage to make the position of the Iraqi government, which expresses the aspirations of most Iraqis, clear."

On the ground, aside from the notorious bombing and then banning of Al-Jazeera, other instances of media repression were numerous. A journalist for the al-Arabiya network, who attempted to get inside Fallujah, was detained by the military, as was a French freelance photographer named Corentin Fleury, who was staying at my hotel. Fleury, a soft-spoken, wiry man, was detained by the U.S. military along with his interpreter, twenty-eight-year-old Bahktiyar Abdulla Hadad, when they were leaving Fallujah just before the siege of the city began. They had worked in the city for nine days leading up to the siege, and were held for five days in a military detention facility outside the city. "They were very nervous and they asked us what we had seen, and looked through all my photos, asking me questions about them," he said as we talked in my room one night. He told me he had photographed homes destroyed by U.S. warplanes.

Despite appeals by the French government to the U.S. military to free his translator and return Fleury's confiscated camera equipment and his photos, there had been no luck in attaining either. (When I had last seen Fleury in February 2005, Hadad was still being held by the U.S. military.)

The military was maintaining a strict cordon around most of the city. Meanwhile, Al-Jazeera continued to run announcements over their satellite station apologizing to viewers for its inability to offer better coverage in Iraq, since its office had been closed indefinitely by the U.S.-backed interim government. Nevertheless, Al-Jazeera did manage to get the word out. One week into the siege, the network reported that Asma Khamis al-Muhannadi, a doctor who had witnessed the U.S. troops and Iraqi National Guard raid the General Hospital, said the hospital had been targeted by bombs and rockets during the initial siege of Fallujah, and troops had dragged patients from their beds and pushed them against the wall. This was in addition to warplanes having bombed the Nazzal Emergency Hospital, killing doctors, nurses, and an unknown number of patients.[5] Al-Muhannadi recounted "I will always remember this. I was taking care of a woman who was giving birth and the baby was still connected to its mother through the umbilical cord. The U.S. soldier asked the National Guardsman to arrest me, and the guard tied my hands with ropes. . . .The two doctors who were with us on the road—there were people from the Red Cross and the Association of Muslim Scholars—were completely stripped of their clothes. They inspected their underclothes completely and their shoes. They even inspected their hair, anything they could think of."[6] Two months later, another doctor from Fallujah, Ahmed Abdulla, verified her story when I interviewed him in Baghdad.

◆ ◆ ◆ ◆

Since I could not get into Fallujah because of the ongoing military cordon, I set out to interview doctors and patients who had fled the city and were presently working in various hospitals around Baghdad. While visiting Yarmouk Hospital looking for more information about Fallujah, I came across several children from areas south of Baghdad.

One of these was a twelve-year-old girl, Fatima Harouz, from Latifiya. She lay dazed in a crowded hospital room, limply waving her bruised arm at the flies. Her shins, shattered by bullets from U.S. soldiers when they fired through the front door of her house, were both covered by casts. Small plastic drainage bags filled with red fluid sat upon her abdomen, where she took shrapnel from another bullet. Her mother told us, "They attacked our home, and there weren't even any resistance fighters in our area." Fatima's uncle was shot and killed, his wife had been wounded, and their home was ransacked by soldiers. "Before they left, they killed all our chickens." A doctor who was with us looked at me and asked, "This is the freedom. In their Disneyland are there kids just like this?"

Another young woman, Rana Obeidy, had been walking home in Baghdad with her brother two nights earlier. She assumed the soldiers had shot her and her brother because he was carrying a bottle of soda. She had a chest wound where a bullet had grazed her, but had struck her little brother and killed him.

Lying in a bed near Rana was Hanna, fourteen years old. She had a gash on her right leg from the bullet of a U.S. soldier. Her family had been traveling in a taxi in Baghdad past a U.S. patrol that very morning, when a soldier opened fire on the car. Her father's shirt was spotted with blood from a head injury from when the taxi crashed.

In another room, a small boy from Fallujah lay on his stomach. Shrapnel from a grenade thrown into his home by a U.S. soldier had entered his body through his back and was implanted near his kidney. An operation had successfully removed the shrapnel, but his father had been killed by what his mother described as "the haphazard shooting of the Americans." The boy, Amin, lay in his bed vacillating between crying with pain and playing with his toy car.

Later that afternoon, I found myself at a small but busy supply center in Baghdad that had been set up to distribute goods to refugees from Fallujah. Standing in an old, one-story building that used to be a vegetable market, I watched as people walked around wearily to obtain basic foodstuffs, blankets, or information about housing. "They kicked all the journalists out of Fallujah so they could do whatever they want," said Kassem Mohammed Ahmed, who had escaped from Fallujah three days before. "The first thing they did was bomb the hospitals because that is where the wounded have to go. Now we see that wounded people are in the street and the soldiers are rolling their tanks over them. This happened so many times. What you see on the TV is nothing. That is just one camera. What you cannot see is much more."

There were also stories of soldiers not discriminating between civilians and resistance fighters. Another man, Abdul Razaq Ismail, had arrived from Fallujah one week earlier and had been helping with the distribution of supplies to other refugees, having received similar help himself. Loading a box with blankets to send to a refugee camp, he said, "There are dead bodies on the ground and nobody can bury them. The Americans are dropping some of the bodies into the Euphrates River near Fallujah. They are pulling some bodies with tanks and leaving them at the soccer stadium."

Another man sat nearby nodding his head. He couldn't stop crying. After a while, he said he wanted to talk to us. "They bombed my neighborhood and we used car jacks to raise the blocks of concrete to get dead children out from under them."

Another refugee, Abu Sabah, an older man in a torn shirt and dusty pants, told of how he escaped with his family, just the day before, while soldiers shot bullets over their heads, killing his cousin. "They used these weird bombs that first put up smoke in a cloud, and then small pieces fell from the air with long tails of smoke behind them. These exploded on the ground with large fires that burned for half an hour. They used these near the train tracks. When anyone touched those fires, their body burned for hours."

This was the first time I had heard a refugee describing the use of white phosphorous incendiary weapons by the U.S. military, fired from artillery into Fallujah. Though it is not technically a banned weapon, it is a violation of the Geneva Conventions to use white phosphorous in an area where civilians may be hit. I heard similar descriptions in the coming days and weeks, both from refugees and doctors who had fled the city.

Khalil, a forty-year-old refugee I interviewed, after confirming that incendiary weapons had been used in the city by the U.S. military, told me, "When the Americans came to our city, we refused to accept any foreigner coming to invade us. We accept the Iraqi National Guards but not the Americans. Nobody has seen any Zarqawi. If the Americans don't come in our city, who do Fallujans attack? Fallujans don't attack other Iraqis. Fallujans only attack the American troops when they come inside or near our city." Rather than weeping like many others I interviewed, Khalil was seething in anger, "If we have a government, it should solve the suffering of the people. Our government does not do this, instead it is always attacking us. It is a dummy government. They are not here to help us. The ministers of defense and interior claim that we are their family. Why then do they collapse our houses on our heads? Why do they kill all of us?"

Several doctors I interviewed had told me they had been instructed by the interim government not to speak to any journalists about the patients they were receiving from Fallujah. A few of them told me they had even been instructed by the Shia-controlled Ministry of Health not to accept patients from Fallujah.

That night I interviewed a spokesman for the IRC, who told me none of their relief teams had been allowed into Fallujah, and the military said it would be at least two more weeks before any refugees would be allowed back into their city. Collecting information from doctors in the city, he had estimated that at least eight hundred civilians had been killed so far in the siege.

The second assault on Fallujah was a monument to brutality and atrocity made in the United States of America. Like the Spanish city of Guernica during the 1930s, and Grozny in the 1990s, Fallujah is our monument of excess and overkill. It was soon to become, even for many in the U.S. military, a textbook case of the wrong way to handle a resistance movement. Another case of winning the battle and losing the war.

A boy in Fallujah killed by U.S. forces. November 2004. Photo: Unknown Photographer.

CHAPTER 16

INTO OBLIVION

It was Friday, November 19, a day of prayer, and Harb and I agreed to take a much needed day off. Emotionally exhausted from the draining task of interviewing refugees from Fallujah, I celebrated the break by sleeping in as long as I could.

After my usual breakfast of hard-boiled eggs, bread, and cheese, washed down with thick, Arabic coffee, I shuffled downstairs and across the street to the nearby Internet café. There had been no bombs or gunfire in the vicinity that morning, and I was surprised to be feeling something similar to relaxation.

Just then my cell phone began to ring and Harb's name appeared on the LED screen. I found it odd that he was calling when it was the prayer hour at mosques across Iraq.

"I am being held at gunpoint by American soldiers inside Abu Hanifa mosque, Daher," he yelled. "Everyone is praying to God because the Americans are raiding our mosque during Friday prayer!" His frantic voice was nearly drowned out by the deafening roar of hundreds of people in a confined area repeatedly hailing, "*Allahu Akbar,*" which reverberated off the mosque walls and through my telephone before the line went dead.

Harb soon called back. He made several short calls, updating me on the atrocity one scene at a time. After each new bit of information, he hung up. Each time, I tried to finish typing before he called back. "They have shot and killed at least four people while they were praying, and nearly twenty are wounded now. I cannot believe this. I can't let them see me calling you." He lowered his voice. "I am on my stomach now and they have their guns on everyone, there are more than a thousand people inside the mosque and it is sealed. We are on our bellies and in a very bad situation."

Several long minutes dragged by as I waited for his next call. There was no way I could call him, since his ringing phone could have been a death sentence.

Harb called back. "We were here praying and now there are over fifty of them with their guns on us," he whispered. "They are holding our heads to the ground, and everything is in chaos. They are roughing up a blind man now."

He called back a few minutes later and told me that the soldiers had released the women and children, along with men who were related to them. He spoke with me from outside the mosque this time. He was released only because a boy approached him and requested that he act as his father. Harb asked me to hold on and hung up the phone. Shortly thereafter he phoned me from his home in tears. "Daher, I cannot believe what has happened. I will go back to see what is happening now." I urged him not to go, but he insisted. "This is my mosque and my people. I must go and see what is happening to them."

It was now 2:15 p.m. and the mosque was well into its third hour of being sealed. Harb began to interview people he was with and simultaneously described the scene to me. "People were praying and the Americans invaded the mosque," says Abdulla Ra'ad Aziz, who had been released along with his wife and children. "Why are they killing people for praying? After the forces entered, they went to the back doors of the mosque and we heard many bullets being fired from their guns. There are wounded and dead. I saw them myself."

All the people interviewed were in a state of high agitation and stress.

Some of the people who had been at prayer were ordered by the soldiers to carry the dead and wounded out of the mosque. "One Iraqi National Guardsman held his gun on people and yelled, 'I will kill you if you don't shut up,'" said Rana Aziz, a mother who had been trapped in the mosque. She was now waiting outside for her brother, who was still inside.

She said someone asked the soldiers if they were going to be taken hostages. "A soldier yelled at everyone to 'Shut the fuck up,'" she told Harb. Suddenly, she laughed through her tears. "The Americans have learned how to say shut up in Arabic, '*Inche*.'"

Twenty-year-old Hammad Mohammed told Harb, "My uncle's coffin was taken inside the mosque to be blessed, and the Americans raided the mosque and went to the imams' room. Then they went to the back doors and we heard shots. It was a gun bigger than a Kalashnikov. I saw four killed and nine wounded." Harb then broke off the interview to tell me, "Doctors and staff are standing outside but the Americans are refusing to let them inside. They can do nothing, and the Americans are not letting them inside while there are wounded people suffering inside the mosque."

Just like in Fallujah, soldiers denied the IRC ambulances and medical teams access to the mosque. As doctors negotiated with American soldiers outside, more gunfire was heard from inside the mosque. Shortly thereafter about thirty men were led out with hoods over their heads and their hands tied. Soldiers loaded them into a military vehicle and took them away around 3:15 p.m. A doctor with the IRC confirmed four dead and nine wounded worshipers. Harb entered the mosque to find pieces of brain splattered on one of the walls and large bloodstains covering the carpets in several places.

Later that evening, Harb came to my hotel to see me. Distraught and crying, he recounted the story once again. He had managed to tape the entire raid with the small recorder we used for interviews. It had been in his pocket, and he had switched it on the minute the soldiers entered the mosque. After listening to the entire recording, he said, "I am in a very sad position. I do not see any freedom or any democracy for Iraq. If this could lead to a freedom, it is a freedom with blood. It is a freedom of emotions of sadness. It is a freedom of killing. You cannot gain democracy through blood or killing. This is neither democracy nor freedom."

A few days later, Harb and I were trapped in the usual snarl of traffic on Baghdad's streets. We were on our way to conduct interviews when an Iraqi police truck raced past on the wrong side of the road, its sirens blaring. In the back stood several men in black clothes and black face masks. We had been noticing this from time to time, but by late November it had become more common. Harb had recently mentioned that several families in his primarily Sunni neighborhood had talked of similarly attired men coming in the middle of the night to kidnap and assassinate certain people. Salam had told me the same thing was occurring in his predominately Shia neighborhood, where most of the people supported Muqtada al-Sadr.

It was already clear that Operation Phantom Fury had succeeded in spreading the resistance across much of Iraq, rather than breaking "the back" of it, as marine General John Sattler had declared it would do.[1]

When *Newsweek* magazine released an article about the Pentagon considering the use of "Special-Forces-led assassination or kidnapping teams in Iraq," it came as no surprise to the Iraqi people. There were other reasons for the discussions on the imminent use of "the Salvador option."[2]

By no coincidence, John Negroponte was the U.S. ambassador to Iraq at this time. This was the same man that the Honduras Commission on Human Rights in 1994 had accused of widespread human rights violations when he was the U.S. ambassador to Honduras from 1981 to 1985. According to a CIA working group set up in 1996 to look into the U.S. role in Honduras, the violations Negroponte oversaw in Honduras were carried out by operatives trained by the CIA. Records reveal that his "special intelligence units," better known as "death squads," were comprised of CIA-trained Honduran armed units that kidnapped, tortured, and killed thousands of people suspected of supporting leftist guerrillas.

Retired colonel James Steele was at the time adviser to the training of Iraqi security forces. Steele, who reported to Negroponte, and whose official title was Counselor for Iraqi Security Forces, had been stationed in Central America in the 1980s as commander of the U.S. military adviser group in El Salvador from 1984 to 1986, around the time that Negroponte was in Honduras. These death squads were a well-known and brutal feature in Guatemalan politics during the 1980s. There, soldiers wore uniforms during the day and used unmarked cars at night to kidnap and kill those who were hostile to the right-wing regime. During the early 1980s, the Reagan administration funded and trained Nicaraguan contras based in Honduras, with the goal of ousting the Sandinista regime in Nicaragua. Steele also has the distinction of smuggling weapons to the Contras in Nicaragua and lying about it to the Senate Intelligence Committee, as has been documented in the final report of the Iran-Contra special prosecutor.[3] The money used to equip the Contras had been obtained from illegal American arms sales to Iran, a scandal that should have toppled Reagan.

Following the Central American model, the Pentagon proposal was to send U.S. Special Forces teams to advise, support, and train Iraqi death squads. These death squads were hand-picked from the Kurdish Peshmerga, Shi'ite Mehdi Army, and Badr Army militias, to target Sunni resistance leaders and those who supported them. It was a move sure to deepen sectarian and ethnic tensions. The well-trained and heavily armed Kurdish Peshmerga militia had long since controlled northern Iraq. The Shia Badr Army was an organization backed, armed, and funded by Iran, that had entered Iraq just after the March 2003 invasion. The Mehdi Army, the armed wing of Shia cleric Muqtada al-Sadr, while not well armed or trained, was the largest of these militias. We had already seen evidence of their activities in November 2004. (Not surprisingly, since he was a U.S. pawn and CIA asset from the beginning, Iyad Allawi was vigorously supportive of this policy, which so quickly spun out of control that a September 2005 UN human rights report held the interior ministry forces largely responsible for the organized campaign of detentions, torture, and killings in Iraq.[4])

The fact that the United States organized and backed these death squads was strong enough that in April 2006 U.S. Representative Dennis Kucinich penned a letter to Secretary of Defense Donald Rumsfeld that read:

Dear Secretary Rumsfeld:

I am writing to request a copy of all records pertaining to Pentagon plans to use U.S. Special Forces to advise, support and train Iraqi assassination and kidnapping teams. . . .

About one year before the *Newsweek* report on the "Salvador Option," it was reported in the *American Prospect* magazine on January 1, 2004, that part of $3 billion of the $87 billion Emergency Supplemental Appropriations bill, which had hoped to get funds for operations in Iraq, and had been signed into law on November 6, 2003, was designated for the creation of a paramilitary unit manned by militiamen associated with former Iraqi exile groups. According to the *Prospect* article, experts predicted that creation of this paramilitary unit would "lead to a wave of extrajudicial killings, not only of

armed rebels but of nationalists, other opponents of the U.S. occupation and thousands of civilian Baathists." The article further described how the bulk of the $3 billion program, disguised as an Air
Force classified program, would be used to "support U.S. efforts to
create a lethal, and revenge-minded Iraqi security force." One of the
article's sources, John Pike, an expert of classified military budgets
on www.globalsecurity.org [stated], "The big money would be for
standing up an Iraqi secret police to liquidate the resistance."[5]

Even as far back as late November 2004 there was compelling evidence of how the U.S. was directly contributing to creating civil war
in Iraq by this secretive "security" strategy. This is only to be expected. The strategy of divide and rule has been used throughout
history by colonial powers, and had been extensively used during
the first British occupation of Iraq eighty-five years earlier.

(By fall 2006, with Iraq in the throes of a brutal civil war, these
U.S.-trained and U.S.-backed sectarian death squads had become
the leading cause of death in Iraq.[6])

◆ ◆ ◆ ◆

In early December, an Iraqi friend of mine managed to enter Fallujah as part of an IRC aid convoy that was allowed passage through
one of the U.S. checkpoints. By this time, the military had set up
checkpoints that used biometrics. All residents of Fallujah were required to undergo retina scans and be fingerprinted for a bar-coded
ID badge. They were all searched at gunpoint after waiting hours in
long lines. Speaking on condition of anonymity, a woman I shall call
Suthir, upon returning to Baghdad, said, "I need another heart and
other eyes to bear it because my own are not enough to bear what I
saw. Nothing justifies what was done to this city."

The U.S. military had not given a date when the hundreds of

thousands of refugees from Fallujah would be allowed to return to their city. "There was no reconstruction anywhere. I just saw more bombs falling and black smoke everywhere. There is not a single house or school undamaged there."

Later that afternoon, an Iraqi friend who had worked with me as translator, stopped by my hotel. She had just returned from Fallujah and brought me a disc that contained photographs that had been taken by an Iraqi man. He was granted permission to photograph some of the bodies to enable families that had fled the city to identify their loved ones who had remained inside. The seventy-five photographs he had shot were of bodies either partially or mostly eaten by dogs, with bloated stomachs in various stages of decomposition, bodies with charred skin, and others buried in the rubble of bombed homes. Some of the photos showed people shot to death while still in their beds.

Fighting continued to rage around Baghdad. Car bombs had long since become a daily event. One morning Harb called to tell me his neighborhood had been once again closed since the Hamid al-Alwan mosque, a small Shia mosque in his predominantly Sunni area of Adhamiya, had been targeted by a car bomb. Witnesses reported that the car had been left there at 6:00 a.m. and later detonated remotely. After the first blast, people in nearby homes, hearing the screams of the wounded, ran outside to help. As a group formed around the wreckage, a second, much larger explosion went off. In the end, fourteen were killed and nineteen wounded. Residents took it upon themselves to evacuate most of the wounded and dead to nearby al-Numan Hospital. Ambulances failed to arrive until forty-five minutes after the blast.

It was interesting to note that while the U.S. military were usually among the first to arrive on the scene at bombings, they never showed up for this one. Nor did the ING, which had a base in the ex-presidential palace less than a half mile from the bombing.

Meanwhile, the director of Fallujah General Hospital had been shot and wounded by soldiers when he and two other doctors were attempting to enter Fallujah in an ambulance to provide aid to families trapped there. They had gone into the city after having been granted permission by both the military and the Ministry of Health. Reported at length by Arab outlets, the news largely escaped the attention of most Western outlets.

Around the same time, Al-Jazeera started telecasting photographs dated from May 2003, depicting U.S. soldiers torturing Iraqis, including close shots of men with bloodied mouths and guns held to their heads. The pictures had been uploaded to the Internet by the wife of a soldier who had returned to the United States from Iraq. John Hutson, a retired rear admiral who served as the U.S. Navy's judge advocate general from 1997 to 2000, clearly said that the photos suggested possible Geneva Conventions violations, as international law prohibits souvenir photos of prisoners of war. "It is pretty obvious that these pictures were taken largely as war trophies," he said.[7]

With more people managing to escape Fallujah and others returning from survey visits undertaken to check on their city, more horror stories emerged. Several eyewitness reports from refugees indicated that U.S. soldiers in Fallujah were tying the dead bodies of resistance fighters to tanks and driving around displaying their "trophies." Refugees spoke of indiscriminate killings by U.S. forces during the peak fighting of the previous month in their largely annihilated city.

One of my fixers arranged an interview with Burhan Fasa'a, an Iraqi journalist who worked for the popular Lebanese satellite TV station, LBC. My fixer brought Fasa'a and his friend Khalil, who requested that his last name not be used, to a nearby hotel, where we sat in a quiet lobby for the interview. Fasa'a, a gaunt man with a distant look on his face, was in Fallujah for nine days during the most intense combat. He shook my hand, thanking me for meeting with him, and appeared shaken by his experiences. He began his account by describing how U.S. soldiers had been very impatient with people who could not understand English.

"The Americans did not have interpreters with them," Fasa'a said, "so they would enter houses and kill people because they did not follow or speak English. They entered a house where I was staying with twenty-six other people, and they shot people because [the people] didn't obey orders, but that was because those people could not understand a word of English. Soldiers thought the people were defying their orders, so they shot them. But the truth was that the people just could not understand them." He told me that U.S. troops had detained him. They had interrogated him specifically about working for the Arab media and held him for three days. Like the other prisoners, he had slept on the ground without blankets. He said prisoners were made to go to the bathroom in handcuffs, and had use of only one toilet, which was in the middle of the camp. "During the nine days I was in Fallujah, none of the wounded women, kids, and old people were evacuated," he said. "They either suffered until they died, or somehow survived."

Khalil said he had witnessed the shooting of civilians who were waving white flags as they tried to exit the city. "They shot women and old men in the streets. Then they shot anyone who tried to approach the dead bodies. There are bodies the Americans threw in the river." He had personally witnessed U.S. troops dispose of dead Iraqis in the Euphrates. "And anyone who had stayed on knew for certain that they would be killed by the Americans, so they tried to escape by swimming across the river. Even people who could not swim attempted it. They drowned rather than staying in the city and be killed by the Americans."

It was at this time that Associated Press photographer Bilal Hussein reported civilians being massacred as they attempted to flee the city. After running out of basic necessities and deciding to flee the city at the height of the U.S.-led assault, Hussein ran to the Euphrates. "I decided to swim," Hussein told colleagues at the AP, who wrote up his harrowing story, "but I changed my mind after seeing U.S. helicopters firing on and killing people trying to cross the river." Hussein said he had seen soldiers kill a family of five as they tried to swim across the river. He had to bury a man by the riverbank with his bare hands. "I kept walking along the river for two hours and I could still see some U.S. snipers ready to shoot anyone who might swim," Hussein recounted. "I quit the idea of crossing the river and walked for about five hours through orchards."[8]

A Pulitzer Prize–winning photo journalist, Hussein, who had been with the AP since 2004, was later detained by the U.S. military in Ramadi on April 12, 2006. He was held in a military detention center in Iraq, without charge or trial until September 2006. The military accused him of collaborating with "insurgents." But Frank Smyth from the Committee to Protect Journalists, told reporters, "There's no evidence that he collaborated with insurgent activity, collaborating being providing material assistance. Journalists can have contact with the other side and that cannot be a crime."[9]

Hussein's detention added greatly to the stress of journalists not "embedded" with the U.S. military. Any of us, at any time, could have been detained by the military and accused as Hussein had been.

◆ ◆ ◆ ◆

Harrowing accounts from Fallujah continued unabated. One of my trusted fixers, who I will call Ahmed, arranged a trip for me to accompany him with a small supply of medical aid to hospitals at Amiriyat al-Fallujah, a small town roughly six miles east of Fallujah, and Saqlawiyah, to the northwest.

Our driver, who I also will not name, arrived at my hotel early on a cold, gray morning. The road toward Fallujah was mostly empty, aside from a random military patrol or civilian vehicles packed with families either returning from or going toward the besieged city. Countless craters lined the road approaching Amiriyat al-Fallujah, but thankfully we arrived at the hospital unscathed. We found out from local doctors that the main hospital in Amiriyat al-Fallujah had been raided twice recently by U.S. soldiers and members of the ING.

"The first time was November 29 at 5:40 a.m., and the second time was the following day," said a doctor at the hospital who did not want to give his name for fear of U.S. reprisals. In the first raid, about 150 U.S. soldiers and at least forty members of the ING had stormed the small hospital. "They were yelling loudly at everyone, doctors and patients alike," the young doctor said. "They broke the gates outside, they broke the doors of the garage, and they raided our supply room where our food and supplies are kept. They broke all the interior doors of the hospital, as well as every exterior door." The doctor had been interrogated about resistance fighters, he said. "The Americans threatened to do here what they have done in Fallujah if I did not co-operate with them," he said. Another doctor, also speaking on condition of anonymity, said that all the doors of the clinics inside the hospital were kicked in. All the doctors, along with the security guard, had been handcuffed and interrogated for several hours.

Two doctors took us behind the hospital to where three damaged ambulances were parked. Pointing to one of the vehicles that had a shattered back window, one of them said, "When the Americans raided our hospital again last Tuesday at 7:00 p.m., they smashed one of our ambulances." His colleague pointed toward the two other bullet-riddled ambulances. "The Americans have snipers all along the road between here and Fallujah," he said. "They shoot at our ambulances if we make any attempt to go to Fallujah."

Afraid to stay too long, we thanked them for their time, left a few boxes of medical supplies with them, and circumnavigated Fallujah to arrive at the small town of Saqlawiyah. Just as we arrived at the tiny hospital there, a desperate Dr. Abdulla Aziz told us that occupation forces had blocked all medical supplies from entering or leaving the city. "They won't let any of our ambulances go to help people in Fallujah," he said. "We are out of supplies and they won't let anyone bring us more." It was the same tactic the military had employed during the April siege of Fallujah. In the aftermath of that siege, Dr. Abdul Jabbar, an orthopedic surgeon at Fallujah General, had told me, "The marines have said they didn't close the hospital, but essentially they did. They closed the bridge that connects us to the city, and closed our road. The area in front of our hospital was full of their soldiers and vehicles. Who knows how many civilians we could have saved who died instead." He witnessed troops firing on civilian ambulances and the clinic he had been working in. "Some days we couldn't leave, or even go near the door because of the snipers. They were shooting at the front door of the clinic."

By this time, the IRC had estimated that as many as ten thousand people remained trapped inside the city, many in severe need of medical care. The IRC had been able to deliver some supplies to Fallujah in recent days, but the U.S. military had ordered them out of Fallujah again because of ongoing military operations. I phoned the United States Agency for International Development (USAID), the official aid agency of the U.S. government, in Baghdad to ask what its plan was regarding reconstruction projects in the city, since it had announced its intention to assist the people of Fallujah in reconstruction efforts. Unable to find someone there who would talk with me, one of their spokespeople in the United States, Susan Pittman, told me there were no civilians in the city. "I don't believe that there is anyone in there yet," she told me, as I listened in disbelief. Rebuilding "assessments" would be carried out once military operations were completed, she added.

Many of my contacts inside Fallujah told me that the U.S. military was power blasting streets with water, excavating dirt, and trucking it out of the city from areas where certain munitions were used. Residents claimed these were efforts to conceal the use of illegal weapons. Meanwhile, doctors were starting to say that they had treated civilians hit by incendiary weapons. (Pentagon spokesperson Lieutenant Colonel Barry Venable admitted that white phosphorous had been used by the military in Fallujah, when he spoke to reporters in November 2005, after enough evidence provided by military personnel and other journalists had forced the issue into public awareness. The Pentagon admitted that the restricted weapon had been used and that it may well have hit civilians.[10] Less than two weeks later, a Pentagon spokesman went out of his way to tell reporters that white phosphorous would still be used in Iraq if the need arose.[11])

Iraqi medical personnel in Fallujah estimated that of all the bodies they had logged in their database, at least 60 percent were women and children. The first medical teams to respond had collected more than seven hundred bodies, five hundred and fifty of them women and children, in barely one third of the city. Hence, nearly 80 percent were women and children.

Refugees were also reporting the "firing of houses" by U.S. and Iraqi military personnel. According to witnesses, occupation forces, along with their Iraqi colleagues, were going house by house and burning up everything inside the homes and shooting holes in water tanks atop the houses.

The U.S. military claimed that twelve hundred resistance fighters had been killed, and seven hundred to one thousand captured in Fallujah from early November to December. The U.S. puppet interim Prime Minister Iyad Allawi had the audacity to claim that all twelve hundred killed were resistance fighters, and that not one civilian had been killed in Fallujah. During the first week of Decem-

ber, the military was toying with the idea of making Iraqi men returning to Fallujah work for pay in military-style battalions that
would reconstruct buildings and the water system, depending on
the men's skills. There would also be "rubble-clearing" platoons. The
stated intent of this plan was to make Fallujah a "model city."

(In one of the first signs of the fierce anti-American and anti-occupation sentiment that prevailed in the city after Operation Phantom
Fury came to an end, more than thirty thousand residents of Fallujah
demonstrated in the city on January 2, 2005, refusing to live under military occupation and demanding that the United States leave their city.)

Concurrently, hospitals across Iraq were under a different kind of
siege. Despite the promises of reconstruction and billions of dollars
given to contractors, the situation had long since passed the point of
catastrophe.

Baghdad Medical City in Baghdad, the largest medical complex
in the country, had recently received a new coat of paint. But inside
the hospital, doctors were infuriated at the lack of medicine, supplies, and any real reconstruction. Dr. Hammad Hussein, a resident
of ophthalmology at the center, standing inside his office as patients
clogged the hallway outside, told me, "I have not seen anything
which indicates any rebuilding here other than the new pink and
blue colors with which our building and the escape ladders have
been painted. What we lack is medicines. I will be prescribing medication and the pharmacy simply does not have it to give to the patient. In addition, the hospital is short of wheelchairs, half the lifts
are in disrepair, and the family members of patients are being forced
to work as nurses because of the shortage of medical personnel."

Over at Yarmouk Hospital, Harb and I found new desks and
chairs in some of the offices. The new desk delivered to Dr. Aisha
Abdulla sat in the corridor outside her office. "They should build a
lift so patients who can't walk can be taken to surgery, and instead we

have these new desks," she told us. "How can I take a new desk when there are patients dying because we don't have medicine for them?"

Bechtel Corporation had been hired to deliver an assessment of all damage following the invasion and to identify priority reconstruction projects. Bechtel carried out repair work in about fifty primary health-care centers before handing the rest over to USAID. USAID spent nearly a year selecting contractors to rebuild health-care centers and hospitals before awarding one of the largest contracts to ABT Associates Incorporated, a large government and business consultancy firm based in Massachusetts. The initial ABT contract was worth more than $22 million, according to the USAID Web site. The contract was to support the Iraqi health ministry with medical equipment and supplies, distribute grants to health organizations for critical supplies, and determine specific needs, particularly those of vulnerable groups such as women and children. USAID said it had provided considerable assistance to the Ministry of Health in providing health care for pregnant women and children, supporting immunization programs, and refurbishing local health clinics. More than one hundred such facilities had been improved, according to the USAID spokesman in Baghdad, David DeVoss.

On December 2, I spoke with DeVoss in connection with a story I was writing about the crumbling Iraqi health system. I called him to ask if I could get information on completed or ongoing ABT reconstruction projects in the health-care sector in Iraq. He asked my name, and after I told him, he inquired, "You are the guy who did that "When American Soldiers Raid a Mosque" story? You didn't verify any of that information, did you?" I was taken aback but responded, "Of course it's verified—with both witnesses at the scene and Iraqi Red Crescent workers there. I personally interviewed IRC workers at a later date to confirm, as well. But what does this have to do with information regarding ABT?" He replied curtly, "Because that determines what information I will give you."

He quickly backtracked, knowing he had crossed the legal line about providing public information to a journalist. When I pressed him further, his explanation was, "We have information on what USAID has done regarding clinics. We don't have information on what contractors have done. The goal is the end product, not what the specific contractor is working on. I cannot give you that information."

Meanwhile, according to a study conducted by the UN Development Program, Norway's Fafo Institute for Applied International Studies, and Iraq's Health Ministry, the number of children suffering from malnutrition had doubled since the March 2003 invasion. About 8 percent of Iraqi children below the age of five suffered from chronic diarrhea and protein deficiency. Diarrhea caused mainly by unsafe water was responsible for 70 percent of child deaths in Iraq.[12]

◆ ◆ ◆ ◆

By the middle of December, I was traumatized by what I had witnessed over the previous six weeks. Harb was unable to make it out of his neighborhood, which once again had been sealed by the military. "Everything is *insh'Allah* now, Daher," he told me when I told him I would see him again after a short break in Jordan. "Everything is up to God."

Luckily for me, Salam was able to collect me and drive me to Baghdad International Airport, where I made my way past the countless security guards to the departure gate.

Slumping down into my seat, I languidly watched out my window as we taxied to the runway and then sped down the tarmac.

An eighty-year-old man carries his belongings past a barrier placed in the road by the U.S. military as part of their campaign of collective punishment against residents of the al-Dora region of Baghdad. The military sustained repeated attacks by the Iraqi resistance and responded by blocking roads, cutting off electricity and water, and destroying the only nearby fuel station. January 2005.

CHAPTER 17

DYING FOR DEMOCRACY

After a brief respite with some friends in Jordan, I was drawn back to Iraq, in 2005. In Baghdad, I promptly settled back into the hotel inside a guarded compound where I had stayed previously. Knowing full well that sooner or later this one, too, would be attacked by a car bomb, I assured myself that since there were no contractors residing in my hotel, the odds were I would be all right. I hoped that this would help, since there had already been several attacks on hotels where Western contractors, particularly security contractors, were residing. Long after I left Baghdad, this compound was indeed car bombed, causing serious damage.

Once again, stories of atrocities committed by the U.S. military began to flow in from my sources. In mid-January, my Iraqi colleague Suthir phoned to tell me that the people of the al-Dora region on the outskirts of Baghdad were being subjected to collective punishment. It was not a new tactic. The U.S. military had been using it for well over a year. The previous January, I had visited a farm in this beautiful rural area, where date palms and orange trees lined the banks of the Tigris. The military had left unexploded mortars in the fields of the farmer Hamid Salman Halwan when he failed to provide any information about resistance fighters. I had noticed similar tactics being used in

Samarra during my first trip there. The military conducted home demolitions each time their patrols were struck by roadside bombs.

At al-Dora, eerily close to the place I had visited a year back, the military faced many attacks by the resistance. In retaliation, they began to plow down date palm orchards, blasted the only existing gas station with a tank, cut off the supply of electricity, and placed massive concrete barriers to block the roads.

As Suthir, my driver, and I drove deeper into the farming area along a thin, winding road that paralleled the Tigris River, a wolf trotted across the road. Rounding a bend, we saw a large swathe of date palms that had been bulldozed to the ground. Huge piles of them had been pushed together, doused with fuel, and burned. "The Americans were attacked from this field. Later they returned and started plowing down all the trees," explained a local mechanic named Kareem, who approached us when he saw us taking photos. "None of us knows any fighters. They are coming here from other areas to attack the Americans, but we are the ones to suffer."

Mohammed, a fifteen-year-old secondary school student, was standing near his home when we approached him. "There is a grave of an old woman they bulldozed," he said. Indicating the adjacent road, he added, "They destroyed our fences, and now wolves are attacking our animals. They destroyed much of our farming equipment, and worse, they cut our electricity." He bent down to pick up a wrapper of an MRE [U.S. Army rations, "Meal, Ready-to-Eat"] on the ground, dropped by the soldiers who had bulldozed the orchard. "We need electricity to run our pumps to be able to irrigate our farms. At the moment we are having to carry water in buckets from the river instead and this is very difficult for us. They say they are going to make things better for us, but things are worse. Saddam was better than this, even though he executed three of my relatives."

We walked a little way down the road and Ahmed, a thirty-eight-year-old farmer, began to talk with us. He had been detained during a home raid on August 13, 2003. "I don't know why I was arrested," he said. Ahmed talked of his journey through the military detention system for ten months. He experienced everything from mock executions to being bound and having his head covered for days on end, at a camp near Basra in the scorching summer temperatures. "At that camp, they hung a sign that said 'The Zoo,'" he told us. During detention he witnessed sexual humiliation and regular beatings of other prisoners. "I watched American soldiers force naked Iraqi women into a cell. I heard the screams as the soldiers raped the women."

Sheikh Hamed, a rotund, well-dressed middle-aged man, came to us and suggested we move off the road in case a patrol came through and began shooting again. After we moved aside, he told us, "These are our grandfathers' orchards. Neither the British nor Saddam behaved like this. This is our history. When they fell a tree, it is like they are killing a member of our family." He said three of his cousins had been executed by Saddam Hussein's regime but he was quick to add, "We don't want this freedom of the Americans. They are raiding our homes and terrorizing us all the time. We are living in terror. They shoot and bomb us every day. We have sent our families to live elsewhere."

We drove a little farther along the Tigris and saw four large concrete blocks rising out of a deep hole that had been blasted in the road. One of the men, who had accompanied us to show us around the area, told us that the road was first blocked when the military blew it up when they were destroying the orchards, and later when they placed the concrete barriers.

People found it tiring and wearisome to walk home from the roadblocks, so they used farm tractors to pull the blocks and reopen the road. The previous day, the military had brought in larger barriers and the road had been sealed yet again. While we stood talking, an eighty-year-old man carrying several bags of food rations gingerly made his way through the barrier and shuffled down the road toward his home.

As we drove back out on the narrow, winding road, two patrols of three Humvees each rumbled past us, heading toward the village we had just visited. Overhead, two helicopters flew the same direction. Back at my hotel, I phoned the military press office in Baghdad and asked for some information on why they were blocking roads, firing weapons, plowing down date palm groves, and disconnecting electricity in the al-Arab Jubour village in al-Dora. The spokesman, who refused to give me his name, said he knew nothing about such things, adding only that there were "ongoing security operations in the al-Dora area."

As the elections slated for the end of January neared, posters of various political candidates and parties papered the walls along the garbage-strewn streets of the capital city. Many of these posters were torn down the same day they were put up, while others were crumpled into piles and burned on the sides of streets. Candidates who were not contesting anonymously, a distinct minority, promised would-be voters that they would call for a timetable of withdrawal of the occupation forces, a promise they would never be able to fulfill. Nevertheless, because of this, for many Iraqis, January 30, the date of the elections, held out the hope of a united and secure Iraq. At the same time, there were others who feared that elections would only accelerate the chaos that reigned across most of the country, worsen security, and divide Iraq further.

Less than a month before the elections, Allawi publicly admitted that the government's draconian security plans would not suffice to provide full security. New plans included the closing of all Iraqi borders from January 29 to 31, disabling mobile and satellite phone services on the day of the elections, apparently to thwart remotely detonated car bombs, banning interprovincial travel in all of Iraq's eighteen provinces, lengthening curfew hours, and severely curtailing the use of vehicles. Security at the polling stations was to be heavy, comprising three security rings around each of the nine thousand polling stations, another promise the government would not be able to fulfill. An indicator of the government's anticipated inability to contain the violence that was sure to accompany the elections was an announcement by the Ministry of Health that it would provide more hospital beds, medical supplies, and staff for the day.

Less than three weeks before the elections, at least eight candidates had been assassinated. With countless others receiving daily death threats, campaigning consisted mostly of political parties employing staff to post leaflets and posters. The election posters were interesting and entertaining. One poster had the smiling face of a man whose sole promise was to restore electricity.

Most Iraqis I spoke with about the polling process were confused by it. This was understandable. With 7,785 mostly unidentifiable candidates populating the lists of eighty-three coalitions of political parties, voters had little idea for whom they would vote. Each coalition list contained between 83 and 275 candidates, contesting on manifestos that championed all sorts of causes. Instead of names, the candidate coalition lists had themes such as "The Security and Stability List," "The Security and Justice List," and the "Iraq List." Most candidate lists did not mention the occupation. The stated agendas on these lists were largely sectarian. Kurdish lists focused on winning control of Kirkuk for the Kurds and obtaining a top government post. Some Shia lists offered federalism and others an Iranian-style regime. The Sunni religious body of the Association of Muslim Scholars called for a boycott of the elections in protest against the destruction of Fallujah. Local pollsters were correctly predicting that roughly 90 percent of the Sunnis would not vote, which later would lead to several Sunni representatives being appointed to the new "government," by U.S. administrators working behind the scenes.

It was expected that by and large the Shia community would be voting on January 30. The revered leader of a large portion of the Shia community of Iraq, Ayatollah Ali al-Sistani, issued a fatwa instructing his followers to vote or burn in hell. "I will vote because Sistani has told us this will help the country," Abdel Hassan, a shoemaker in the predominantly Shia district of Karrada in Baghdad told me. "I am ready to do anything to help my country." Other Iraqis were firmly against the elections. "How can we vote when we don't know any of the candidates," asked a Shia man named Ghassan. "And how can any of them help a country that is occupied by invaders?"

The fear of violence had already led many Iraqis to remain at home on January 30. "We don't know when the next bullet will come, so we are staying in our homes most of the time," Abdulla Hamid, a thirty-five-year-old vegetable vendor and father of five in Baghdad, told me. In the same area, I met Hamoudi Aziz, who drove his car as a taxi to make a living. "I'm not even safe in my own home though there is martial law," he said, "so how am I expected to vote for this crazy parliament?" His view was not uncommon, and was in part the reason that approximately 60 percent of eligible Iraqis would choose not to vote.

By mid-January, the two morgues in the hospitals of Baghdad, along with the main morgue in the capital, were filled to capacity on a nearly daily basis. Our contact at Yarmouk Hospital, Dr. Aisha, chose to defy the Iraqi government order that banned journalists from visiting hospitals unless accompanied by a press officer, and requested that I look into the hospital situation in the city.

When Harb and I arrived at her hospital, one of the larger ones in Baghdad, Dr. Aisha, along with the person in charge of their morgue, took us behind the hospital to the three freezers reeking of decaying bodies, despite the cold temperature inside the rooms. The smell rushed out at us as the doors were opened. Some of the bodies were from Fallujah, obviously picked off the streets. Parts of them had been eaten by dogs. Most had odd discolorations on their skin and other abnormalities. One man's face looked like it had been peeled off his skull, as if he had been dragged behind a moving vehicle for a long distance.

In the next freezer, like the first, bodies were piled on the floor, on gurneys, on shelves, and on each other. Most were uncovered, their eyes staring off into nowhere. I mechanically took photos of halves of bodies, piles of arms and legs, heads, charred bodies, and corpses of small children. Some of the bodies had tags tied to their toes or feet. Most did not.

The morgue manager with us said most of the bodies in this freezer had been shot and were not from Fallujah. The majority, he said, were victims of death squads and militias.

The third freezer was also packed with bodies. Many of them were so decayed or decomposed that they were shrinking into themselves. Harb accompanied me inside each freezer. As he yanked blankets back to expose heads so I could take photos, I could feel his anguish and rage. After we exited the last cooler, we started to walk away from the morgue area.

"That was the most dreadful thing I have ever seen in my life," I said as Harb and I walked out of the hospital toward our car.

◆   ◆   ◆   ◆

The day before the elections, areas like Arasat Street, usually teeming with crowds at the shops, restaurants, and hotel patrons, sat eerily empty in the middle of the day. The few grocery stalls that were open were packed with customers stocking up as if another invasion were imminent. The police were edgy, apprehensive that every car was a potential suicide bomber. Several men in one police car that we passed had all their guns aimed at us until we were out of their sight. When a policeman started firing off rounds over the top of our car after I had taken a photo of him, our venture around Baghdad on that day came to a quick close.

The day before the elections, Allawi announced that martial law would be extended for another month, and a rocket attack on the U.S. embassy inside the Green Zone killed two Americans and wounded four others. Most people I had interviewed said they did not intend to vote, either because they felt that holding elections under foreign occupation made them illegitimate or because they feared for their lives.

The morning of January 30, the first explosions began echoing across the expanse of Baghdad at 7:00, the hour the polling stations opened. Less than an hour later, I stood on the roof of my hotel trying to locate where the attacks were occurring. Blasts clapped across the city at the rate of nearly one every minute. Baghdad was again under siege. By the end of this bloody day, at least thirty Iraqis had been killed and more than two hundred wounded.

Later, while commenting on the number of Iraqis who died that day, Bush said blithely, "Some Iraqis were killed while exercising their rights as citizens."[1] I wondered how the media would have responded if, during an election in the United States, thirty Americans had been killed and he had made the same remark. Would they still have allowed his comment to remain unchallenged?

I soon found out that, despite the unprecedented security measures that saw well over one hundred thousand U.S. and Iraqi security forces deployed to contain the anticipated violence, two U.S. and ten British soldiers were also among the dead. The British troops were on board a C-130 transport plane that was shot down by resistance fighters in Balad, a city just northwest of Baghdad.

A suicide bomber at a security checkpoint in the Mansor district of western Baghdad killed a policeman and wounded two others, while a man wearing a belt of explosives detonated them at a queue of voters in Sadr City, killing himself and at least four others. Nine suicide bombings wreaked havoc in polling stations that day. Many Iraqis who had intended to vote stayed indoors as gunfire echoed around the downtown area of Baghdad and mortar attacks on polling stations continued throughout the day.

Hesitantly, I left my hotel with Harb in order to conduct a few interviews. We set out on foot, as traffic was severely restricted. We caught a ride with some Iraqi journalists to the predominantly Shia Karrada district of Baghdad. There, a shopkeeper named Sabah Rahwani, said, "The high commissioner for elections was appointed by Bremer, so how can we have a legitimate election under these circumstances? This election only serves the interest of the occupier, not Iraqis. This is only propaganda for Bush."

Later, while walking down a side street closer to my hotel, we saw through an open door a man with two young children sitting in the small courtyard of his home. He invited us in for tea when he heard we were journalists. "Yesterday a bicycle bomb killed someone near my house," thirty-two-year-old Ahmed Mohammed told us. "I never intended to vote in this illegitimate election anyway, but if I had wanted to, I would never go out in these conditions."

His sister, Layla Abdul Rahman, a high-school English teacher, joined us in the conversation. "Baghdad looks like it's having a war, not elections. Our streets are filled with tanks and soldiers and our bridges are closed. All we hear is bombing all around us, and for the last two nights there have been many clashes that have lasted longer than usual. We should not have had elections now. It is just not practical with this horrible security." Their neighbor, Abdulla Hamid, overheard us talking and came over. An unemployed computer engineer, the wiry middle-aged man gingerly sat down. Accepting a cup of tea, he said, "How can we call this democracy when I am too afraid to leave my home? Of course there will be low turnout here with all these bombings going on."

He was right. Turnout was extremely low in Baghdad, as it was throughout most of central Iraq. By that afternoon, long before the polls had closed, an official with the Independent Electoral Commission for Iraq (IECI), Adel al-Lami, had declared a 72 percent voter turnout, a figure proudly repeated by some members of the Bush administration.[2] Condoleezza Rice, during an interview on Fox News, said, "The Iraqi people are turning out in large numbers to vote," and agreed that the long lines gave her "goose bumps."[3] Not long after this figure had been announced, IECI spokesman Farid Ayar was asked about its source at a press conference. He backpedaled and said that the turnout was nearer to 60 percent of registered voters. The earlier figure of 72 percent, he said, was only "a guess," just an estimate that had been based on very rough, word-of-mouth estimates gathered informally from the field. He also said it would be some time before the IECI could issue accurate figures on the turnout. "Percentages and numbers come only after counting and will be announced when it is over," he said. "It is too soon to say that those were the official numbers."[4]

Regardless of this public admission, the Bush administration and the corporate media chose to repeat the misleading original figure in numerous reports. Photographs of upheld purple ink–stained fingers of voters were also widely broadcast. "The world is hearing the voice of freedom from the center of the Middle East," Bush proclaimed. The gamble of using the elections to justify the ongoing failed occupation of Iraq did pay off politically for the Bush administration, at least momentarily, with a large boost in Bush's approval ratings. Even the high death toll was hailed as a figure that was "lower than expected," and therefore acceptable, by the Bush administration and establishment media. But this was not the most important misrepresentation by the mainstream media. The press obscured the fundamental fact that, among those who voted, hardly anyone had done so in support of a continuing U.S. occupation of their country. Indeed, most Iraqis voted for precisely the opposite reason. Every Iraqi I spoke with who had voted expressed the belief that the formation of a National Assembly of elected representatives would signal an end to the occupation. And they expected the call for a withdrawal of foreign forces in their country to come soon, as the candidates had promised they would demand.

Viewed from this perspective, the footage aired by mainstream media outlets of cheering, jubilant Iraqis did not quite convey the professed gratitude toward the Bush administration for bringing them "democracy," but a desire for an end to occupation and for genuine self-determination.

(Important questions remained unanswered. After the National Assembly was formed, with more than one hundred and forty thousand U.S. soldiers remaining on the ground in Iraq, why did the Bush administration continue in its refusal to provide a timetable for their withdrawal? What would happen when Iraqis realized that rather than disbanding the existing permanent military bases in their country, the United States was, in fact, constructing more?)

Just prior to the elections, Antonia Juhasz, at the time a scholar at Foreign Policy in Focus, wrote an article that examined a topic that had been ignored amid the election hype: oil. Juhasz wrote,

On Dec. 22, 2004, Iraqi Finance Minister Abdel Mahdi told a handful of reporters and industry insiders at the National Press Club in Washington, D.C., that Iraq wants to issue a new oil law that would open Iraq's national oil company to private foreign investment. As Mahdi explained: "So I think this is very promising to the American investors and to American enterprise, certainly to oil companies."

In other words, Mahdi is proposing to privatize Iraq's oil and put it into American corporate hands. According to the finance minister, foreigners would gain access both to "downstream" and "maybe even upstream" oil investment. This means foreigners can sell Iraqi oil and own it under the ground—the very thing for which many argue the United States went to war in the first place. As Vice President Dick Cheney's Defense Policy Guidance report explained back in 1992, "Our overall objective is to remain the predominant outside power in the [Middle East] region and preserve U.S. and Western access to the region's oil." While few in the American media other than Emad Mekay of Inter Press Service reported on—or even attended—Mahdi's press conference, the announcement was made with U.S. Undersecretary of State Alan Larson at Mahdi's side. It was intended to send a message—but to whom? It turns out that Abdel Mahdi is running in the Jan. 30 elections on the ticket of the Supreme Council for the Islamic Revolution [in Iraq] (SCIRI), the leading Shiite political party. While announcing the selling-off of the resource which provides 95 percent of all Iraqi revenue may not garner Mahdi many Iraqi votes, it will unquestionably win him tremendous support from the U.S. government and U.S. corporations. Mahdi's SCIRI is far and away the front-runner in the upcoming elections, particularly as it becomes increasingly less possible for Sunnis to vote because the regions where they live are spiraling into deadly chaos.[5]

It is also worth noting that the list of political parties Mahdi's SCIRI belonged to, the United Iraqi Alliance (UIA), included the Iraqi Governing Council (IGC), led by none other than Ahmed Chalabi, an old friend of the Bush administration who had provided the faulty information necessary to justify the illegal invasion of Iraq. In addition, the UIA had the blessing of the Iranian-born Shia cleric Grand Ayatollah Ali al-Sistani, who had conveniently issued the fatwa instructing his followers to vote or burn in hell.

Juhasz continued:

> Thus, one might argue that the Bush administration has made a deal with the SCIRI: Iraq's oil for guaranteed political power. The Americans are able to put forward such a bargain because Bush still holds the strings in Iraq. Regardless of what happens in the elections, for at least the next year during which the newly elected National Assembly writes a constitution and Iraqis vote for a new government, the Bush administration is going to control the largest pot of money available in Iraq (the $24 billion in U.S. taxpayer money allocated for the reconstruction), the largest military and the rules governing Iraq's economy. Both the money and the rules will, in turn, be overseen by U.S.-appointed auditors and inspector generals who sit in every Iraqi ministry with five-year terms and sweeping authority over contracts and regulations. However, the one thing which the administration has not been able to confer upon itself is guaranteed access to Iraqi oil—that is, until now.[6]

Having the numbers, of course the UIA was brought into the seats of power by the elections, and with it, Mahdi, an economist trained in France, who had returned to Iraq on April 12, 2003, after thirty-four years of exile. He promptly was brought to power by representing SCIRI on the IGC assembled by Bremer. After the June 28, 2004, "transfer of sovereignty," he was named finance minister of the Bremer-appointed Iraqi interim government. As finance minister,

Mahdi made trips to Washington, D.C., and met with both George W. Bush and Dick Cheney in 2003 and 2004. During his 2003 visit, he gave a speech at a conservative think tank, the American Enterprise Institute, where he said that Iraq was making "a good start on a broad range of structural and legal reforms" to its economy.[7] These "reforms" were the Bremer "100 Orders," which Mahdi was already actively implementing, laws that opened Iraq's economy to 100 percent foreign ownership businesses and banks, gave complete immunity for U.S. contractors and soldiers from Iraq's laws, and allowed unlimited repatriation of profits earned in Iraq by foreign companies. Soon Mahdi was named as the Bush administration's second choice for prime minister of the transitional government, after CIA-asset Iyad Allawi.

When the newly formed government eventually chose the highest seats, Mahdi missed winning the position of prime minister by just one vote. He eventually landed in the position of vice president of the permanent government, and continued working on pro-Western oil company production-sharing agreements (PSAs).

The problems with the elections were not limited to Baghdad. Bombings at polling stations occurred in Hilla, Mosul, Kirkuk, Basra, and Baquba. In Samarra, where a roadside bomb struck a U.S. patrol, there was no sign either of voters or of the police on the streets, according to one of my contacts there. "Nobody will vote in Samarra because of the security situation," Taha Hussein, head of Samarra's local governing council, told reporters.[8] In Fallujah, even according to the U.S. military, less than 3 percent of the residents who had returned to the city voted. The polling station was located inside a U.S. base.[9]

While voter turnout in the Kurdish-controlled north and the Shia-dominated southern region was heavy, most polling stations in the capital city and central Iraq remained relatively empty. The hope of many Iraqis that the elections would bring security and stability began to fade before the day was even over. This wasn't helped by the fact that a few hours before the polling stations had even opened, during his weekly radio address, George W. Bush had announced that "as democracy takes hold in Iraq, America's mission there will continue." His administration had also recently announced that U.S. troops would remain in Iraq until at least 2006.

The following day, we arrived at Yarmouk Hospital to find every available bed occupied with patients who were victims of polling day violence.

Upstairs, in a dirty, hot room that smelled of stale sweat, rubbing alcohol, and dirty clothing, we found an Iraqi police colonel whose chest was covered in bandages. He was writhing in pain and moaning with every breath. His legs from the knees down were nearly completely hidden from view due to the thick bandages that held together what was left of his shins. Standing near the foot of his bed, Dr. Aisha told me, "We gave him first aid and requested a transfer because we don't have any specialists left." The colonel's face was scrunched up with the continuous pain. "We sent him to a neurological hospital that could not treat him because all their specialists have left the country," Dr. Aisha continued. The colonel was returned to Yarmouk untreated. He had been guarding a polling station when a suicide bomber detonated nearby. The shrapnel had turned his legs into hamburger and split his chest open.

"I asked him not to leave the house, not to obey the Americans," his wife, who was standing nearby with their little boy and girl, said desolately, "But he said that he had to go or the Americans would cut his salary. And also because he said it was his duty." She looked over to him as another whimper escaped his contorted face, then looked back at me with anger flashing in her weary eyes. "The Americans told him he should die with his countrymen. God damn them for what they have done to my husband. God damn them for what they have done to Iraq."

Walking toward the next room down a grimy hallway lined with broken windows, Dr. Aisha explained, "He will probably lose his legs. All we have are rotator doctors and residents since all our specialists left the country to escape being kidnapped. I have been here two days straight without sleep."

In the next room was another policeman. His abdomen had been blown open by a mortar blast at a polling station. He held a blue bandage to his face, which had caught some shrapnel. Tubes ran from his stomach off one side of the bed.

In a nearby bed was a twenty-seven-year-old voter, Amir Hassan. His polling station had been mortared and he had caught shrapnel near his waist. He was waiting for some pain medication that did not exist. "We asked the Americans for supplies," Dr. Aisha told me later when we exited the room, "but they didn't help us. How can we continue like this? When an American private is badly wounded they fly him to Germany or America. Here we have high-ranking police officers and Iraqi soldiers being brought to this dirty hospital with no specialists."

◆ ◆ ◆ ◆

Voting, seen by many Iraqis as a hopeful action that would lead to an end to the occupation and the beginning of true self-governance for the first time in decades, soon came to be seen as a hopeless and futile act that would only deepen and prolong their suffering.

Prior to the elections, many Iraqis I interviewed had expressed fears that their monthly food rations would be discontinued if they did not vote. Many told me they had been forced to sign voter registration forms in order to pick up their food supplies. Their experiences on the day of polling underscored their suspicions about the questionable methods used by the U.S.-backed Iraqi interim government to increase voter turnout.

Just days before the election, Amin Hajar, a fifty-two-year-old auto mechanic, who owned a garage in central Baghdad, told me, "I'll vote because I can't afford to have my food ration cut. If that happened, my family and I will starve to death." When he had gone to pick up his monthly food ration before polling day, he had been forced to sign a form stating that he had collected his voter registration as well. His fear was that the government would use this information to track those who did not vote.

I phoned the IECI and the Ministry of Trade, which was responsible for dispensing the precious monthly food rations, for a statement, but neither call was returned.

IECI officials quickly lowered their earlier estimates of voter turnout. In places where there had been a large turnout, the motivation behind the voting and the voting process both appeared questionable. The Kurds were voting for autonomy, if not independence. In the south and elsewhere, Shias were competing with Kurds for a bigger say in the 275-member National Assembly. In some places such as Mosul, the turnout was heavier than expected, but many of the voters came from outside the city, and identity checks on voters appeared lax. Others spoke of vote-buying bids. Nonetheless, the Bush administration lauded the success of the Iraq election.

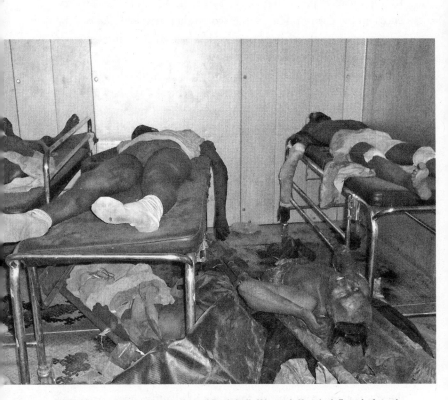

Bodies in a cooler at the morgue of Baghdad's Yarmouk Hospital. Even before the January 30 elections, morgues across the capital city were filled to capacity on nearly a daily basis. January 2005.

CHAPTER 18

COMING "HOME"

FEBRUARY 2005

Despite the media frenzy, it was evident that the violence had not and was not going to subside after the elections. Apprehensions of a civil war were growing among Iraqis. Thousands of Iraqis were fleeing the country each month as tensions percolated.

I felt there was little room for error in the randomness of the violence and that it was only a matter of time before something happened to me and my dear friend Harb. The pattern of the growing number of kidnappings was that interpreters were found dead soon after the reporters who were associated with them were detained for ransom or for the ridiculously impossible demands of the kidnappers that Iraq be decolonized. My worst fear was that the same might happen to Harb. I feared this even more than myself being kidnapped. I knew it was time for me to leave, even though it was unlikely that I would be able to come back and work as I had, and I had no idea if or when I would see Harb and my other Iraqi friends again.

Back in the United States, part of me felt confined. While my body walked the streets of my home country, my heart and mind so often still wandered in war-ravaged Iraq. Coming home from the war in Iraq, I had found another kind of duality. It seemed to me that the war I had left was going on at home on many fronts—and yet most people seemed almost blissfully unaware of it.

Several months after my return, I had just concluded a tour of presentations on Iraq and was on a train from Philadelphia to New York when I read in the morning papers that at least four car bombs had detonated in Baghdad. I phoned Harb. The connection was poor, but the moment he heard my voice, he responded with his usual mirth, "How are you, my friend?" I might as well have been in another universe. "I just wanted to know that you're all right, *habibi.*"

I asked Harb if the most recent car bombs had been close to his home. "There have been ten car bombs in Baghdad today, habibi, at least thirty people killed with more than seventy wounded. It's becoming unbearable, even for those of us who have known so much suffering for so long." I found, to my amazement, that I was wiping my tears and fighting the crazy desire I had been unable shake off all those months, to return to Baghdad.

"Please stay safe, habibi, and I will see you soon," I told him as my train approached New York. "*Insh'Allah,* I will stay safe and will see you soon, habibi."

"*Insh'Allah,*" he replied. Then he said in a rush that there was gunfire nearby and that he had to go. I waited for him to hang up first. It was a kind of ritual. Only then did I push the button on my phone, set it down, and leave Iraq once again for this country of mine where I had never quite landed.

Just beyond the window, trees and houses raced past as the train sped along. I watched the peaceful American countryside zip by, filled with the knowledge that Harb, having just dropped his wife and children off at her father's for safety, was trying to make his way home through streets full of fighting and criminal gangs, was living under the constant threat of more car bombs in the night, and with a military cordon around his neighborhood. He was concerned that his home would be looted if he stayed away, and felt it was worth the risk to return to his neighborhood to guard his belongings, even though the area had been sealed off by U.S. soldiers.

Of course, it was just a regular day for him in Baghdad.

For ten weeks I had traveled along each coast, giving presentations on the war in Iraq, often to large crowds hungry for information. It was heartening to see so many people, so concerned, and angry about what was being done in their name—and with their tax money. Upon returning from a presentation in Vancouver, Canada, I was waiting for a U.S. border agent to scan my passport. I watched him languidly flicking through my many pages of Jordanian, Iraqi, Lebanese, and Egyptian visas, staring at the Arabic script and stamps. "What were you doing in the Middle East?" he asked. Instantly I felt a surge of anger and glanced up at the signs all across the border station informing non-U.S. citizens that they would have their photos taken upon entry and their index fingers placed on a scanner—solely for our safety and security, of course. I had that natural human urge to tell him it was none of his damned business where I had been. I checked myself, and simply said, "I'm a journalist." He looked at me, handed me my passport, and I came "home" yet again.

Not too long after that, I received an email from a friend in Baghdad who had just spoken to a teacher friend in Fallujah who had crossed another kind of "border" there, also guarded by U.S. soldiers—a border around her own city. She had had to undergo a retinal scan mandated by the U.S. military and had all of her ten fingers printed in order to obtain the necessary identification badge, which, unfortunately, she lost while shopping in a Baghdad market. When she tried to return to Fallujah without it, ING soldiers would not let her back in.

"She told them she had lost her ID in Baghdad at the market, that she wanted to go home, that they have to let her in, but they refused," my friend wrote. "A neighbor of hers inside Fallujah was there and told them she was his neighbor, but they refused. She called her husband with her neighbor's mobile and he came to the checkpoint with her papers, to prove that she was his wife and that he lived in Fallujah, but they still refused to let her in." She was crying, my colleague said, as she related her woes to him. She had lost nine relatives during the U.S. military assault on the city in November 2004. "I want you to tell your friends and your audience about this. Please ask them what would happen if they were prevented from getting inside their city although the people inside knew they were a teacher who had to get to their school?" My friend also wanted me to ask my audiences what U.S. citizens would do if our country were invaded and the only ID that was recognized was the one given by the invading forces—and not any of the several regular documents of identification members of the audience possessed.

Not surprisingly, most U.S. citizens know nothing about such occurrences in Iraq, thanks to the corporate media, which has done such a fantastic job of whitewashing the impossible conditions in Iraq.

In 1968, in the Vietnamese village of My Lai, American troops massacred more than four hundred innocent civilians, the majority of whom were women, children, and the elderly. In Fallujah, during the November siege of the city, according to an Iraqi NGO, an estimated five thousand innocent civilians, the majority of whom were women, children, and elderly, were slaughtered. Five thousand innocent civilians, who, under the Geneva Conventions, an occupying power is required by law to protect, died in what was essentially a "free-fire zone."[1]

In an article titled "Conditions of Atrocity," Robert Jay Lifton, a psychiatrist, cited both My Lai and the Iraqi prison of Abu Ghraib as examples of what he called

> atrocity-producing situations . . . so structured, psychologically and militarily, that ordinary people, men or women no better or worse than you or I, can regularly commit atrocities. In Vietnam that structure included "free-fire zones" (areas in which soldiers were encouraged to fire at virtually anyone); "body counts" (with a breakdown in the distinction between combatants and civilians, and competition among commanders for the best statistics); and the emotional state of U.S. soldiers as they struggled with angry grief over buddies killed by invisible adversaries and with a desperate need to identify some "enemy."

> This kind of atrocity-producing situation surely occurs in some degree in all wars, including World War II, our last "good war." But a counterinsurgency war in a hostile setting, especially when driven by profound ideological distortions, is particularly prone to sustained atrocity—all the more so when it becomes an occupation.[2]

AFTERWORD

On February 10, 2005, I traveled to Rome to provide testimony at a tribunal regarding Western media complicity in the U.S.-led invasion of Iraq. The World Tribunal on Iraq (WTI) was an international peoples' initiative seeking the truth about the war and occupation in Iraq. The tribunal had already held meetings focusing on different aspects of the invasion and occupation, in cities such as Brussels, London, Mumbai, New York, Hiroshima, Copenhagen, Stockholm, and Lisbon. The WTI found much of the Western media guilty of deceiving the international community and inciting violence with its reporting of Iraq.

The informal panel of WTI judges at the tribunal accused the governments of the United States and Britain of impeding journalists in performing their task, as well as producing lies and misinformation. The judges found that the mainstream media reportage on Iraq was guilty under article six of the Nuremberg Tribunal, set up to try Nazi crimes, which states: "Leaders, organizers, instigators and accomplices participating in the formulation or execution of a common plan or conspiracy to commit any of the foregoing crimes (crimes against peace, war crimes and crimes against humanity) are responsible for all acts performed by any persons in execution of such a plan."

Though I was exhausted and suffering symptoms of PTSD (Post-Traumatic Stress Disorder), providing testimony in front of the WTI panel that could help highlight the guilt of the mainstream media was an important moment for me. It was, after all, the complicity of the media that had initially led me to Iraq. While the majority of people in the United States remained largely ignorant of how complicit the corporate media truly was, the majority of the rest of the world appeared to understand this. This fact was underscored when later that summer I provided testimony at the culminating session of the WTI, in Istanbul, Turkey. The huge meetings were attended by more than three hundred journalists from around the globe, but not a single representative from the U.S. mainstream media.

Meanwhile, the situation in Iraq continued to decline. The results of a survey taken by the respected group World Public Opinion, released on September 27, 2006, found that more than 70 percent of Iraqis wanted the U.S. military to leave within a year, and by a wide margin Iraqis believed U.S. forces provoked more violence than they prevented. Iraqis who supported attacks on U.S. forces had jumped to 61 percent, up from 47 percent less than a year earlier.[1] By October 2006, the number of attacks against American troops had reached "unprecedented levels," according to the U.S. military.[2] The Pentagon's quarterly report released on November 30, 2006, stated that U.S. military and Iraqi security forces were being attacked more than eight hundred times every week, an average that had risen over 100 percent since the summer of 2005, and since January 2006, sectarian executions had increased more than fivefold.[3] Yet, as from the very first day of the invasion, it was the Iraqi people who continued to pay the highest price.

On October 11, 2006, the Johns Hopkins Bloomberg School of Public Health and Medicine, in coordination with Iraqi doctors from al-Mustansiriya University in Baghdad, published the horrifying results of their scientific study of "excess deaths" in Iraq. Published in the peer-reviewed, prestigious *Lancet* medical journal in the United Kingdom, the study found that 655,000 excess deaths (2.5 percent of the entire population of Iraq) had occurred since the invasion and occupation in March 2003.[4]

Eight days after the study was published, in another blatant example of censorship, the office of U.S.-backed Iraqi Prime Minister Nouri al-Maliki instructed the Iraq Health Ministry to stop providing mortality figures to the UN. According to the prime minister's directive, the prime minister's communications director would be responsible for "centralizing and disseminating such information in the future."[5]

Meanwhile, Iraqi medics announced that as many as half of the 655,000 deaths in Iraq would have been preventable had it not been for the fact that even the most basic treatments were lacking. More than two hundred doctors, nurses, and pharmacists had been killed and more than eighteen thousand others—over half of all Iraqi doctors—had fled the war-torn country.[6] Doctors had been begging the international community to help stem the soaring death rate and assist in easing the suffering of their people but found that governments, along with the international medical community, ignored their plight.

With billions of dollars allocated for reconstruction missing, due to a combination of criminal activity, corruption, and incompetence, it was not surprising that Iraqis were without the essentials of basic medical treatment. The country had never recovered from the genocidal sanctions. Even common aids like gauze, aspirin, and medical tape continued to be scarce. The group Medact reported, "Easily treatable conditions such as diarrhea and respiratory illness caused 70 percent of all pediatric deaths," and said that "of the 180 health clinics the U.S. hoped to build by the end of 2005, only four have been completed and none opened."[7]

Dr. Bassim al-Sheibani and his colleagues at the Diwaniyah College of Medicine told reporters, "Emergency departments are staffed by doctors who do not have the proper experience or skills to manage emergency cases. Medical staff . . . admit that more than half of those killed could have been saved if trained and experienced staff were available. Many emergency departments are no more than halls with beds, fluid suckers, and oxygen bottles."[8]

As if that were not bad enough, hospitals had been a place of refuge for those hoping to escape the rampant violence. Now Iraqis were going out of their way to avoid them. Public hospitals in Baghdad were controlled by the Shia who had given death squads free access to enter and kill Sunni patients. Abu Nasr, whose cousin was injured in a car bomb and then dragged from his hospital bed and riddled with bullets, told the *Washington Post*: "We would prefer now to die instead of going to the hospitals. I will never go back to one, never. The hospitals have become killing fields."[9]

By the autumn of 2006, 68 percent of Iraqis had no access to safe drinking water and a mere 19 percent had functional sewage systems.[10] In December 2006, Iraq's minister of labor and social affairs, Mohammed Radhi, said that unemployment remained at approximately 50 percent.[11] In January 2007, it was announced that Iraq's inflation rate averaged 70 percent throughout 2006.[12] Both electricity and oil production remained far below prewar levels and had never exceeded them.

With Iraq's infrastructure in shambles, in November 2006, San Francisco–based Bechtel Corporation announced its pullout from Iraq. The company announced it had received $2.3 billion of its original budget of $3 billion, a figure that included both money the company claimed to have spent on projects, as well as its undisclosed profit margin. Yet, according to the Iraqi government, an estimated $100 billion was required over four to five years in order to rebuild its shattered infrastructure. Not surprisingly, on October 31, 2006, at a news conference in Kuwait, Iraqi government spokesperson Ali al-Dabbagh announced, "The situation in Iraq surpasses Iraq's ability to finance development projects."[13]

On February 26, 2007, Iraq's cabinet approved a draft of an oil law that would set guidelines for nationwide distribution of oil revenues and foreign investment in Iraq's giant oil industry. The law would grant regional oil companies the power to sign contracts with foreign companies for exploration and development of oil fields, and open the door for investment by foreign oil companies.[14] If passed by Iraq's parliament, this law will open Iraq's currently nationalized oil industry to private foreign oil companies with terms never seen before in the Middle East. It is worth noting that the consulting company BearingPoint, which is based near the CIA headquarters in Maclean, Virginia, was commissioned by USAID to advise the Iraqi Ministry of Oil on drawing up a new hydrocarbon law.[15] The U.S.-designed Iraqi law sets up an oil and gas council that could theoretically be populated by employees of multinational oil corporations and other U.S. corporate advocates, and could allow PSAs (whose wording was changed to "Exploration and Risk Contracts" in the latest draft of the law) in which American firms would enjoy an initial 70 percent profit from Iraqi oil extraction.[16] After BearingPoint had prepared the early draft of the oil law, it was sent to the White House, several Western petroleum corporations, the British government, and then to the International Monetary Fund. During this time, most Iraqi legislators and the general public knew little to nothing about it.[17] The law, as well as the drafting process, was immediately criticized by analysts and labor groups, who warned that the bill is skewed in favor of foreign companies. The law specified that up to two-thirds of Iraq's known oil reserves could be developed by multinational corporations under contracts lasting up to thirty-five years. At the time of this writing, the law was fully expected to be ratified by the Iraqi parliament because powerful faction leaders in the government had already cleared it.[18] Iraq's vice president, Abdel Mahdi, when he was the minister of finance, had already said that this law would be "very promising to the American investors and to American enterprise, certainly to oil companies."[19] The law mirrors proposals that were originally written by the Bush administration before the invasion even began. Over a course of several meetings between December 2002 and April 2003, members of the U.S. State Department's Oil and Energy Working Group agreed that Iraq "should be opened to international oil companies as quickly as possible after the war" and that the best way to facilitate this would be via production-sharing agreements.[20]

The guidelines that form the basis of the current proposed oil law, which could give foreign companies control of two-thirds of Iraq's oil, are based on proposals submitted by Iraq's U.S.-appointed Prime Minister Iyad Allawi. He recommended that the "Iraqi government disengage from running the oil sector" and that all undeveloped oil fields in Iraq be turned over to private international oil companies using PSAs. In October 2006, *Petroleum Economist* magazine reported that U.S. oil companies had put the passage of this oil law before their security concerns as the deciding factor over their entry into Iraq.[21]

As far as the other reason for the occupation, the geostrategic positioning of the U.S. military, we need only look at the Quadrennial Defense Review released in February 2006. That report tells us that the

U.S. military must be prepared to fight "multiple overlapping wars" and to "ensure that all major and emerging powers are integrated as constructive actors and stakeholders into the international system."[22]

Adding insult to injury, during the autumn of 2006, Iraq, in a state of nearly complete and total political and economic collapse, was forced to pay more than $21.4 billion in "war reparations" to some of the richest countries and corporations in the world, on top of $41.3 billion previously paid in recompense for the 1991 Iraq War, in which Saddam Hussein invaded Kuwait.[23]

◆ ◆ ◆ ◆

Most of the Iraqis I met in Iraq have either fled or been killed. Salam had long since fled after receiving a death threat. His brother, whom I'd met during my last trip in Iraq, was later gunned down in broad daylight. I had been pleading with Harb to leave for months. His reply was always, "*Habibi*, my heart is in Baghdad. I can never leave." But by fall 2006, the situation had become so intolerable that he had taken his wife and young sons to Damascus. Ghreeb, who had assisted us in entering Fallujah during the April assault, had been killed by unknown gunmen. Dr. Aisha from Yarmouk Hospital, whose brother was killed, his body dropped off at her hospital after she had returned from a speaking tour in the United States, fled the country and applied for political asylum. Suthir, who had taken me to al-Dora to chronicle the collective punishment being meted out there during my last trip, also fled with her family. Hamoudi was attempting to find political asylum as well. Sheikh Adnan and a few others I met during my time in Iraq who remain, do so under conditions that resemble something akin to prison or house arrest.

By February 2007, Iraq was experiencing the largest exodus in the Middle East since Palestinians were forced to flee their homes in

1948 amid the creation of Israel. The UN High Commission for Refugees (UNHCR) announced that fifty thousand Iraqis every month were abandoning their homes. UNHCR regional representative Stephanie Jaquemet announced that two million Iraqis had fled abroad and another 1.5 to 2 million were displaced within Iraq.[24] By spring 2007, at least one out of every six Iraqis had fled their homes since the invasion of March 2003. Ken Bacon, the president of Refugees International, told a U.S. Senate Judiciary Committee hearing in January 2007, "This is the fastest growing refugee crisis in the world. The U.S. has a special obligation to help, since the violence in Iraq and the growing displacement comes in the aftermath of our invasion and occupation."[25] At the same hearing, the Bush administration's senior refugee official, Assistant Secretary of State Ellen Sauerbrey, said that the Bush administration, which was spending roughly 30 million dollars per day on military operations in Iraq, had only earmarked 20 million dollars for Iraqi humanitarian needs in bilateral aid for all of 2007.[26] By January 2007, the Bush administration had only granted refugee status to 466 Iraqis since 2003. In February, the Bush administration announced it would take in seven thousand Iraqi refugees, roughly the number flooding out of Iraqi borders every four days, but did not say who would be chosen and how.[27]

While my hope of going to Iraq to bring truthful information back to U.S. citizens was only partially achieved, mainstream outlets in Europe and other areas of the world ran many of my articles. Meanwhile, U.S. censorship remains largely intact. The national television and radio appearances I have made in countries like England, Italy, Denmark, Canada, Greece, and Turkey had no equivalent in the United States. Internet and independent media outlets remain my primary outlets in my home country.

If the people of the United States had the real story about what their government has done in Iraq, the occupation would already have ended. As a journalist, I continue to hold out hope that if people have knowledge of what is happening, they will act accordingly. If people in my country could hear the stories of life under occupation and put themselves into the Iraqis' stories, they would understand. I hold that hope because the stories of Iraq are our story now. Whether we accept that or not, it is the truth. The water from the Euphrates runs through all our veins.

NOTES

INTRODUCTION

1. "New SEC Chairman Sworn-in," White House Press Release, February 18, 2003, www.whitehouse.gov/news/releases/2003/02/20030218-1.html.
2. Denis Halliday, "End Sanctions: Ten Years After the Gulf War, UN Should Stop Punishing People of Iraq," *Gazette* (Canada), January 16, 2001; Michael Jansen, "Denis Halliday: Iraq Sanctions Are Genocide," *Daily Star* (Lebanon), July 7, 2000; Nyier Abdou, "Scylla and Charbydris: An Interview with Denis Halliday,"*Al-Ahram*, December 30, 2002.
3. Hans M. Carlson, "A Watershed of Words: Litigating and Negotiating Nature in Eastern James Bay, 1971–75," *Canadian Historical Review* 85, no. 1 (March 2004): 63–84.

1. ENTERING IRAQ

1. Anthony Shadid, "3 Journalists Killed by U.S. Strikes; Military Says Forces Fired at from Hotel," *Washington Post*, April 9, 2003.
2. Charles Hanley, "Baghdad Tunnel Blast Slightly Wounds Two U.S. Soldiers; Shiite Headquarters Attacked," Associated Press, October 22, 2003.
3. Colin Nickerson and Vivienne Walt, "U.S. Forces Kill 46 in Iraq Battle: Fighting Follows Convoy Ambush," *Boston Globe*, December 1, 2003.
4. Derrick Z. Jackson, "Do Americans Know the Score?" *Boston Globe*, December 3, 2003.
5. Jeffrey Brown, "Planting News in the Iraqi Media,"*Jim Lehrer NewsHour*, PBS, www.pbs.org/newshour/bb/middle_east/july-dec05/media_12-02.html.
   The transcript begins with Jeffrey Brown asking: "Is the U.S. military

crossing a line by planting good news stories in the Iraqi media? Such reports have been circulating for several days. This afternoon, Senate Armed Services chairman John Warner met with military officials and said it's still unclear to him what media coverage the U.S. military in Iraq may have paid for and whether traditionally accepted journalistic practices were violated.

Warner: I'm still concerned about any actions that would undermine our nation and the practice of journalism.

Brown: According to published reports, a Washington-based public relations company called the Lincoln Group was contracted by the military to translate articles written by Americans into Arabic, and then place them, often through payments, in Iraqi news organizations both print and television. These included articles and stories that did not disclose their American sponsorship. In Baghdad yesterday, Major General Rick Lynch had this to say: 'We do empower our Operational Commanders with the ability to inform the Iraqi public, but everything we do is based on facts, not based on fiction.'"

6. Charles Clover, Nicholas Pelham, and Peter Speigel, "U.S. Accused of Provoking Shootout in Samarra," *Financial Times*, December 2, 2003.

7. Vivienne Walt, "Civilian Deaths Raise Iraqi Fears/Anger," *Boston Globe*, December 3, 2003.

8. Eric Schmitt, "Pentagon and Bogus News: All Is Denied,"*New York Times*, December 5, 2003.

2. PEERING INTO AN ABYSS

1. Michael Dobbs, "Halliburton's Deals Greater Than Thought," *Washington Post*, August 28, 2003.

2. The fourth pillar of Islam, fasting, is practiced during the month of Ramadan. Ramadan is the ninth month of the Islamic calendar and is considered the most venerated, blessed, and spiritually beneficial month of the Islamic year. Fasting, charity, prayers, and self-accountability are stressed at this time. Other religious observances associated with Ramadan are also kept throughout the month. God prescribes daily fasting for all able, adult Muslims during the whole month of Ramadan, beginning with the sighting of the new moon.

3. *Health and Environmental Consequences of Depleted Uranium Use in the U.S. Army: Technical Report*, AEPI, June 1995, cited in Dr. Doug Rokke, "Commentary on Army DU Medical Management Policy," www.traprockpeace.org/rokke_du_army_policy.html.

4. *STP 21-1-SMCT: Soldiers' Manual of Common Tasks*, cited in Rokke, "Commentary on Army DU."

3. GROWING FURY AND UNREST

1. "Saddam: Betrayed, Drugged and Traded," Al-Jazeera, December 21, 2003, http://english.aljazeera.net/English/archive/archive?ArchiveId=42318.
2. Yvonne Ridley, "Blood-Feud Rebels Seized and Drugged Dictator, Then Left Him for Americans," *Sunday Express*, December 21, 2003.
3. "The Capture of Hussein," *New York Times*, December 13, 2003; "Finally, Three Words: We Got Him—The Capture of a Tyrant," *Australian*, December 13, 2003.
4. David M. Walker, "Stablizing Iraq: An Assessment of the Security Situation," Government Accountability Office, available at: www.gao.gov/new.items/d061094t.pdf.
5. http://icasualties.org/oif/prdDetails.aspx?hndRef=12-2003.
6. "Collateral Damage," *Washington Post* "Fog of War" resources, www.washingtonpost.com/wp-srv/inatl/longterm/fogofwar/index/cdamage.htm.

4. KEBABS IN FALLUJAH

1. Theola Labbe and Vernon Loeb, "Wolfowitz Unhurt in Rocket Attack; Baghdad Hotel Hit; Helicopter Is Downed in Separate Incident," *Washington Post*, October 26, 2003.
2. Sameer N. Yacoub, "Bremer Survives Ambush on Convoy; Blast at Shiite Party Office Kills," Associated Press, December 19, 2003.
3. "Coalition Provisional Authority Briefing with Brigadier General Mark Kimmitt, Deputy Director for Coalition Operations, and Daniel Senor, Senior Adviser, Coalition Provisional Authority," Federal News Service Defense Department Briefing, January 2, 2004.

5. CRAVING HEALTH AND FREEDOM

1. Rory McCarthy, "U.S. Pays Up for Fatal Iraq Blunders," *Guardian* (UK), November 26, 2003.
2. "Bechtel, USAID, and the Iraq Infrastructure Reconstruction Program: Accomplishments and Challenges," Bechtel Assessment Report, June 2003, www.bechtel.com/PDF/Accomplishments_and_Challenges.pdf; David Baker, "Bechtel Ends Iraq Rebuilding After a Rough 3 Years," *San Francisco Chronicle*, November 1, 2006, www.sfgate.com/cgi-bin/article.dgi?f=/c/a/2006/11/01/BECHTEL.TMP.

3.   The uprising began after encouragement from the U.S. military and government was broadcast over the CIA-run radio station the Voice of Free Iraq. Statements read by an ex-member of Saddam Hussein's Revolutionary Command Council, Salah Omaral-Ali, who had been personally expelled by the former dictator, included, "Rise to save the homeland from the clutches of dictatorship," and "Start a revolution now, before it's too late."

4.   Thomas E. Ricks and Kate Spayd, "A Measure of Success in Iraq; Commanders See Signs of Progress, and New Pitfalls," *Washington Post,* January 23, 2004.

5.   Ibid.

7. REENTERING THE INFERNO

1.   Sameer N. Yacoub, "Iraqis Drag 4 U.S. Bodies Through Streets," Associated Press, March 31, 2004.

2.   Severin Carrell and Robert Fisk, "Occupiers Spend Millions on Private Army of Security Men," *Independent* (UK), March 29, 2004.

3.   Human Rights Watch, "Violent Response: The US Army in al-Falluja," June 2003, www.hrw.org/reports/2003/iraqfalluja.

4.   Thom Shanker, "Hussein's Agents Behind Attacks, Pentagon Finds," *New York Times,* April 29, 2004.

8. SARAJEVO ON THE EUPHRATES

1.   "Coalition Provisional Authority Briefing with Brigadier General Mark Kimmitt, Deputy Director for Coalition Operations, and Dan Senor, Senior Adviser, CPA," Federal News Service Defense Department Briefing, April 9, 2004.

2.   Mustafa Abdel-Halim, "U.S. Forces Want Al-Jazeera Out of Fallujah," Islam Online, April 9, 2004, www.islamonline.net/English/News/2004-04/09/article6.shtml.

3.   "Residents Start to Flee Besieged Iraq Rebel Bastion," Agence France-Presse, April 9, 2004.

4.   These figures are tallied on the Iraq Coalition Casualty Count website, which tracks entries based on news articles and press releases confirmed by the Department of Defense, www.icasualties.org/oif/prdDetails.aspx?hndRef=4-2004.

5.   T. E. Lawrence, "A Report on Mesopotamia." *Sunday Times,* August 22, 1920.

6.   Robert Fisk, *The Great War for Civilisation: The Conquest of the Middle East,* (New York: Knopf, 2005), 145.

7.   "Four Civilians Killed in Iraq Worked for N.C. Security Firm," Associated Press, March 31, 2004; "Hamas Chief Killed in Air Strike," BBC, March 22, 2004, http://news.bbc.co.uk/2/hi/middle_east/3556099.stm.

8.   Human Rights Watch, "Needless Deaths in the Gulf War: Civilian Casualties During the Air Campaign and Violations of the Laws of War," 1991, Introduction and Summary of Conclusions.

9.   Chris Hughes, "Two Killed in New Iraq Demo Shooting," *Daily Mirror,* May 1, 2003.

10.   Human Rights Watch, "Violent Response."

11.   UN Office of the High Commissioner for Human Rights, "Basic Principles on the Use of Force and Firearms by Law Enforcement Officials," September 7, 1990, Special Provision 9.

9. RAIDING MOSQUES, TORTURING IRAQIS

1.   "President Addresses the Nation in Prime Time Press Conference," April 13, 2004, White House Press Release, www.whitehouse.gov/news/releases/2004/04/20040413-20.html.

2.   George W. Bush interview, Al-Hurra Network, May 5, 2004, www.state.gov/p/nea/rls/rm/32282.htm.

10. THE AFTERMATH IN FALLUJAH

1.   Patrick Cockburn and David Usborne, "Burning with Anger: Iraqis Infuriated with New Flag That Was Designed in London," *Independent* (UK), April 28, 2004.

2.   "Fallujah Brigade Provides Route Security for Marines," Centcom Press Release, May 11, 2004.

3.   Ibid.

11. SHATTERED DREAMS

1.   The Coalition Provisional Authority website, "Regulation 6," www.iraq-coalition.org/regulations/index.html#Regulations (accessed May 15, 2007; site now discontinued).

2.   Paul Haven, "Shi'ites to Hold Majority in Iraqi Political Council," Associated Press, July 6, 2003.
3.   "Soccer Balls Given Out in Ramadi, Karbala, and Hilla," CPA Press Release, May 21, 2004, www.cpa-iraq.org/pressrelease/20040522_soccer_hillah.html (accessed May 15, 2007; site now discontinued).

12. "NOBODY HERE LIKES THE OCCUPIERS"

1.   "U.S. Forces in Iraq Detain Three After Raid,"Associated Press, November 21, 2004.
2.   BBC World News, June 22, 2004.
3.   "U.S. Troops in Iraq: 72% Say End War in 2006," Zogby International, February 28, 2006, www.zogby.com/news/ReadNews.dbm?ID=1075.
4.   Edmund Sanders, "Joint U.S.-Iraqi Patrols Are Getting Off on Wrong Foot," *Los Angeles Times*, July 5, 2004.
5.   Hamza Hendawi, "Insurgents Launch Series of Attacks in Sunni Muslim Dominated Iraq," Associated Press, June 24, 2004.

13. LEAVING THE VOLCANO
FOR THE EYE OF THE HURRICANE

1.   Fouad Ajami, "Iraq May Survive, but the Dream Is Dead," *New York Times*, May 26, 2004.

14. SPIRALING INTO OCCUPIED IRAQ

1.   "President Outlines Steps to Help Iraq Achieve Democracy and Freedom," George W. Bush speech at U.S. Army War College, Carlisle, Pennsylvania, May 24, 2004, www.whitehouse.gov/news/releases/2004/05/20040524-10.html.
2.   "Iraq: Shortage in Food Rations Raises Concern," Integrated Regional Information Network, July 25, 2005, www.irinnews.org/report.aspx?reportid =25298.
3.   Bush, "President Outlines Steps."
4.   Antonia Juhasz, "The Hand-Over That Wasn't: How the Occupation of Iraq Continues," Foreign Policy in Focus, July 2004, www.fpif.org/papers/0407 iraqtransf.html.
5.   Ibid.

6.   Ibid.
7.   Anthony Cordesman, "Economy Hurting Iraq More Than Violence," Inter Press Service, November 9, 2004, www.globalpolicy.org/security/issues/iraq/attack/consequences/2004/1109economy.htm.
8.   Robert H.Reid, "Insurgents Launch Deadly Attacks Across Central Iraq as US Prepares for Fallujah Attack," Associated Press, November 6, 2004.

15. OPERATION PHANTOM FURY

1.   "US, Iraqi Forces Continue Push into Fallujah, Now Control 70% of City," *Frontrunner,* November 11, 2004.
2.   Richard Oppel Jr., "Early Target of Offensive Is a Hospital," *New York Times,* November 8, 2004.
3.   "Humanitarian Aid Barred from Fallujah," Al-Jazeera, November 16, 2004.
4.   "Keep Government Line on Fallujah, Iraq Media Body Says," Reuters, November 11, 2004.
5.   "US Strikes Raze Falluja Hospital," BBC News, November 6, 2004.
6.   "'Medical Assistant' Paints Horrors of US 'Raid' on Al-Fallujah," BBC Monitoring International Reports, November 15, 2004.

16. INTO OBLIVION

1.   Michael Hirsh and John Barry, "The Salvador Option: The Pentagon May Put Special-Forces-led Assassination or Kidnapping Teams in Iraq," *Newsweek,* January 14, 2005.
2.   Ibid.
3.   David Corn, "From Iran-Contra to Iraq," *Nation,* May 7, 2005.
4.   Mussab al-Khairalla, "UN Raises Alarm on Death Squads and Torture in Iraq," Reuters, September 8, 2005.
5.   Kucinich to Rumsfeld, April 5, 2006, http://kucinich.us/floor_speeches/iq_rumsfeld_letter4may.php.
6.   Gilbert Burnham et al., "Mortality Before and After the 2003 invasion of Iraq: Cluster Sample Survey," *Lancet* 368, no. 9545 (October 21, 2006): 1421–28. The first *Lancet* report published October 29, 2004, found 84 percent of violent deaths in Iraq were caused by coalition forces, whereas the 2006 report found that 31 percent of violent deaths were caused by coalition forces. The leading cause of violent death shifted from coalition forces to death squads, criminal gangs, and other armed groups.

7.   "U.S. Investigates Fresh Abuse Photos," Al-Jazeera, December 6, 2004, http://english.aljazeera.net/News/archive/archive?ArchiveId=8033.

8.   Katarina Kratovac, "AP Photographer Flees Fallujah: Witnesses US Helicopter Kill Fleeing Family of 5," Associated Press, November 15, 2004.

9.   Alan J. Mccombs, "U.S. Holds Iraqi Journalist for Five Months," UPI, September 19, 2006.

10. "U.S. Defends Use of Phosphorous Bombs in Fallujah," Reuters, November 17, 2005.

11. "Top Military Official Calls White Phosphorus 'Legitimate Tool,'" State News Service, December 1, 2005.

12. Karl Vick, "Children Pay Cost of Iraq's Chaos: Malnutrition Nearly Double What It Was Before Invasion," Washington Post Foreign Service, November 21, 2004.

17. DYING FOR DEMOCRACY

1.   "President Congratulates Iraqis on Election," White House Press Release, January 30, 2005, www.whitehouse.gov/news/releases/2005/01/20050130-2.html.

2.   The IECI was established by the U.S.-run CPA in May 2004. There was no independent monitoring body to confirm or support the validation of interim results from the commission.

3.   Chris Wallace, "Condoleezza Rice Interview," Fox News Sunday, January 30, 2005.

4.   "Iraq Electoral Commission Backtracks on Turnout," Reuters, January 30, 2005; Rory McCarthy, "Iraqi Voters Defy the Bombers," Guardian (UK), January 31, 2005.

5.   Antonia Juhasz, "Of Oil and Elections," AlterNet, January 27, 2005, www.alternet.org/story/21100.

6.   Ibid.

7.   Miriam Fam, "Iraqi Officials Say No Results or Turnout Figure Expected Soon," Associated Press, January 31, 2005.

8.   Dahr Jamail, "Iraq: Voters Turn Out on a Bloody Day After Embassy Is Hit," Inter Press Service, January 30, 2005.

9.   Scott Peterson, "Fallujans Welcome Security, Await Electricity," Christian Science Monitor, February 8, 2005, www.csmonitor.com/2005/0208/p01s02-woiq.html.

18. COMING "HOME"

1. Ali al-Fadhily and Dahr Jamail, "Terrified Soldiers Terrifying People," Inter Press Service, January 9, 2007.
2. Robert Jay Lifton, "Conditions of Atrocity," *Nation*, May 31, 2004, www.thenation.com/doc/20040531/lifton.

AFTERWORD

1. S. Kull et al., "The Iraqi Public on the U.S. Presence and the Future of Iraq," WorldPublicOpinion.org poll, conducted by the Program on International Policy Attitudes, September 27, 2006, http://www.worldpublicopinion.org/pipa/pdf/sep06/Iraq_Sep06_rpt.pdf.
2. Borzou Daragahi, "More Than Ever, Insurgents Are Targeting U.S. Forces," *Los Angeles Times*, November 1, 2006.
3. "Measuring Security and Stability in Iraq," Department of Defense, November 30, 2006, www.defenselink.mil/pubs/pdfs/9010Quarterly-Report-20061216.pdf.
4. Burnham, "Mortality After the 2003 Invasion of Iraq."
5. Colum Lynch, "Iraq Aims to Limit Mortality Data: Health Ministry Told Not to Release Civilian Death Toll to U.N." *Washington Post*, October 20, 2006.
6. Sumedha Senanayake, "Iraq: Health Care System on Verge of Collapse," Radio Free Europe/Radio Liberty, October 27, 2006.
7. Jeremy Laurance, "Medics Beg for Help as Iraqis Die Needlessly," *Independent* (UK), October 20, 2006.
8. Quoted in Ibid.
9. Amit R. Paley, "Iraqi Hospitals Are War's New 'Killing Fields': Medical Sites Targeted by Shiite Militiamen," *Washington Post*, August 30, 2006.
10. Laurance, "Medics Beg for Help."
11. "Unemployment at 50%, Says Minister," *Azzaman*, December 15, 2006, www.azzaman.com/engligh/index.asp?fname=news%5C2006-12-14%5Ckurd.htm.
12. "Iraq Inflation Hits 70 percent in 2006," Agence France-Presse , January 28, 2007.
13. Haitham Haddadin, "Iraq Says Needs $100 Bln to Rebuild Infrastructure," Reuters, October 31, 2006.
14. Edward Wong, "Iraqi Cabinet Approves Draft of Oil Law," *New York Times*, February 26, 2007.
15. Stephen Foley, "Shock and Oil: Iraq's Billions & the White House Connection," *Independent* (UK), January 14, 2007.

16. "Investment Still a Risk with Iraq Oil Law," United Press International, February 27, 2007.
17. Nicola Nasser, "US-tailored Iraqi Oil: Alarm for Producers and Consumers," Al-Jazeera, January 23, 2007.
18. Emad Mekay, "New Oil Law Seen as Cover for Privatization," Inter Press Service, February 27, 2007.
19. Emad Mekay, "U.S. to Take Bigger Bite of Iraq's Economic Pie," Inter Press Service, December 23, 2004.
20. Antonia Juhasz, "It's Still About Oil in Iraq," *Los Angeles Times,* December 8, 2006.
21. Editorial, "Waiting for the Green Light," *Petroleum Economist,* October 1, 2006.
22. Quadrennial Defense Review Report, United States Department of Defense, February 6, 2006, www.defenselink.mil/pubs/pdfs/QDR20060203.pdf.
23. Editorial, "Reparations That Are Now an Absurdity," *Independent* (UK), October 27, 2006.
24. Patrick Cockburn, "Iraqis Abandon Their Homes in Middle East's New Refugee Exodus," *Independent* (UK), February 27, 2007.
25. Jim Lobe, "U.S. Offers Scant Help to Fleeing Refugees," Inter Press Service, January 17, 2007.
26. Ibid.
27. Charles Recknagel, "U.S. Plans to Take in 7,000 Refugees," Radio Free Europe/Radio Liberty, February 15, 2007.

ACKNOWLEDGMENTS

Harb al-Mukhtar—translator, fixer, driver, and most of all, friend. Without your consistent dedication to our work and willingness to put yourself in harm's way by working with me, most of these stories would never have been told. I also wish to humbly thank Ahmed Ayad, Salam Talib, Jabran Mansoor, Hamoudi, Maki al-Nazzal, and Hannah.

Jeff Pflueger designed, built, maintained, and then expanded www.dahrjamailiraq.com to meet demand that exceeded our wildest dreams. Without your expertise, ideas, and suggestions (many of which averted certain disaster), the stories of the Iraqi people could never have reached as far as they have. I cannot thank you enough for your work, and for being my friend.

A big thank you to James Longley for introducing me to Akeel, and for reassuring me of the rightness of my decision to enter Iraq the first time. Christian Parenti, your work suggestions and companionship have meant very much to me. Jo Wilding, thank you for your fearlessness and thirst for justice. Many thanks also to Antonia Juhasz, Dr. Robert Jay Lifton, Noam Chomsky, Howard Zinn, Amy Goodman, Denis Moynihan, Dori Smith, Dirk Adriaensens, Julia Guest, Mark Manning, Robert Knight, Imad Mortada, and Mike Ferner.

A special thanks to Nigel Parry, Ali Abunimah, and the rest of the www.electroniciraq.net crew. I could not have hoped for a better launching pad. Brian Dominick and Jessica Azulay for all the hard work and support from the *New Standard*; you helped me take the work to another level. I also wish to thank my editor at *Inter Press Service*, Sanjay Suri, for providing such a great platform, and your assistance in getting the stories out, particularly with regard to Fallujah.

Joanna and Fran Macy and my friends in Santa Cruz, thank you for being there for me when the walls finally came down. Thank you Anita Barrows, for so, so much. Nora Barrows-Friedman, you are my sister in solidarity and dear friend.

Thanks to my parents for your patience and enduring the tremendous worry I caused you during my time in Iraq. Your openness to tolerating that with grace, and then just your openness, is a model to me. Thank you Jon and Elizabeth Worden, for your kindness, warmth, and generosity.

Thank you James Jamail, for your guidance from afar. There will never be a forgetting and the lessons from you continue.

Duane French, for showing me there are no barriers; and for teaching me the value of risk, disobedience, and always questioning the powers that be.

Karen Button, a heartfelt thank you for being such a great friend, teacher, and ally.

Effusive thanks to all those who have helped organize presentations to get this information out to the people of the United States; there are so many I am indebted to. I'd especially like to thank Debra Ellis, Gerri Haynes, Maureen Aumand, and my friends in Alaska. Paul Prebys and Ruth Sheriton, you and the rest of the clan up there remain an inspiration to me.

Camilo Mejía and Dr. Sami AlBanna, your editorial assistance is deeply appreciated.

Rich Kambak, for pushing me forward through my indecision and doubt. Bhashwati Sengupta, there I no way I could have written this without you.

A big thanks to my agent Laura Gross and to my fantastic editor Anthony Arnove. I also wish to personally thank Dao Tran, Rachel Cohen, and Julie Fain for all your hard work in helping this book be what it is. Also, thank you, Sarah Macaraeg for all your great organizing work.

To my partner America Worden; thank you for being in my life, and helping me tell these stories. Your emotional and moral support was unwavering throughout my writing of this book, as well as my overseas travels. You taught me the meaning, power, and importance of story. Thank you from the bottom of my heart for being in mine.

INDEX

ABT Associates Incorporated, 256
Abdul Kareem, Ezzedin, 178–180
Abdulla, Ahmed, 235
Abdulla, Aisha, 195, 255–256, 264–265, 273–274, 289
Abed, Ali, 191
Aberle, Josslyn, 80–81
Abizaid, John, 69
Abrahim, Khalid Mohammed, 183
Abrahim, Walid Mohammed, 183–184
Abu Ghraib, 135; prison, 14, 80, 81, 154, 165, 184–188, 195, 281
Abu Hanifa mosque, 120, 121; raided by U.S. military, 145–147, 175, 182, 241–244
Adhamiya, 120, 156, 166, 183
Adnan, Sheikh, 203, 289
Adwar, 55
Ahmed, Kassem Mohammed, 236–237
Ahmed, Khalil, 41–42
Ahmed, Sabah, 222
Al-Abid, Saduk, 95–96
Al-Adhamiya, 120, 156, 166, 183
Al-Ageialap mosque, 118
Al-Arabiya (television station), 192, 225, 234
Al-Askari, Hassan, 26, 27
Al-Askari shrine, 26–27
Al-Awany, Jaadman Ahmed, 180
Al-Ayoubi, Saladin, 23

Al-Chederchi, Nassir, 166
Al-Dabbagh, Ali, 287
Al-Dhari, Harith, 130
Al-Dora, 28, 75, 150, 258, 259–262
Al-Dulaimi, Adnan Mohammed Salman, 147
Al-Hadith, Ahmed, 221
Al-Hard Al-Mohamudia mosque, 192
Al-Hawza, 112, 118, 119
Al-Hurra (television station), 156
Al-Iraqiyah (television station), 17, 176
Al-Jazeera, 18, 22, 125, 134, 204; bombed and banned, 234; telecasts photos of U.S. torture, 249
Al-Jubure, Jasem Hamza, 88–89
Al-Kaahd school, 79, 131
Al-Kafaei, Hamid, 167
Al-Khadam Shrine, 119
Al-Khoei, Abdul Majid, 112
Al-Lami, Adel, 268
Al-Mahdi, Muhammad, 26–27
Al-Maliki, Nouri, 285
Al-Muhannadi, Asma Khamis, 234, 235
Al-Mukhtar, Harb, 44–50 passim, 101, 104, 151, 197–206, 209–210, 277–279; Abu Hanifa mosque raid and, 241–244; Fallujah trips, 81–83 passim, 191–197; flees to Damascus, 289
Al-Mustansariyah University, 97, 285

Al-Nazzal, Maki, 137–140 passim
Al-Numan Hospital, 150, 248
Al-Nuwesri, Qasim, 196, 197
Al-Sabah, 175–177
Al-Sabah Al-Jadeed, 176–177
Al-Sadr, Muqtada, 112–116 passim, 118–120, 123, 129, 148
Al-Sadr Teaching Hospital, 151
Al-Shahid Adnan Kherala Secondary School for Boys, 61
Al-Sha'alan, hassim, 225
Al-Sheibani, Bassim, 286
Al-Shemany, Sa'adoun, 114
Al-Sistani, Ali al-Husseini, 96–97, 119, 264, 271
Al-Ubadi, Firdu, 233
Al-Zarqawi, Abu Musab, 230, 238
Ali, Amer, 198–199
Allawi, Iyad, 201, 211, 226, 232, 233, 272; admits government's security plans insufficient, 262–263; announces continuation of martial law, 266; says no citizens killed in Fallujah, 254; submits oil privatization proposals, 288; supports death squad formation, 246
Alwhan, Amer, 203
American Enterprise Institute, 90
American Prospect, 246–247
Amin, Faiq, 198
Amiriyah district (Baghdad), 60–64
Amiriyat al Fallujah, 251–252
Amman, 11–15 passim, 102–103, 108
Andrews, Julian, 132
Annan, Kofi, 97, 223
Army Corps of Engineers, 37
Army War College, 220
Arzaga Water Project, 94
Association of Muslim Scholars, 235, 264
Atia, Jabbar, 186
Ayar, Farid, 268
Ayoub, Tareq, 18
Aziz, Abdul, 161

Aziz, Abdulla, 253
Aziz, Abdulla Ra'ad, 242
Aziz, Hamoudi, 264
Aziz, Rana, 243
Azziz, Raad Ali Abdul, 134

Ba'ath Party, 19, 79, 132, 179
Backus, Ken, 200
Bacon, Ken, 290
Badr Army, 245–246
Baghdad, 7–11, 17–22, 33–40 passim, 54–55, 112; Adhamiyah district, 130, 146, 150, 156; al-Amiriyah district, 60–64; car bombings, 28, 278–279; Convention Center, 89; demonstrations after capture of Saddam Hussein, 57–60; elections and, 259–268, 275; history (as capital), 23; Karrada district, 122, 267; Khadamiyah neighborhood, 117–119 passim, 167; Old Baghdad, 54, 81; pro-occupation demonstrations in, 43. *See also* Al-Dora; Black Zone; Firdos Square; Green Zone; Red Zone; Sadr City; Yarmouk Hospital
Baghdad International Airport, 15, 209–210, 217–218; closed during siege of Fallujah, 230, 232
Baghdad Medical City, 20, 255
Baquba, 129, 160, 166, 201–206, 222–223, 232
Barakat, Hajji, 81–83 passim
Bassam, Mahnouz, 134
Bearing Point, 287
Bechtel Corporation, xiii, 90–95 passim, 221, 256; pulls out of Iraq with $2.3 billion, 286–287
Bechtel, Riley, 91
Black Zone, 113
Blackwater USA, 108–109, 110
Bloomberg School of Public Health and Medicine, 284–285
Bolivia, 90
Brandl, Gary, 222

Bremer, L. Paul III, 34, 221, 233, 271; Bechtel Corporation and, 91; convoy attacked, 67–68; de-Ba'athification program and, 180; election delay and, 96, 97; Fallujah assault and, 127; Iraqi Governing Council and, 181–182; Muqtada al-Sadr and, 112; Saddam Hussein capture and, 57

Bremer Orders, 181, 220–221, 233, 272

Bridge to Baghdad, A, 134

Brown, Jeffrey, 293–294

Bush, George H. W., 96

Bush, George W., xv, 1, 144, 217, 268–269, 272; comments blithely on Iraqi deaths, 266; doesn't apologize for Abu Ghraib atrocities, 156; says U.S. mission in Iraq will continue, 273; says U.S. wants prosperity for Iraqi people, 220; says "we did not seek this war," 213

CIA, 195, 211, 233, 245, 296

CNN, 143

CPA. See Coalition Provisional Authority

Caliph al-Mu'tasim, 23

Camp Babil, 92

Carroll, Jill, 10

Center for Strategic and International Studies, 221

Chalabi, Ahmed, 165

Cheney, Dick, 37, 270, 272

Christian Science Monitor, 10

Chuwader General Hospital. 196–197

Clemmon, Christy, 162

Coalition Provisional Authority (CPA), 34, 54, 67, 88, 89; Fallujah and, 161, 194; gives soccer balls to Iraqi children, 187; Iraq Ministry of Health and, 200; Ramadi and, 179; usurpation of IGC authority, 181–182. See also Bremer Orders; Office of Human Rights and Transitional Justice

Cockburn, Patrick, xiv

Committee to Protect Journalists, 251

Committee for the Liberation of Iraq, 90

Contras (Nicaragua), 245

Cordesman, Anthony, 221–222

Couso, José, 18

Dabag, Nazim, 56

Democracy Now!, xv

Dempsey, Martin, 67–68

Department of Defense, 26; Quadrennial Defense Review, 288–289

DeVoss, David, 256–257

Dhari, Sheikh, 130

Diwaniyah, 94–95

Diwaniyah College of Medicine, 286

Dominick, Brian, 80

Dulaimi, Adnan Mohammed Salman, 147

El Salvador, 244–245

Enders, David, 44, 154–155

Export Council, 91

Fafo Institute for Applied International Studies, 257

Fahdil, Sabar, 180

Faisal, Hajji, 204

Fallujah, xi–xii, xiv, 13, 16, 81–83; 2004: attack of John Abizaid in; 2004, 69; Blackwater mercenaries killed, 107–109; U.S. siege, April 2004, 106, 111–142, 143–151 passim, 159–166 passim, 180; civilian aid mission to, 130–140; end of siege, 162, 167–172, 174; post-siege (June–November), 191–206, 222–226 passim; U.S. siege, November 2004, 229–258; 2005: elections and, 272

Fallujah Brigade, 162

Fallujah General Hospital, 126, 230, 233, 249; raided by U.S. troops, 234–235

Fallujah (play), xiv

Fasa'a, Burhan, 249–250

Ferner, Mike, 103

Firdos Square, 35, 124, 144

Fisk, Robert, xiv
Fleury, Corentin, 234
Foreign Claims Act, 88

Geneva Conventions, 133, 166, 238, 249, 280
Ghani, Abbas, 115
Global Risk Strategies, 218
Gordon, Lee, 130–131, 134
Gordon, Michael, xv
Gouda, Abu, 222
Green Zone, 17, 30, 155, 162, 190; barraged by mortar fire, 232
Guatemala, 245
Guest, Julia, xii

Hadad, Bahktiyar Abdulla, 234
Haditha, 223–224
Hajar, Amin, 275
Hakeem, Hayda, 85–86
Half, Hammed Nawf, 40–42, 45
Halliburton, 37–38, 221. See also KBR
Halliday, Denis, 3
Halwan, Hamid Salman, 76, 259
Hamadi, Dhasin Jassim, 193
Hamed, Faris, 162
Hamdalide, Alla, 168
Hamid, Abdulla (vegetable vendor), 264
Hamid, Abdulla (computer engineer), 268
Hamid al-Alwan mosque, 248
Hamilton, Robert B., 42
Hammed, Lilu, 185–186
Hamza al-Jubure, Jasem, 88–89
Harouz, Fatima, 235
Harris Corporation, 176–177
Hashim, Ayad, 86–88
Hassam, Sheikh, 118, 119
Hassan, Abdel, 264
Hassan, Adel, 167
Hassan, Amir, 274
Hersh, Seymour, xiii–xiv, 80, 154
Hilla, 91–93

Hillman, James, 7, 127, 229
Hodges, Michael C., 78
Honduras, 244–245
Hughes, Chris, 132
Human, Abdul, 203
Human Rights Watch, 110, 132
Husain, Taha, 272
Hussein, Hammad, 255
Hussein, Aziz, 165
Hussein, Billal, 250–251
Hussein, Saddam, 1, 22, 27, 83, 121, 153 capture of, 55–59; Fallujah and, 110; toppling of statue of, 2, 35, 124
Hussein, Uday, 56
Hutson, John, 249
Hydro Quebec, 4

IMF, 287
Imam Adham Islamic College, 146
Imam Adham mosque, 232
Imam Ali Shrine, 148, 156
Independent Electoral Commission for Iraq (IECI), 268, 275
International Committee for the Red Cross, 92, 94, 235
International Monetary Fund, 287
INTERSOS, 134
Iran, 246
Iran-Contra scandal, 245
Iraq Ministry of Health, 148, 161, 200–201, 238, 249, 257, 263; instructed to stop providing mortality figures, 285
Iraq Ministry of Oil, 287
Iraq Ministry of Trade, 275
Iraqi Civil Defense Corps (ICDC), 164, 167–170, 191–194 passim
Iraq Coalition Casualty Count, 296
Iraqi Governing Council, 96, 98, 115, 148, 179, 271; authority usurped by CPA, 181–182; new flag proposal, 165–167
Iraqi National Guard (ING), 232, 234, 235,

238, 248, 279; Abu Hanifa mosque raid and, 241; Amiriyat al-Fallujah hospital raid and, 252

Iraqi Red Crescent, 162, 232–233, 238; Abu Hanifa mosque raid and, 243; second siege of Fallujah and, 253

Islamic Party, 159, 188, 232

Islamic Republic News Agency, 55

Ismail, Abdul Razaq, 237

Jabbar, Abdul, 171, 172, 253

James Bay, 4

Japan, 122

Jassin, Ahmed Saadoun, 170

Johns Hopkins Bloomberg School of Public Health and Medicine, 284–285

Jordan, 133, 217. *See also* Amman

Jordan-Iraq border, 15–16

Juhasz, Antonia, 220–221, 269–270, 271

KBR, 37–38, 218

Kadel, Salman Hassan, xiii, 92–93

Kareem, Ezzedin Abdul, 178–180

Kellogg Brown & Root. *See* KBR

Kerbala, 128

Khalid, Walid, 204

Khalil, Omar, 120

Khalil, Samah, 42

Khasil, Salam, 120

Khoei, Ayahtollah, 112

Kimmitt, Mark, 77, 127, 162, 201–202, 206

Kirkuk Airport Detention Center, 79

Kissinger Associates, 34

Korea, 122

Kucinich, Dennis, 246–247

Kufa, 112, 118–119

Kurdish Patriotic Front, 55–57 passim, 166

Kurdistan, 224

Kurds: elections and, 272, 275

Kut, 123, 124, 128

Kuwait, 90

LBC (television station), 249

Lancet, 285, 299–300

Larson, Alan, 270

Lawrence, T. E., 130

Leachman, Gerald, 130

Letter to the Prime Minister, A, xii

Lifton, Robert J., 281

Lincoln, Group, 294

LOGCAP, 37

Longley, James, 14

Lynch, Rick, 294

MI6, 233

Mahajan, Rahul, 111, 113, 129, 134

Mahdi, Abdel, 270, 271–272, 288

Mahmoud, Qahtan, 204

Mainscum, Francois, 4

Marsh Crisis Consulting, 34

Martinez, David, 134

Medact, 285–286

Mehdi Army, 112–114 passim, 119, 136–137, 196, 197; U.S. Special Forces and, 245–246

Mekay, Emad, 270

Mikhail, Baha, 53–55, 69

Miller, Judith, xv

Mohammed, Ahmed, 267

Mohammed, Hammad, 243

Mohammed, Hassan Mehdi, 95

Mohammed, Ismail Mahmoud, 25

Muhammed, Abdul, 164

Muher, Abu, 160

Mujahed, Khaled Abu, 159–160

Munir, Ayad Nihad Ahmed, 187–188

Munir, Nihad, 187–188

My Lai, 280–281

NPR, 143

Nadhme, Wmidh Omar, 151–152

Nagem, Hussin Hamsa, 93

Najaf, 93–94, 118–119, 123

Naqshabandi, Abbas, 24–26

Nasariyah, 122
Nasr, Abu, 286
National Public Radio, 143
Nazzal Emergency Hospital, 223, 235
Negroponte, John, 244–245
New York Times, xiii–xiv, xv, 26, 109, 143; parrots U.S. military propaganda, 230
New Yorker, 154
Newsweek, 244, 246
Nicaragua, 245
Noor, Salam Fahim, 94–95
Nuremberg Tribunal, 283

Obeidy, Rana, 236
Oday, Ibrahim Ahmed, 40–42, 45
Oday, Sabah Ahmed, 40–42, 45
Office of Human Rights and Transitional Justice, 89
Omaral-Ali, Salah, 296
"Operation Iraqi Freedom," 2
"Operation Iron Grip," 77
"Operation Phantom Fury," xiv–xv, 225, 229–240
"Operation Vigilant Resolve," 111–126

Pace, Peter, xiii, 22
Palestine, 152
Parenti, Christian, 72, 74, 196–206 passim
Pari, Simona, 134
Patriotic Union of Kurdistan (PUK), 55–57 passim, 166
Perlez, Jane, xiv
Peshmerga, 245–246
Petroleum Economist, 288
Pike, John, 247
Pilger, John, xiv
Pittman, Susan, 253
Powell, Colin, 67
President's Export Council, 91
Project for the New American Century, 90

Program Management Office (PMO), 221–222
Protsyuk, Tara, 18
Public Citizen, 89

Queen Alia International Airport, 11–13 passim

Radhi, Mohamed, 286
Rahman, Abdul, 168
Rahman, Layla Abdul, 267–268
Rahwani, Sabah, 267
Ramadi, 16, 45–50, 178–182, 223; execution of civilians in, 40–43 45–47
Rasul, Kosrat, 56
Red Crescent Society, 145, 171. *See also* Iraqi Red Crescent
Red Cross, 92, 94, 235
Red Zone, 30
Refugees International, 290
Republican Palace, 17
Rice, Condoleeza, 268
Rumsfeld, Donald, 26, 34, 68, 246–247

SAIC, 26, 176
Sabah, Abu, 237
Sadr City, 112–113, 115–116, 121, 123, 125; suicide bombing in, 267. *See also* Chuwader Hospital
Sadr, Mohammed Bakr, 118
Sadr, Mohammed Sadiq, 118
Sadr, Muqtada al, 112–116 passim, 118–120, 123, 129, 148
Saladin al-Ayoubi, 23
Salam, Addel, 161
Saleh, Jassmim Miuhamad, 162
Salim, Ezzedin, 181
Salon, 154
Samarra, xiii, 22–31, 72, 223, 272
Samir, Jilal, 186

Sanchez, Ricardo, 21, 123, 135
Saqlawiyah, 253
Satar, Khassem Mohammed Abdel, 192–193
Sattler, John, 244
Saudi Arabia, 83
Sauerbrey, Ellen, 290
Science Applications International Corporation, 26, 176
Senate Judiciary Committee, 290
Senor, Dan, 68
Shi'ites, 26–27, 95, 96; elections and, 263–264; Sunnis and, 113, 120, 123–124, 156. *See also* Badr Army; Supreme Council for the Islamic Revolution in Iraq
Shultz, George, 90
Shupp, Mike, 233
Sistani, Grand Ayatollah, 96–97, 119, 264, 271
60 Minutes II, 154
Smyth, Frank, 251
Steele, James, 245
Suari, Assad Turkey, 115, 116
Sunnis, 147, 155, 264, 270; Shi'ites and, 113, 120, 123–124, 156
Supreme Council for the Islamic Revolution in Iraq, 270–271
Swannick, Charles, 69
Syria, 102, 152

Talabani, Jalal, 55
Talib, Salam, 219–220
Templer, Victor, 117–118
Tharir Square, Fallujah, 194
Tikrit, 78, 79
Toretta, Simona, 134

USAID, 90, 253, 256–257, 287
U.S. Army Corps of Engineers, 37
U.S. Army War College, 220
U.S. Department of Defense, 26; Quadrennial Defense Review, 288–289

U.S. State Department, Oil and Energy Working Group, 288
United Iraqi Alliance (UIA), 271
United Nations, 97, 223, 233, 285; Development Program, 257; High Commission for Refugees, 290; UNICEF, 92
United States Agency for International Development, 90, 253, 256–257, 287

Venable, Barry, 254
Voice of Free Iraq, 296

Warner, John, 23, 294
Whitaker, Max, 89–90
Wilding, Jo, xii, 44; Fallujah aid mission and, 129, 130, 134, 140
Wolfowitz, Paul, 67–68
World Public Opinion, 284
World Tribunal on Iraq (WTI), 283–284

Yarmouk Hospital, 149, 195, 235, 255, 273, 276
Yassin, Sheikh, 130

Zarqawi, Abu Musab, 230, 238
Zayer, Ismail, 175–177
Zogby International, 200
Zoman, Sadiq, 66, 78–81

ALSO FROM HAYMARKET BOOKS

Welcome to the Terrordome: The Pain, Politics, and Promise of Sports
Dave Zirin • This much-anticipated sequel to *What's My Name, Fool?* by acclaimed sportswriter Dave Zirin breaks new ground in sportswriting, looking at the controversies and trends now shaping sports in the United States—and abroad. Always insightful, never predictable. ISBN 978-1-931859-41-7.

In Praise of Barbarians: Essays Against Empire
Mike Davis • No writer in the United States today brings together analysis and history as comprehensively and elegantly as Mike Davis. In these contemporary, interventionist essays, Davis goes beyond critique to offer real solutions and concrete possibilities for change. ISBN 978-1-931859-42-4.

Sin Patrón: Stories from Argentia's Occupied Factories
The lavaca collective, with a foreword by Naomi Klein and Avi Lewis • The inside story of Argentina's remarkable movement to create factories run democratically by workers themselves. ISBN 978-1-931859-43-1.

Between the Lines: Readings on Israel, the Palestinians, and the U.S. "War on Terror"
Tikva Honig-Parnass and Toufic Haddad • This compilation of essays—edited by a palestinian and an Israeli—constitutes a challenge to critially rethink the Israeli-Palestinian conflict. ISBN 978-1-931859-44-8.

No One Is Illegal: Fighting Racism and State Violence on the U.S./Mexico Border
Justin Akers Chacón and Mike Davis • Countering the chorus of anti-immigrant voices, Davis and Akers Chacón expose the racism of anti-immigration vigilantes and put a human face on the immigrants who risk their lives to cross the border to work in the United States. ISBN 978-1-931859-35-3.

A Little Piece of Ground
Elizabeth Laird • Growing up in occupied Palestine through the eyes of a twelve-year-old boy. ISBN 978-1-931859-38-7.

The Communist Manifesto: A Road Map to History's Most Important Political Document

Karl Marx and Frederick Engels, edited by Phil Gasper • This beautifully organized and presented edition of *The Communist Manifesto* is fully annotated, with clear historical references and explication, additional related texts, and a glossary that will bring the text to life. ISBN 978-1-931859-25-7.

Subterranean Fire: A History of Working-Class Radicalism in the U.S.

Sharon Smith • Workers in the United States have a rich tradition of fighting back and achieving gains previously thought unthinkable, but that history remains largely hidden. *In Subterranean Fire*, Sharon Smith brings that history to light and reveals its lessons for today. ISBN 978-1-931859-23-3.

Soldiers in Revolt: GI Resistance During the Vietnam War

David Cortright with a new introduction by Howard Zinn • "An exhaustive account of rebellion in all the armed forces, not only in Vietnam but throughout the world."—*New York Review of Books*. ISBN 978-1-931859-27-1.

Friendlly Fire: The Remarkable Story of a Journalist Kidnapped in Iraq, Rescued by an Italian Secret Service Agent, and Shot by U.S. Forces

Giuliana Sgrena • The Italian journalist, whose personal story was featured on *60 Minutes*, describes the real story of her capture and shooting in 2004. Sgrena also gives invaluable insight into the reality of life in occupied Iraq, exposing U.S. war crimes there. ISBN 978-1-931859-39-4.

The Meaning of Marxism

Paul D'Amato • A lively and accessible introduction to the ideas of Karl Marx, with historical and contemporary examples. ISBN 978-1-931859-29-5.

Revolution and Counterrevolution: Class Struggle in a Moscow Metal Factory

Kevin Murphy • Murphy's wealth of research and insight deliver an exciting contribution to the discussion about class and the Russian Revolution. ISBN 978-1-931859-50-9.

The Women Incendiaries: The Inspiring Story of the Women of the Paris Commune Who Took up Arms in the Fight for Liberty and Equality

Edith Thomas • *The Women Incendiaries* tells the often over-looked story of the crucial role played by women during the Paris Commune of 1871, one of history's most important emxperiments in working-class democracy. ISBN 978-1-931859-46-2.

The Dispossessed: Chronicles of the *Desterrados* of Colombia

Alfredo Molano • Here in their own words are the stories of the Desterrados, or "dispossessed"—the thousands of Colombians displaced by years of war and state-backed terrorism, funded in part through U.S. aid to the Colombian government. With a preface by Aviva Chomsky. ISBN 978-1-931859-17-2.

Vive la Revolution: A Stand-up History of the French Revolution

Mark Steel • An actually interesting, unapologetically sympathetic and extremely funny history of the French Revolution. ISBN 978-1-931859-37-0.

Poetry and Protest: A Dennis Brutus Reader

Aisha Karim and Lee Sustar, editors • A vital original collection of the interviews, poetry, and essays of the much-loved anti-apartheid leader. ISBN 978-1-931859-22-6.

The Bending Cross: A Biography of Eugene Victor Debs

Ray Ginger, with a new introduction by Mike Davis • The classic biography of Eugene Debs, one of the most important thinkers and activists in the United States. 978-1-931859-40-0.

What's My Name, Fool? Sports and Resistance in the United States

Dave Zirin • What's My Name, Fool? offers a no-holds-barred look at the business of sports today. In humorous and accessible language, Zirin shows how sports express the worst, as well as the most creative and exciting, features of American society. ISBN 978-1-931859-20-5.

Literature and Revolution

Leon Trotsky, William Keach, editor • A new, annotated edition of Leon Trotsky's classic study of the relationship of politics and art. ISBN 978-1931859-16-5.

ABOUT HAYMARKET BOOKS

Haymarket Books is a nonprofit, progressive book distributor and publisher, a project of the Center for Economic Research and Social Change. We believe that activists need to take ideas, history, and politics into the many struggles for social justice today. Learning the lessons of past victories, as well as defeats, can arm a new generation of fighters for a better world. As Karl Marx said, "The philosophers have merely interpreted the world; the point however is to change it."

We take inspiration and courage from our namesakes, the Haymarket Martyrs, who gave their lives fighting for a better world. Their 1886 struggle for the eight-hour day, which gave us May Day, the international workers' holiday, reminds workers around the world that ordinary people can organize and struggle for their own liberation. These struggles continue today across the globe—struggles against oppression, exploitation, hunger, and poverty.

It was August Spies, one of the Martyrs who was targeted for being an immigrant and an anarchist, who predicted the battles being fought to this day. "If you think that by hanging us you can stamp out the labor movement," Spies told the judge, "then hang us. Here you will tread upon a spark, but here, and there, and behind you, and in front of you, and everywhere, the flames will blaze up. It is a subterranean fire. You cannot put it out. The ground is on fire upon which you stand."

We could not suceed in our publishing efforts without the generous financial support of our readers. Many people contribute to our project through the Haymarket Sustainers program, where donors receive free books in return for their monetary support. If you would like to be a part of this program, please contact us at info@haymarketbooks.org.

Order these titles and more online at www.haymarketbooks.org or call 773-583-7884.